BEYOND THE FAÇADE

BEYOND THE FAÇADE

POLITICAL REFORM
IN THE ARAB WORLD

MARINA OTTAWAY

JULIA CHOUCAIR-VIZOSO

EDITORS

Carnegie Endowment for International Peace
1779 Massachusetts Avenue, N.W.
Washington, D.C. 20036
202-483-7600, Fax 202-483-1840
www.CarnegieEndowment.org

Typesetting by Oakland Street Publishing
Printed by United Book Press

Library of Congress Cataloging-in-Publication Data
Beyond the facade : political reform in the Arab world / Marina Ottaway,
Julia Choucair-Vizoso, [editors].
    p. cm.
  Includes bibliographical references and index.
  ISBN 978-0-87003-239-4 (pbk. : alk. paper) — ISBN 978-0-87003-240-0
(cloth : alk. paper) 1. Democratization—Arab countries. 2. Arab
countries—Politics and government—1945- I. Ottaway, Marina. II.
Choucair-Vizoso, Julia. III. Title.

  JQ1850.A91B49 2008
  320.917'4927--dc22

2007045680

CONTENTS

ACKNOWLEDGMENTS

This collection of essays on political reform in Arab countries is the result of many meetings and much collective discussion by the research staff of the Middle East Program at the Carnegie Endowment for International Peace, of comments and contributions by scholars in other institutions, and of course of the individual efforts of the authors. Our thanks go to all of them.

The essays and the book also owe much to the contributions of the innumerable individuals who generously gave their time and shared their insights with the authors. The inquisitiveness of visiting researchers can be a real burden for people who already have overloaded schedules and we sincerely thank all those who helped us, even if the names are too numerous to mention.

Carnegie Endowment junior fellows also contributed to this project in various ways during the last two years. In particular, Dina Bishara provided invaluable research support on several countries and Michael Grosack proved to be a careful and reliable editor.

The staff of the publications department steered the manuscript through production smoothly and competently. Our special thanks go to Ilonka Oszvald for her painstaking editing and always willing assistance.

The Endowment is deeply grateful to the Carnegie Corporation of New York, the Ford Foundation, the John D. and Catherine T. MacArthur Foundation, the Rockefeller Brothers Fund, and the United Kingdom's Department for International Development (DFID) for their generous support of our Middle East work.

FOREWORD

Political reform in the Middle East and North Africa has been the subject of a seemingly endless, but nonetheless important, discussion. Most Arab governments admit that some political change is needed, and there has been considerable intellectual and public discussion about what it should look like. But when reform has come, it has been a poor match for high-pitched rhetoric. No country in the region has experienced fundamental political progress: some have regressed. It has become difficult to tell whether real political transformation is under way, or if there has simply been enough talk and cosmetic reform to create that impression.

History provides no clear model for distinguishing between the two. Reform is a long, bumpy, and idiosyncratic process, highly dependent on local context and individual leadership. What has been missing until now has been a study of recent political change in this critical region that is deep and detailed enough to do justice to each country's unique experience, yet broad enough to spot general trends.

In this volume Marina Ottaway and Julia Choucair-Vizoso provide exactly that. Analyzing ten countries, they delve into the sources of political change in each, noting the continuing obstacles to greater democratization and describing the likely forms that real reform would take.

From these detailed studies, trends emerge important for policy makers and scholars alike. Ottaway and Choucair-Vizoso do not see a true political paradigm shift—the hallmark of real reform—in any of the ten countries they examine. That shift would be a redistribution of power from the executive—as distinct from the benevolent acts of an enlightened ruler—to parliament, creating real checks and balances. Instead, they see reforms orchestrated from the top, carefully designed so as not to undermine the power of the ruling elite or risk letting the political genie out of the bottle.

The United States and other countries seeking to advance democracy have had limited impact in the Arab world, in part because of the weakness of domestic forces for reform and in part because of their own mistakes. Ultimately, real change only comes from within, but the United States and Europe could help by tailoring their advice and their pressure to the conditions in each country, rather than indulging in soaring rhetoric about democracy even while ignoring gross human rights violations when it seems politically expedient.

These essays paint a vivid picture of how long and difficult the path of political change will be in the Arab world. They also show, however, that even the most conservative countries can no longer protect themselves from the ferment of new currents and trends.

This collection of essays is part of a large body of work on political processes in the Middle East and North Africa undertaken by the Washington-based Middle East Program and by the Beirut-based Carnegie Middle East Center. The work includes research on all political actors that seek, in their own way, to bring about change in their countries—moderate Islamic movements and parties, secular political parties, and reform advocates in incumbent regimes.

—JESSICA T. MATHEWS
President, Carnegie Endowment for International Peace

EVALUATING MIDDLE EAST REFORM: SIGNIFICANT OR COSMETIC?

Marina Ottaway

A re Arab countries reforming politically? Are they becoming more democratic? Can they be helped, or coerced, from the outside to open up their political systems and become more democratic?

Such questions have received ample attention from policy makers and analysts in recent years. Two factors in particular served as catalysts for this unprecedented level of interest in political reform and democracy in the Arab world. The first was the publication of the first United Nations Development Program (UNDP) *Arab Human Development Report* in 2002, which pointed to the existence of a "democratic deficit" in Arab countries.[1] Although the report was not particularly original in its diagnosis and reflected ideas that had long been discussed among Arab intellectuals and foreign scholars, its publication by the UNDP moved discussions of the problem from the halls of academia to the pages of newspapers. The report was not welcomed by all and in fact inspired resentment on the part of many Arab governments, but it could not be ignored.

The second factor that intensified discussions about Arab political reform and democracy was the change in U.S. policy toward the Middle East triggered by the terrorist attacks of September 11, 2001. The attacks forced the Bush administration to focus on the threat posed by radical organizations that used Islam as their political ideology. These groups were already well known among specialists and policy makers. Until September 11, however, this threat had not come to the attention of the general public, nor was it a major determinant of U.S. policy in the region.

The September 11 drama prompted rethinking in U.S. policy where earlier intelligence reports and security estimates had not. That the hijackers came

1

predominantly from Saudi Arabia, a country long viewed as a reliable U.S. ally, was particularly shocking. It suggested at the very least that the Saudi royal family was not as firmly in control as it had been in the past. At worst, it raised questions concerning whether the Saudi government's policies were directly or indirectly the cause of terrorism. Questions of Saudi involvement led to finger pointing, ranging from accusations of lax control over Wahhabi religious organizations and the activities they funded in other Muslim countries to outright accusations that the Saudi government encouraged Islamist extremism. The explanation eventually embraced by the Bush administration was less harsh. The Saudi government was responsible for the rise of terrorist organizations in the Kingdom not because it directly supported such groups, but because its authoritarianism and its poor economic policies were creating social conditions that favored the growth of terrorism. Lack of democracy and economic opportunities among young Saudis caused frustration that manifested itself in the form of terrorist activities. Other Arab authoritarians were creating similar conditions in their countries. To contain terrorism the United States needed not only to rely on good intelligence and security measures but also to address the root causes of the problem by promoting democracy and economic reform. Thus was born the Bush administration's "freedom agenda" for the Middle East.

The U.S. decision to promote democracy in the Middle East in turn intensified long-standing debates about democracy among Arab intellectuals. Many reacted with indignation at the arrogance with which the Bush administration tried to impose political choices on Arab countries and questioned the United States' moral authority to do so. Although objecting to U.S. policy, a large number of intellectuals, however, agreed that Arab countries needed to put their political houses in order and that democracy should not be rejected just because the United States was proposing it.

Most important, some governments started responding to U.S. criticism by taking steps toward political reform. But how important are these changes? Are they meaningful reforms, as the governments claim, or are they simply placebos offered by authoritarian regimes in an attempt to pacify domestic and international public opinion, as the opposition often argues? In other words, are the reforms significant or cosmetic? If the reforms introduced so far are not significant, what steps would be? Can the international community help make them more significant? Answering these questions is a demanding task because what constitutes significant rather than cosmetic change varies from country to country depending on the prevalent conditions and past experiences. It is also an important task not only in trying to assess the significance of the change taking place but also in helping policy makers focus their efforts.

"Significant" reform does not mean perfect reform. The goal of the essays in this book is not to provide a list of all the changes that each country would have to introduce to become a full-fledged democracy. Such an endeavor would be easy but essentially futile. A list of such changes could be readily derived from any textbook that discusses the characteristics of democratic systems. But we know that the process of democratization is slow and quirky—even a country that eventually democratizes successfully will follow a convoluted path. The challenge is thus not to describe a perfect process that will almost certainly not take place, but to distinguish partial steps that start altering the distribution of power and the character of the political system from those that are only window dressing.

The following discussion seeks to suggest parameters by which the significance of reforms can be judged, thus providing the conceptual framework for the case studies that follow.

A History of Change

Most Middle Eastern countries have a long history of political change, including at times democratic reform. Egypt and to a lesser extent Syria experienced promising periods of democratic opening before World War II. Most of the independence movements in the region incorporated democratic demands in their agenda. Although the 1950s and 1960s saw the triumph of Arab nationalism in most countries outside the Gulf—leading to the imposition of single party systems in many—the following decades witnessed a slow return to more pluralistic political systems in most countries.

During the 1990s, however, Arab political systems remained stagnant, seemingly untouched by the wave of change that swept across much of the world after the fall of socialist regimes in the Soviet Union and Eastern Europe. After sitting out the first period of reform after the end of the Cold War, many Arab countries paradoxically started opening up to the possibility of political change in the late 1990s when doors were closing elsewhere. There is a lot of debate about the reasons for this new political vitality, particularly the relative importance of domestic factors and outside pressure, but the change is undeniable.

There is a new willingness on the part of most Arab governments to admit that some political change is needed. Even the most conservative among them are willing to say that Arab countries are bound to evolve politically, although in their own fashion and at their own pace. Arab intellectuals are speaking up about the need for change more openly than before, although it is not clear whether the spirited discussions taking place reach a broader and more mainstream audience than in the past. Debates about reform and democracy have become a growth industry in the Arab press. Democratic manifestos have been issued in rapid succession at meetings of civil society organizations, business groups, and even governments, creating a new and confusing array of declarations—the Sana'a Declaration, the Alexandria Declaration, and the Beirut Declaration are only some of a long list of new democratic manifestos.

The concrete steps taken by Arab governments to reform their political systems do not come even remotely close to matching the rhetoric. Many of the signatories of the eloquent declarations issued by "civil society" are not organizations but individuals who work for or with the same governments they supposedly want to reform. Intellectuals engaging in the debate over democracy in the press are careful not to cross redlines that would bring down the ire of intolerant regimes upon them. Concrete change, in other words, remains limited at best. Furthermore, it is already clear that the process of change will not be linear. In some countries, particularly in Egypt, reverse trends toward greater authoritarianism are beginning to appear.

These contradictory trends make it difficult for analysts to judge the real extent of change in the region. Are Middle Eastern countries experiencing the beginning of a real process of transformation that may lead to the emergence of democratic systems in a region hitherto known for its authoritarianism or semiauthoritarianism? Or is all the talk a smokescreen to hide political stagnation, and are the modest steps taken by some governments simply cosmetic reforms that produce the impression of change without actually altering the lopsided distribution of power to which Arab regimes owe their longevity?

The answers given to these questions from various quarters are usually more influenced by politics than rigorous analysis. Many Arabs chafing under the control of unpopular regimes tend to dismiss all changes as purely cosmetic, and they resent the approval expressed by Western governments and organizations for the steps enacted by Arab regimes. Regime supporters portray even modest measures as momentous indications of change, as does the Bush administration, anxious to convince the American public that its policies are working and that U.S. pressure is turning the Middle East into a more democratic region that is less of a danger to the United States.

A more balanced, less political appraisal of the significance of reform measures being enacted by Middle East regimes can be reached by addressing two issues: First, what is the difference between significant and cosmetic reform in general? And second, how is it possible to ascertain in practice whether specific steps undertaken by a government or by the opposition are significant components of a process of democratization or merely cosmetic measures?

The Democratization Conundrum

What makes it difficult to assess the significance of the reforms being enacted is that democratization is not an event but a process, usually quite lengthy— President Bush has described it in various speeches as a generational task. Even in retrospect, it is not always clear when and how the process started in a given region or country. When did the process of democratization start in the old democracies of Europe? With the signing of the Magna Carta? With the enclosure movement in Great Britain? With the French Revolution? Or did it begin when the voting franchise was extended beyond the narrow limits of the landowning class? And when did the United States become a democratic country? Volumes continue to be written on such issues.

Even more recent and seemingly clear-cut examples, such as the transformation of Central Europe in the late 1980s and 1990s, are not so simple. The fall of the Berlin Wall or the surge of crowds in Wenceslas Square in Prague were undoubtedly turning points, but they were not a beginning, because much had happened before. Furthermore, the beginning of a process of democratization is not always followed by success. Thus, democratization may start with seemingly insignificant changes, while apparently significant changes may not lead anywhere.

The processes of gradual democratization are particularly difficult to analyze. In the case of Mexico, some analysts have chosen to interpret the transfer of power from the Institutional Revolutionary Party (PRI) as the final outcome of a slow process of transformation that started in the early part of the twentieth century. The change, however, could just as plausibly be read as the result of a much more recent process triggered by the worldwide changes of the 1990s.

It is also clear from even the most superficial analysis that countries democratize in different ways: some more gradually, some suddenly; some as the result of deep socioeconomic change, others as the result of political upheaval. There may be some similarities in the final stages of the transformation in some countries, but there is certainly no universal pattern. Efforts to impose a standardized template on democracy promotion efforts during the 1990s have made this clear. The standardized models are more useful in helping democracy promoters organize and justify their interventions than in understanding how and why countries do or do not become democratic.

Nor can the significance of specific reforms be judged on the basis of whether they are found in a checklist of the characteristics of a democratic system. The regular holding of multiparty elections, for example, is indisputably one characteristic of a democratic system, but plenty of countries have learned the art of holding multiparty elections without allowing a real challenge to the incumbent government. Such elections are not a sign of democratization. Equal rights for all citizens, including women, are basic to the definition of a democratic system. Again, it is possible for an intelligent authoritarian to make concessions on women's rights without bringing the country closer to democracy. In other words, we cannot judge the significance of reforms by juxtaposing them with a checklist of what a democratic country must have. This is true both because countries can make a lot of progress toward democracy without scoring well on the checklist for a long time—the United States, for example, had moved far along the road to democracy before equal rights legislation was proposed—and because seemingly important reforms can be meaningless in the wrong context.

It is particularly important not to confuse all positive change taking place in a country with democratization. Economic reform does not automatically lead to democratization, and countries with abundant state control of and interference with the market can be democratic, as the history of Western Europe after World War II shows. More recently, China has introduced breathtaking economic reforms without moving significantly in the direction of democracy. Singapore has educated its population, created a legal environment favorable to investment, and introduced many other positive changes thought to be conducive to democracy, but it is not moving toward democracy. Indonesia, in contrast, has seen some real change in the political realm in a socioeconomic environment that, by frequently used standards, is extremely unfavorable. Positive change can occur on many different fronts without democratization, and there can be democratization while other conditions are poor.

The Idea of Paradigm Shift

One way to approach the difficult problem of differentiating between significant and cosmetic reform is to borrow the concept of a paradigm shift from the world of the natural sciences. Thomas Kuhn has argued that major scientific advances are the result not of cumulative incremental change but of scientific revolutions that lead scientists to abandon fundamental assumptions underlying their former work and to adopt a new paradigm, or set of assumptions, that looks at phenomena in a different light. It is these paradigm shifts that allow major progress to be made in the natural sciences.

In the same way, the transition from an authoritarian to a democratic system requires a political paradigm shift, an abandoning by those controlling the government, and often also by their opponents, of old assumptions about the fundamental organization of the polity, the relation between the government and the citizens, and thus the source, distribution, and exercise of political power. Paradigm shifts do not always lead to democracy. The Russian Revolution entailed a paradigm shift with worldwide implications, but it was most certainly not a shift toward democracy. Former Egyptian President Gamal Abdel Nasser and the Free Officers brought about a political paradigm shift in Egypt that had repercussions throughout the Arab world, but again democracy was not part of this shift. Yet while there can be and have been paradigm shifts without democracy, there can be no democracy without a preceding paradigm shift.

Absent such a paradigm change, a country can still show some progress toward a less repressive political system without making real progress toward democracy. An authoritarian regime can become more benevolent—for example, by avoiding the most extreme forms of repression (often because the regime concludes that such measures are counterproductive). A government may even liberalize a little, for example, by permitting limited criticism of high officials in the press. As long as these changes are benevolent acts of the ruler rather than the recognition of inalienable political rights of the citizens, no paradigm shift has taken place. The wave of post–Cold War political transitions provides numerous examples of political reforms without paradigm shift, leading to the rise of semiauthoritarian regimes.

The idea of a paradigm shift as the central element of the process of democratization is rather different from the usual concept of how transitions occur offered by students of democratization and adopted by democracy promoters. In the more common approach, democratization is seen as a three-phase process: a period of liberalization, followed by a transition represented by the holding of competitive multiparty elections, followed finally by a prolonged period of democratic consolidation. The problem with this conceptualization of the process of democratization is that many countries experience a period of liberalization and hold competitive elections without truly democratizing. They erect the façade of democracy but not the building behind it, and become what I have called elsewhere semiauthoritarian countries. These countries have not experienced a paradigm shift but have simply superimposed the formal processes expected by the international community on the old assumptions about how power is generated and exercised.

What leads to political paradigm shifts? In the Middle East, the dominant assumption is that only incumbent regimes have the power to launch a meaningful reform process. The assumption is widely shared by Arab governmental and nongovernmental elites as well as important segments of the public. It is also eagerly embraced by outsiders who want to promote democracy without risking destabilization, including U.S. government agencies and nongovernmental organizations. On the part of Arab groups, the assumption is based on a mixture of political prudence and cultural traits. People who live in authoritarian countries have, by definition, little experience with grassroots organizing and are used to seeing the government as the source of all problems and all solutions. Although most Arab countries have known periods of some political openness and, outside the Gulf states, have some experience with democratization, citizens tend to look to the authorities for solutions; those who do not are more likely to advocate violent, radical change rather than incremental reform. But the focus on change from the top is also the result of political expediency for many Arabs, as it is for many Westerners. Change from the top protects the interests of citizens for whom the status quo is morally reprehensible but materially safe and even rewarding. Change from the top also safeguards the interests of foreign countries that are concerned about stability and advocate democracy not as a means to bring about sweeping change, which can be dangerous, but as a means to create mildly reformist regimes deemed to be more flexible and thus more stable than authoritarian ones.

The focus on reforms introduced by the government is justified by the understanding that, ultimately, a change in the political paradigm of a country requires action by the government, whether the old or the new one, because it is the government that can change the rules of the political game and enact a new system. Even in the rare cases where political change takes a revolutionary form, the new system is established by those who seized control of the state, and thus control of governing. But political change that affects the distribution of power in a country rarely comes solely at the initiative of the government—from the top down—without any prompting. Reform is usually a response to pressures within the society that make change imperative. In assessing the significance of the changes taking place in a country, it is thus important to look not only at the initiatives taken by the government but also at actions by nongovernmental actors, such as political parties, civic organizations, social movements, and labor unions, that may affect the balance of power and put real pressure on the government to reform. Not all steps taken by such independent organizations are significant in terms of democratic change; there are cosmetic activities here as well. The growth of political parties with a large membership is undoubtedly a significant change. The signing of a democracy manifesto by a small number of intellectuals is a cosmetic though morally gratifying step, unlikely to trigger a political paradigm shift.

Until the end of the Cold War, and even more recently in the Middle East, a discussion of reform from the top and pressure from below would have exhausted the possibilities about the sources of paradigm change. At present, with the issue of political reform in the Arab world high on the agenda of the United States and the European Union, the question also needs to be asked whether a political paradigm change can result from external pressure. Events of the last few years show that external pressure can easily trigger cosmetic reform. Many Arab regimes have been quite responsive to U.S. pressure. For example, several countries have tried to refurbish their reformist credentials by amending family codes to improve the rights of women or by appointing women to important, visible positions. Some are experimenting with elections, at least local ones, although usually in such a way that makes it extremely unlikely, if not outright impossible, for candidates or parties hostile to the government in power to acquire control.

What we have not witnessed so far is any example of outside pressure convincing the incumbent government to expose itself to competition that might result in its ouster from power. Nor is it clear whether the United States and other outsiders pushing for reform really want to see the enactment of measures that could lead to a political paradigm change with unforeseeable consequences. Modest, even cosmetic, change often accommodates the political requirements of both incumbent governments and outsiders better than far-reaching measures with unpredictable consequences.

Assessing the Significance of Reforms

Defining reforms that could lead to paradigm shifts as significant and those that do not as cosmetic does not answer the question of how to distinguish between the two in practice. Several problems arise in judging the significance of reforms in practice.

The first is the time frame. Reforms should be judged on the basis of the likelihood that they will make a difference in a relatively short period of time. It is true that democratization is a long process, and that democratic consolidation takes decades at best. But in judging the significance of specific steps supposedly taken by governments or opposition groups to facilitate democratization, it is necessary to use a much shorter time frame. Presumably, if a government is committed to democratic change, it will take steps that have an effect in the short run, not in the distant future. Although any precise number will be arbitrary, reforms that are not likely to have an impact within five years should not be considered significant. For example, the amendment of a party registration law that may have an impact on elections scheduled four or five years in the future should be considered significant because it could contribute to change in the distribution of power, and thus to paradigm change, in the foreseeable future. But the appointment of younger ministers or the promotion of younger officials to high positions in a ruling party cannot be considered a significant sign of change solely because it indicates the rise of a new generation that at some point might take it upon itself to reform the system. The time frame is simply too long, and the supposed process of generational change too vague to see such appointments and promotions as indications that change is indeed underway.

The second problem is whether a measure has a direct impact on political reform or whether it would become significant only if all parts of a chain of events fell into place. For example, the lifting of emergency laws to free up political activity is undoubtedly a significant reform by the government, and the formation of a coalition of political parties a significant step taken by the opposition. Both could lead to a paradigm shift in the foreseeable future. The privatization of state industry, however, cannot be considered significant from the point of view of political paradigm shift because the political impact of such a measure would at best be indirect and contingent on many other pieces falling into place. If privatization were honestly conducted and led to real economic growth, if economic growth were of such a nature that it facilitated the formation of a large middle class rather than the emergence of a small number of robber barons, and if the process continued long enough, a political paradigm shift could develop in the end. But there are too many uncertainties and contingencies in the chain to allow the analyst to define privatization as a significant step toward political paradigm change.

Finally, there is the problem of unintended consequences and the "slippery slope." Reform processes that start out as limited and carefully orchestrated from the top may have unintended consequences leading to a paradigm shift at some point. The repression of the Prague Spring in 1968 triggered a series of reactions that are indirectly connected to the velvet revolution of 1989. Yet, it would make little sense to see the repression of the Prague Spring as the beginning of democratization in Czechoslovakia. Again, there are too many contingencies and intervening variables in the slippery slope scenario.

To be sure, it is only in retrospect that it becomes truly clear whether or not reforms have led to paradigm change. The observer of contemporary phenomena has to be content with evaluating the potential for change, knowing full well that it will not be automatically realized. Furthermore, not all significant reforms are relevant to democratization. Reforms that could lead to democracy must favor the emergence of a political system that, following Robert Dahl's definition in *Polyarchy: Participation and Opposition,* is responsive, or almost completely responsive, to its citizens, allowing them to formulate and express preferences.[2] Focusing on responsiveness rather than on institutional arrangements as the defining characteristic of a democracy makes it easier to separate changes that are steps toward democracy from those that are purely formal. For example, the question is not simply whether elections are held regularly, but whether such elections lead to the formation of responsive governments that are not all-powerful and are thus obliged to respond to their constituents' demands to remain in office.

Significant, political paradigm-changing democratic reforms are thus those that affect, or at least have the potential for affecting, the distribution of power in a country and make power subject to a popular mandate. Such reforms must contribute to limiting the power of the executive, allowing the emergence of other centers of power and introducing an element of pluralism. The countries of the Middle East at the present time are characterized by an extraordinary concentration of power in the hands of an executive—a king, a ruling family, a religious establishment, a strong president. This is the fundamental problem of democracy in the entire region. The only true exceptions at this point are Lebanon, where power is allocated—both constitutionally and in political reality—among different political institutions and religious communities, and Iraq, where U.S. intervention has destroyed the strongman paradigm, leaving no political system capable of generating power and creating a power vacuum, violence, and instability.

The changes in the distribution of power and thus in the responsiveness of the political system do not have to be complete or even particularly extensive for specific changes or reforms to be considered significant. Certainly, a new political paradigm does not have to be elaborated for change to be considered significant. Even in the natural sciences, the shift starts with the challenging of the old assumptions, not with the consolidation of a new model.

In conclusion, significant reforms are those that have the potential for leading to a democratic paradigm shift in a fairly short time period, without the interference of a long chain of intervening variables that may or may not materialize, and equally without the interference of unforeseen circumstances. Although the possibility that a complex chain of events will lead to democratization cannot be ruled out, or that apparently insignificant change will put the country on a slippery slope toward major transformation, we cannot judge the significance of specific reforms by assuming that such a chain of events will unfold.

Significant reform can occur from the top down, if a government enacts measures that start breaking down its monopoly over power. Significant change can also occur from the bottom up, when strong new organizations with a political agenda form. Ideally, that political agenda should be a democratic one, but even the growth of a political organization with an agenda that falls short of democracy can be important in breaking down the power of the old regime. A country where a nondemocratic government is being challenged by other political forces, even if they do not embrace a democratic agenda, is closer to pluralism than one in which a government is unchallenged or challenged only weakly. Anything that leads to autonomous activities and organizing is part of the process of breaking down power at the core.

Even significant reforms, however, may not lead to a paradigm change and democratization. In assessing the significance of reforms, analysts cannot predict the ultimate outcome of a long-term process because too many new factors can intervene. Analysts can only try to ascertain whether the steps taken at a given time are significant and thus have the potential to contribute to democratization. Assessing present significance does not mean predicting future outcomes. For example, a constitutional amendment that increases the power of the parliament is a significant measure, although in the future its potential for changing the balance of power in the country may be voided by electoral maneuvering that ensures that the ruling party controls the overwhelming majority of the seats. The decision to allow political parties to register is significant, although there is no guarantee that those parties will succeed in developing strong constituencies. There is no guarantee that a reform introduced by the government, or an initiative introduced by independent organizations, will eventually lead to paradigm change but that does not mean that such reforms and initiatives should be dismissed as purely cosmetic changes.

Cosmetic reforms are measures that do not affect the distribution of power, do not make the government more open to challenges, and thus do not have the potential for leading directly to paradigm change. Furthermore, cosmetic reforms are deliberately designed to give the appearance of change while precluding its possibility. When a government decides to allow the election of half the members of parliament while maintaining the right to appoint the other half, it is carrying out a cosmetic reform.

Cosmetic reforms may be introduced more often in response to the pressure of the international community when domestic pressure is still limited. Confronted with the mobilization of significant domestic constituencies, governments are likely to either resort to repression or introduce significant change. It is the distant external actors who may be satisfied with façade changes.

Reform in Practice

The ten countries analyzed in this book are quite different from one another. Inevitably, so are the types of reforms their governments have introduced, the nature of the political actors involved, and the process that has determined the extent and type of change taking place. Together, the ten cases offer a broad, though not exhaustive, overview of the variety and complexity of the issues involved in a political reform process.

Political change has been pervasive in most of the countries studied in this volume. But change has not followed a clear direction, and progress toward greater openness has often been undone by reversals. Furthermore, in countries where the political space is more open now than it was even a few years ago—where debate is more lively and participation by citizens the highest— the changes stop well short of a paradigm change.

Morocco and Kuwait are the two most encouraging models of reform analyzed in the book, with a pluralistic and competitive process for electing parliament, lively media, public debates, and reasonable protection of individual rights and liberties, as illustrated by the studies of Marina Ottaway and Meredith Riley on Morocco and of Paul Salem on Kuwait. Yet in both countries the power of the executive remains disproportionately larger than that of other government branches, with the Moroccan king not subject to any constitutional limitations on his power and the Kuwaiti ruling family still fighting the authority of parliament.

Yemen, one of the least developed countries in the Middle East and North Africa region and thus one many analysts would expect to be quite resistant to political reform, also has a very active political scene, with an opposition willing to enter into cross-ideological alliances between Islamist and secular parties and a government that has made a conscious decision not to crush or eliminate some opposition groups even when it has been in a position to do so. Nevertheless, the president and ruling party in Yemen maintain the ability to manipulate the system and avoid any true challenge to its power, as Sarah Phillips shows.

Egypt represents a much more disturbing case where promising advances toward a greater political openness and a more dynamic political system have been quickly reversed, as shown in the analyses by Michele Dunne and Amr Hamzawy. Egypt thus offers a stark reminder of the reversibility and uncertainties of reform processes.

Saudi Arabia demonstrates why political reform needs to be evaluated on a case-by-case basis, keeping in mind the starting point and the overall context. It is easy to dismiss Saudi Arabia as a country where no political reform is taking place. Power is still firmly controlled and exercised within the labyrinthine confines of the royal family and the religious establishment, independent political and even civil organizations are nonexistent, and space for free political activities or even personal lifestyle choices is exceedingly limited. Yet Saudi Arabia should not be dismissed as an example of complete stagnation: Because the society has been so closely controlled, even small changes become significant, and Amr Hamzawy's analysis shows that many small changes are taking place.

Paradoxically, Jordan and Syria, studied by Julia Choucair-Vizoso and Ellen Lust-Okar, respectively, are in many ways politically more stagnant, although more open socially. They are neither moving toward greater openness and reform nor closing down the political space drastically. Rather, they appear to be drifting politically. Stagnation in both cases is explained not just by domestic factors but by the regional context as well.

Algeria, Lebanon, and Palestine have all experienced political ferment as well as violent turmoil. All three cases are extremely complex, and as a result they are often misrepresented. Algeria could certainly be analyzed, like many other countries, in terms of the relationship between government and opposition parties, the changing role of institutions, and the dynamics of political participation. But Hugh Roberts shows that the real story in Algeria is the struggle between military and civilian elites, which has resulted in greater power for civilian elites but not in a broadening of political participation. Julia Choucair-Vizoso shows that two parallel processes are unfolding in Lebanon as well. One is a battle for political reform—where issues such as reform of the electoral law and economic restructuring dominate—and the other is the continuation of the old strife among different confessional groups. The weight of the different issues is in constant flux, with the strife among confessional groups and their foreign allies most prominent in 2007. Similarly, in Palestine, a relatively successful push to set up viable political institutions to control the territories and eventually a Palestinian state was ultimately defeated by fighting between Hamas and Fatah, each backed by its respective foreign allies. Reforms were remarkably successful, Nathan Brown shows, but in the end the process came to naught, destroyed by fighting between Hamas and Fatah.

Understanding the peculiarities of each country, the nature of their political players, and the processes through which they try to exert their influence is thus the first step toward evaluating the significance of the political changes taking place in the Arab world.

Taken together, the ten case studies also offer broader lessons that challenge facile assumptions about the process of democratic transformation and the role that outsiders can play in promoting them.

Notes

1. United Nations Development Program, *Arab Human Development Report 2002: Creating Opportunities for Future Generations* (New York: Oxford University Press, 2003).

2. Robert Dahl, *Polyarchy: Participation and Opposition* (New Haven, CT: Yale University Press, 1972).

THE UPS AND DOWNS OF POLITICAL REFORM IN EGYPT

Michele Dunne and Amr Hamzawy

The political opening in Egypt that began in 2004, but then slipped into reverse in 2006, has been unlike any seen in the country in a half century. So far it has resulted in Egypt holding its first-ever presidential election, conducting parliamentary elections that were significantly fairer and more transparent than in the past, and making broad revisions to its constitution. Political dissidents swept away most of the taboos on criticizing the regime, and the Muslim Brotherhood now commands the largest share any single opposition group has held in parliament since the Free Officers' coup in 1952. Yet new constitutional amendments make it almost impossible for the Brotherhood to form a legal political party and enshrine in the constitutional provisions of Egypt's emergency law that set aside basic human rights and political liberties. Is Egypt experiencing the typically uneven progress of a country edging toward democratization, or did it merely undergo a brief liberal episode that will not fundamentally change the way political power is exercised?

Egypt's history of start-and-stop liberalization and the mixed results of top-down political reform steps so far give ample reason for skepticism. But Egypt is in the throes of a leadership transition that offers the possibility of greater openness to change. There are also longer-term implications of recent developments—for example, expected civilianization of the presidency and legitimization of monitoring of government performance by civil society—that contain the seeds of broader change. Whether they bear fruit depends in part on external actors, especially the United States, which can choose to either direct the Egyptian regime's attention repeatedly to internal calls for change or support the regime in ignoring or responding minimally to such calls.

Political Reform Until 2000

Compared with other Arab countries, Egypt has a lengthy history of political participation, albeit one marked by episodes of expansion and contraction in liberties. Egypt's nineteenth-century rulers established a number of different consultative assemblies whose members were appointed or, in some cases, elected indirectly. They also founded a judiciary and adopted a corpus of laws drawing on both Islamic and European legal traditions. Egypt's 1882 constitution provided for an elected parliament with legislative powers, but British occupation short-circuited that process and the country did not have its first elected assembly in place until 1924. Although Egypt gained its nominal independence in 1922, British forces and advisers remained for another thirty years. During this period a three-way struggle among the king, the British, and a parliament dominated by the liberal Wafd Party made for a chaotic political scene. King Fuad dissolved the parliament numerous times and abrogated the relatively liberal 1923 constitution in 1930, but public demands forced his successor, Faruq, to restore it unchanged in 1936. Tensions rose with the increased British military presence in Egypt during World War II, leading to a series of rigged elections and a rapid succession of cabinets from 1936 to 1952.

In 1952 a group of young officers carried out a bloodless coup, overturning the semiconstitutional monarchy and eventually ousting British forces. The Free Officers also abrogated the 1923 constitution and abolished all political parties. New constitutions in 1956 and 1964 provided for a measure of political participation, but Egypt was effectively a single-party system, in which dissent was repressed harshly, until the death of President Gamal Abdel Nasser in 1970. Anwar al-Sadat brought about partial economic and political liberalization and allowed the emergence of a few tame opposition parties in the 1970s while also quietly encouraging the formation of Islamist groups as a counterbalance to then-popular leftist forces. Furthermore, Sadat tolerated the resurfacing of the Muslim Brotherhood (which played an active role in politics in the 1930s and 1940s but had been declared illegal by Nasser in 1954), but did not alter its illegal status. Opposition to al-Sadat grew increasingly vociferous from 1977 onward due to controversial economic reform steps as well as his initiative to make peace with Israel. He responded with repressive measures such as Law 95 of 1980, known as the Law of Shame, which criminalized many forms of expression. In September 1981 he arrested over a thousand of his critics from all parts of the political spectrum—a step often seen as one of the factors leading to his assassination by an Islamist military officer that October.

Upon Sadat's assassination President Hosni Mubarak released Sadat's critics but also renewed the state of emergency under which Egypt had been ruled on and off since the 1950s, suspending many of the safeguards for civil liberties and human rights provided in the 1971 constitution. Political party life during the 1980s was reasonably lively, with the reemergence of the Wafd Party and active election participation of the Muslim Brotherhood through alliances with various legal parties. Elections in 1984 and 1987 produced parliaments with opposition representation of about 20 percent. A 1990 court-mandated switch from an electoral system based on proportional representation to an individual district system, however, unseated the 1987 parliament and hurt opposition parties' chances in subsequent elections.

The 1990s saw the rise of increasingly assertive Islamist opponents to the regime, including two extremist groups, al-Jamaa al-Islamiyya and al-Jihad, that carried out a series of violent attacks on government officials, secular intellectuals, foreign tourists, and Christians. Partly in an effort to keep Islamists in check, Mubarak took steps during this period that hurt the ability of all Egyptians to express themselves politically in either formal political institutions or more informal venues.[1] The 1993 Syndicates Law, 1995 Press Law, and 1999 Nongovernmental Associations Law curtailed freedoms of association and expression by imposing new governmental regulations and harsh penalties for violations. The security services used their vast authorities under the state of emergency to limit the activities of opposition parties and to subject the Muslim Brotherhood to systematic pressures. By the late 1990s not only had parliamentary politics become stagnant and virtually irrelevant to the life of the country, but alternative avenues for political expression were severely hampered as well.

Sources of Change

Just as it seemed that political life was moribund in the late 1990s, a series of internal and external developments began to alter the context within which the Egyptian political game was played. As President Mubarak began his fourth six-year term in 1999, he promised to uphold a Supreme Constitutional Court ruling calling for judicial supervision of elections. Mubarak pledged at that time to hold free and fair parliamentary elections in 2000, implicitly acknowledging that previous elections were flawed. At the same time, speculation among Egyptians about presidential succession was rising. Mubarak was then aged 71 and his younger son Gamal, a banker by profession, was taking an increasingly active role in politics as a spokesman for business interests and youth, first as a nonpartisan activist and later as a member of the ruling National Democratic Party (NDP).

The 2000 parliamentary elections—the first to be supervised by judges—were by most accounts somewhat cleaner and more credible than the 1990 or 1995 elections, which were characterized by widespread fraud and violence. After boycotting the previous elections, the Muslim Brotherhood and opposition parties participated in 2000, giving the elections a more competitive appearance. Widespread arrests of Brotherhood candidates and campaign workers, however, as well as intimidation of voters outside polling stations, marred the elections. Nonetheless, the NDP still suffered a major humiliation at the hands of independent candidates, who won more than half of the 444 seats of the People's Assembly (lower house of the Egyptian parliament) compared with NDP's 38 percent. Ultimately, however, most of the independents—former NDP members passed over for election nomination—later rejoined the NDP bloc, providing the ruling party with a solid 87 percent majority in the assembly.

As the domestic political scene began to change, dramatic events also altered the international and regional context. The 2001 terrorist attacks in the United States; subsequent U.S. invasions of Afghanistan and Iraq in 2002 and 2003; reasonably free elections in Palestine, Iraq, and Lebanon in spite of continued political turmoil; and the U.S. adoption of democratization as a strategic goal for the Arab world all had important repercussions. Proliferating information outlets magnified the impact of these events, which were beamed live and uncensored into Egyptian homes and coffee shops by Arabic language satellite channels and debated in myriad newspapers and blogs.

Modernization of the Ruling Party

The NDP's embarrassingly poor performance in 2000 gave Gamal Mubarak an opening to propose an overhaul aimed at making the NDP look and function more like a modern political party rather than an engine for recruiting support for the regime in exchange for government patronage. Drawing largely on the model of the British Labour Party, Gamal Mubarak designed and led a new Policy Secretariat that began to produce policy papers on a wide range of economic, political, and foreign affairs topics. He recruited a circle of young businesspeople and technocrats, some of whom were later placed in cabinet or party leadership positions. The Policy Secretariat fashioned a pro-reform platform and injected an element of pluralism in the NDP, which began to debate economic and political reform measures in an open manner.

By 2004 Gamal Mubarak's imprint on the NDP was apparent, with the appointment of a cabinet full of his protégés (among them Prime Minister Ahmed Nazif) in July and the holding of a media-friendly party conference in September showcasing the NDP's new image—under the slogan "Citizens' Rights First." Hosni Mubarak's presidential campaign for a fifth term in summer 2005—which featured Western-style stumping, clear promises for significant reform steps, and an attempt to show that the party was not using government resources in the campaign—documented the touch of Gamal and his circle. NDP parliamentary candidates also made an attempt to run more vibrant than usual campaigns in fall 2005 and to show some uniformity in terms of electoral programs and slogans.

Gamal Mubarak's overhaul of the NDP, however, did not substantially change the party's role in Egyptian politics. Its modern image aside, the NDP remained primarily a tool for recruiting support for the regime and continued to depend on the government in securing its representation in the parliament. The reform platform of the Policy Secretariat generated mixed results. In the economic realm, the cabinet of Prime Minister Ahmed Nazif implemented a series of liberalizing measures that had a revitalizing impact on the economy. Politically, however, introduced reforms were either counterproductive or did not help to sustain and deepen the political opening that emerged in 2004.

The shortcomings of the NDP modernization became apparent in the 2005 parliamentary elections, in which the revamped party (in reality, still a blend of old and new guards as well as of different approaches to party politics) fared no better than in 2000. NDP candidates won only 34 percent of races outright and, once again, it was only by reintegrating large numbers of prodigal sons that the party was able to secure its desired two-thirds majority. Moreover, the opposition representatives elected in 2005—28 percent of the People's Assembly—came overwhelmingly from the Muslim Brotherhood, the primary political adversary of the regime, rather than from the secular parties with whom the NDP was accustomed to dealing.

The 2005 election results shocked the NDP. Yet instead of pushing for a further internal shakeup or even a rupture after the elections, the Policy Secretariat seemed unable to generate new modernizing impulses and gradually backslid on the political reform platform it promoted in 2004 and 2005. In 2006 the NDP used its majority in the People's Assembly to postpone the municipal elections for two years (originally scheduled for 2006) and to renew the state of emergency for an additional two years. In 2007 the NDP's majority endorsed wide-ranging amendments of the 1971 constitution, many of which were undemocratically spirited. Furthermore, the 2005 elections brought back the security services as a major player in the political game after a brief period of holding back. Indeed, the regime relied on security brutality against voters to salvage the elections for the NDP. In the immediate aftermath of the elections the security establishment was given a free hand to keep the opposition in check, especially the emboldened Muslim Brotherhood. It also interfered increasingly in the inner workings of the NDP, dictating, for example, some of the most controversial constitutional amendments approved in 2007.

The Opposition Awakens

In 2004 and 2005, the changed political environment motivated the emergence of new factions inside opposition groups and the creation of completely new movements that challenged existing parties to redefine their goals and strategies. As in the NDP, to some extent this development was generational. Throughout the 1970s and 1980s, a generation of activists was maturing inside organizations ranging from the Muslim Brotherhood to leftist and Nasserist groups through participation in student, professional syndicate, and municipal politics. In the Muslim Brotherhood, for example, activists in their 30s to 50s began to press during the 1990s for greater Brotherhood efforts to form a political party and to contest parliamentary elections more openly. Several Brothers led by Abul Ela Madi broke with the Brotherhood to attempt to form the Center (Wasat) Party, which struggled from 1996 onward to attain licensing as a party. Other leaders of the same generation, such as Abdel Monem Abul Fottouh and Essam al-Eryan, remained within the Brotherhood but pushed for clearer articulation of the movement's political platform and greater democracy within the Brotherhood's essentially patriarchal structure, particularly after the deaths of two Brotherhood supreme guides in 2002 and 2004.

Although the new guide chosen was septuagenarian Mahdi Akef, his two deputies—Muhammad Habib and Khayrat al-Shatir—were prominent members of the younger generation. In March 2004 Akef openly embraced many of the younger generation's ideas in a new political program (Reform Initiative of the Muslim Brotherhood) that expressed clearer support for principles of democratic government than the Brotherhood had done in the past.[2] In 2005, after being barred de facto from running a candidate in Egypt's first multicandidate presidential elections, the Brotherhood's open participation in the parliamentary elections was tolerated by the regime. Under the movement's banner and using its slogan "Islam is the solution," the Brothers contested one-third of the 444 seats of the People's Assembly, winning an unprecedented eighty-eight seats (20 percent of the assembly). The Brotherhood's electoral platform called for the gradual implementation of political reforms as the only viable strategy to democratize Egypt and endorsed peaceful participation in legal politics as the movement's strategic choice.

The Muslim Brotherhood was not alone in being pushed by a younger generation to begin challenging the political order more openly. The secular opposition spectrum went through a similar process. Parliamentarian Hamdeen Sabahi left the Nasserist Party to form the Karama (Dignity) Party, which as of summer 2007 was still engaged in an unsuccessful struggle for licensing. Ayman Nour, an assertive young parliamentarian who was ousted from the Wafd Party after a power struggle in 2001, founded the liberal secular Ghad (Tomorrow) Party, which was licensed in 2004 after a lengthy court fight. But Nour's own battles with the regime were just beginning as he and his party became the target of an apparent campaign to discredit a nascent rival. Charged with forging signatures on petitions to found the party, Nour nonetheless ran in the 2005 presidential election and won more than twice as many votes (nearly 8 percent of the total) as Wafd leader Noman Gomaa. In November of the same year, however, Nour lost his parliamentary seat to a former security officer put up by the NDP and in December Nour was convicted of forgery in a highly politicized trial and sentenced to five years in prison. The Ghad Party also began to splinter under the pressure.

Another significant example for the emergence of new opposition parties since 2004 was the establishment of the Democratic Front. In 2006 Osama al-Ghazali Harb, a member of the Shura Council (the upper house of the Egyptian parliament) and a well-known member of the NDP's Policy Secretariat, resigned from the ruling party, frustrated over the slow pace of political reform and the growing dominance of the security services. Attracting a group of elite liberal politicians, young business leaders, and human rights activists, Harb announced a party platform based on the principles of market economy and liberal democracy. The Democratic Front attained licensing in May 2007.

Despite its growing diversity since 2004, Egypt's secular opposition spectrum remained weak. Notwithstanding frequent promises by government officials, legal and political restrictions imposed on the activities of leftist and liberal parties were not lifted or reduced. Yet unlike the more severely repressed Muslim Brotherhood, these parties also contributed to their own weakness. They failed in building up their organizations, reaching out to potential constituencies, and devising convincing electoral platforms. In contrast to the Brotherhood's eighty-eight seats in the 2005 parliamentary elections, all secular parties won a combined eleven seats. The dismal performance in 2005 seemed at first to unleash a total rethinking of approaches and alliances within the secular opposition spectrum. However, throughout 2006 and most of 2007 this process stopped short of leading to new strategies.

In addition to leftist and liberal parties, protest movements and pro-reform networks emerged that moved beyond the limitations of party politics. Such movements appeared to spring forth suddenly in late 2004 and 2005 but actually had their roots in demonstrations organized from 2001 through 2004 to protest regional issues (for example, the Israel–Palestine conflict and the U.S.-led invasion of Iraq) and to criticize Egyptian policy and President Mubarak.

The most dynamic protest movement to emerge during this period was the Egyptian Movement for Change, a loosely structured network of leftists, Nasserists, liberals, and a few Islamists—many of them younger generation activists rather than party leaders—who united in fall 2004 around the idea of pushing for more substantial democratic reforms than the NDP was willing to initiate. The movement held its first demonstration in December 2004 and quickly became known by the one-word slogan the silent demonstrators wore pasted over their mouths: "Kifaya" or "Enough." Immediately recognized as signifying opposition to the continued rule of Mubarak as well as to regime's efforts to position his son Gamal to become the successor, the slogan violated a long-held taboo against criticism of the president. Kifaya went on in 2005 to hold regular protests that gradually increased from several dozen to several hundred participants, ignoring the need to request police permits for such gatherings under the state of emergency. By the end of 2005, however, Kifaya had lost its effectiveness. It failed to expand its pro-reform platform beyond opposition to President Mubarak, who had been reelected for a fifth term, and the rise of Gamal, who had become an increasingly influential figure in Egyptian politics. Existing opposition parties, which Kifaya attempted to inspire to join forces against the regime, remained unable to coordinate effectively among themselves. The public gradually stopped paying attention to the movement's activities and demonstrations dwindled. By 2007, amid an intimidation campaign by the security services, Kifaya had degenerated to an arena of frivolous ideological conflicts between competing factions.

Minor Fissures Within the Establishment

Just as striking as the reactivation of political opposition forces in 2004 and 2005 was the pro-reform activism by members of the judiciary and, to a lesser extent, by members of the ruling party. The Egyptian Judges Club, a largely social body that lobbied episodically on behalf of judicial independence, passed a resolution in May 2005 threatening that it would not supervise upcoming presidential and parliamentary elections unless the government approved a new law strengthening judicial independence and giving judges greater authority over elections. The threat was a potent one because the government could not hold elections without judicial supervision. The minister of justice, an executive branch appointee, responded at first with efforts to compromise with the club on a new draft judiciary law to be sent to parliament in 2006 and agreed to give judges greater authority in supervising elections.

The judges' bold stroke—loudly cheered by opposition movements and civil society—made the government appear off balance and vulnerable. It was a lesson to all that leverage existed even within an authoritarian regime if players were not afraid to use it. However, once the presidential and parliamentary elections were held, the government turned the tide against the judges, employing its traditional mix of punishment and patronage to divide and buy off judges. By the end of 2006, the government succeeded in breaking the resistance of the judges and subjected some of the leaders of the Judges Club to disciplinary measures. Yet the most serious blow to the judges came with the constitutional amendments in 2007. The previous requirement that judges oversee elections was watered down, with the stipulation that an electoral commission be established whose membership includes but is not limited to current and former members of judicial bodies.

Similar to the judiciary, several liberal members of the NDP brought in as part of the modernizing effort spearheaded by Gamal Mubarak, pushed actively in 2004 and 2005 for more assertive reform measures. Apart from Osama al-Ghazali Harb, who broke ranks with the party and resigned to establish the Democratic Front, other members made their dissatisfaction with the modest scope of NDP reform measures known in media interviews. As the ruling party started to backslide on its modest reforms after the 2005 parliamentary elections, however, liberal voices became increasingly marginal. Only two members of the NDP's parliamentary bloc voted against the constitutional amendments approved in 2007. They were accused of disloyalty and expelled from the bloc.

Evaluating Recent Reform Measures

Faced with growing criticism and the need to arrange a smooth leadership succession, President Mubarak and the NDP undertook a flurry of political reform measures during 2005–2007. Most important were a series of constitutional amendments that contained some positive steps but, on balance, took away more liberties than they provided. The first set of reforms in 2005 constituted a limited liberalization of the political system, albeit one that safeguarded NDP control for the foreseeable future. The second set of reforms—including amendments to thirty-four articles of the constitution, passed rapidly in early 2007 over strong objections from the opposition and civil society groups—made clear that the regime would brook no real competition or dissent.[3] The reforms also created several new bodies including an electoral commission and a human rights commission, but it was unclear how independent or powerful they would be.

Amendments and Laws on Political Rights

Between 2005 and 2007, the Egyptian parliament passed a large number of amendments to the constitution and related laws regarding elections for the presidency and for parliament, powers of the various branches of government, and the formation and regulation of political parties (see the appendix for a complete list). These changes contained important positive aspects, such as introducing direct popular election of the president and increasing parliamentary oversight of the executive branch. The amendments, however, also set rules that sharply limited the competition opposition forces—particularly Islamists—can offer in elections, and cast doubt on how fairly elections will be run.

PRESIDENTIAL ELECTION. Direct popular election of the president is the most potentially significant change in the political system introduced by the new legislation, although the parameters established for candidate eligibility effectively hamper competition under current circumstances. Amended Article 76 and the Presidential Election Law give each licensed party the right to put a candidate on the ballot but subject that right to stiff conditions. The amendment passed in 2005 allowed only parties holding at least 5 percent of seats in both the People's Assembly and Shura Council to get on the ballot, a condition no group could meet except for the Muslim Brotherhood, which is not expected to be allowed to register a party any time soon. In 2007 Article 76 was amended again, this time to lower the requirement to 3 percent of seats and to stipulate that any party with at least a single elected deputy may nominate a candidate in elections that take place until the year 2017. But a party may only nominate a candidate that has been on its executive committee for at least a year, thereby effectively preventing parties from forming tactical coalitions shortly before elections.

For political movements that have been denied registration as parties, notably the Muslim Brotherhood, it is even more difficult to contest presidential elections. To get on the ballot, an independent candidate must gather endorsements from 250 elected central and local government officials, including 14 percent of members of the upper and lower houses of parliament. The Brotherhood now holds enough seats in the lower house of parliament, but it does not yet have the required members in the upper house and local councils. The Brotherhood contested the Shura Council elections in June 2007 but did not win a single seat.

Also noteworthy is that Article 77 of the constitution, which allows the president an unlimited number of six-year terms, was left untouched despite repeated calls for introducing term limits from a broad spectrum of opposition and civil society activists.

ELECTORAL COMMISSION. The amendment of Article 88, which removed the constitutional requirement for full judicial supervision of elections in favor of creating an electoral commission, was among the controversial reforms of 2007. Judicial supervision of polling as well as vote counting, first implemented in 2000, had improved the fairness and transparency of elections, particularly in 2005. Ruling party officials argued that such detailed supervision was logistically awkward (which was true), and that Egypt needed to move beyond such requirements to create an independent electoral commission. Critics charged that the change was more properly understood as a punishment for Egyptian judges, who had acted as whistleblowers in the 2005 elections and also had emerged as the most active constituency for political reform within the ruling establishment. In addition, opposition and civil society activists doubted that the new electoral commission would be truly independent and empowered, especially in view of the unimpressive performance of the commissions created in 2005 to supervise the referendum on the amendment of Article 76 and the presidential elections.

Amended Article 88 and the revised Law on Political Rights establish an electoral commission with eleven members: four sitting judges, three retired judges, and four nonpartisan public figures. The People's Assembly will appoint four of the commissioners, the Shura Council three, and judicial bodies the other four. The commission is charged with delineating electoral districts, supervising voter lists (a major problem in Egyptian elections, as most are outdated), supervising voting and counting, announcing election results, and establishing procedures for electoral monitoring by civil society groups. While the law in itself is a step forward in systematizing electoral supervision, there is reason to doubt whether the Egyptian government is committed to building a commission strong and independent enough to resist pressures from the ministry of interior and the ruling party, both of which have committed extensive electoral violations in past elections.

POLITICAL PARTIES. The weakness of political parties and the lack of meaningful competition are among the main impediments to democratization in Egypt, where the political scene has long been dominated by a former single party transformed into a hegemonic party.[4] The NDP maintains tight control of licensing, generally denying recognition to new parties that might offer competition while licensing a few that enjoy limited popular support. From the mid-1990s onward, several parties with potential constituencies— the Ghad, Wasat, and Karama Parties—petitioned for recognition. All met with rejection from the Political Parties Committee of the Shura Council. A court order forced the committee to license the Ghad Party in late 2004. Although the committee rejected in January 2007 the petitions of twelve parties—among them were the Wasat and Karama Parties, it licensed in an unexpected move the Democratic Front in May 2007. However, it was unclear whether the elite-based Democratic Front would be able to garner significant popular support.

The irony of the situation in Egypt is that the movement that functions most effectively as an opposition party—the Muslim Brotherhood—faces a legal situation that makes it almost impossible for it to form a party. A provision against the creation of a political party based on religion already existed in the Political Parties Law, but in 2007 the parliament added an expanded ban to the constitution itself: Article 5 forbids "any political activity or any political party within any religious frame of reference or on any religious basis." Moreover, the parliament amended Article 62 of the constitution to permit a return to a predominately party list system of parliamentary elections, instead of the individual district system instituted in 1990, which independent candidates from the Brotherhood had used to excellent effect.

In addition, barring independent candidates from contesting all but a small number of parliamentary seats would help the NDP restore its own party discipline; renegade NDP members running as independents—and winning—emerged as a major phenomenon in 2000 and 2005 elections.

PRESIDENTIAL AND PARLIAMENTARY POWERS. The central goal of a broad spectrum of opposition and civil society activists in Egypt has been to diminish the overwhelming power of the president and to distribute more power to the legislative and judicial branches of government, and in 2005–2007 the regime made some gestures in this direction. In addition to instituting presidential elections, constitutional amendments modestly expanded the powers of the parliament (heretofore largely a rubber stamp for executive branch initiatives). Article 115 gave the parliament more meaningful budget oversight, specifying that it would vote article by article and be given adequate time for examination. Article 127 gave parliament a clear procedure for voting no confidence in the prime minister (appointed by the president) without the need for a popular referendum. Several articles gave the prime minister slightly more power vis-à-vis the president.

The NDP attached a heavy price, however, to these concessions. Amended Article 136 gave the president the ability to dissolve parliament and removed a previous requirement that such a decision be put to a popular vote. It specified that new parliamentary elections would have to be held within 60 days of dissolution.

Steps on Civil Liberties and Human Rights

The most significant increase of executive power in the constitutional amendments of 2007 was not in the area of political rights, however, but rather human and civil rights. Among the most persistent criticisms of the Egyptian government by domestic and international observers was that Egypt had been ruled under a state of emergency continuously since the assassination of President Sadat in 1981. As part of his 2005 presidential campaign, Mubarak promised to lift the state of emergency and to replace it with a more limited antiterrorism law. He then renewed the state of emergency for an additional two years in spring 2006, citing the need for more time to compile the law and a related amendment to the constitution.

When the constitutional amendments were unveiled in early 2007, amended Article 179 related to antiterrorism drew a loud outcry from Egyptian judges, civil society activists, opposition politicians, and international observers. In several broad strokes, the amended article constitutionalized the very procedures from the emergency laws that had drawn objections. Article 179 gave the president the authority to remand civilians to trial in military courts in cases related to terrorism and allowed the state to suspend human rights protections in other parts of the constitution as it deemed necessary to combat terrorism. Of all the amendments and new laws passed between 2005 and 2007, this was undoubtedly the most potentially damaging, especially in view of the fact that Egyptian authorities had long since established the practice of using emergency courts and other tools supposedly reserved for terrorism cases against political opponents.

The one positive step taken by the government regarding civil and human rights was the 2003 establishment of a National Council for Human Rights.

Populated by individuals with credentials in the field of human rights, the council has produced credible annual reports and made serious recommendations to the government, although it has generally remained quiet when its recommendations went unheeded. The council also has facilitated communication between the government and nongovernmental organizations (NGOs) active in supporting human and civil rights and has worked to legitimate the work of such NGOs. For example, the council cooperated with a coalition of twenty-two NGOs monitoring the 2005 parliamentary elections and publicly asked the government to permit and facilitate such monitoring.

Silver Linings

Despite the troubling, essentially undemocratic nature of many of the reforms passed in 2005–2007, they did plant some seeds that might yet bear fruit in terms of further reform. Two changes that fall under this category are the civilianization of the presidency and the legitimization of civil society monitoring of government performance.

According to the new laws, when the next presidential election comes—in 2011 or before if President Mubarak leaves office—the NDP must nominate a candidate who has been in the party's senior leadership for at least a year. Such a process effectively excludes active military or security officers, who are barred from party membership, from being presidential contenders. Even if Mubarak chooses a vice president, who would have been the heir apparent before the constitutional amendment, that person cannot become the NDP candidate unless he also holds a senior party office. Thus the process of presidential succession has changed fundamentally, increasing the likelihood that after Mubarak, Egyptians will have their first civilian leader since 1952. The immediate effect of the change is to facilitate the succession of Gamal Mubarak, a key member of what is now a small circle of potential nominees, but if it remains in place it may have longer term positive effects by distancing the military from politics and diminishing the pharaonic aura around the presidency.

The creation of semigovernmental institutions such as the National Council on Human Rights and the electoral commission also has had the effect, perhaps unintended, of legitimizing political activism by civil society groups. The National Council on Human Rights played a key role in persuading the government to sanction the presence of thousands of poll monitors trained and organized by NGOs. The monitoring not only greatly increased the public profile of such organizations but also constituted indirect acknowledgment by the government that such groups have a legitimate role to play in political affairs. Although such organizations remain relatively small and weak due to their inability so far to cultivate mass membership and support, they have been greatly emboldened by the experience of election monitoring. In the longer term, they are likely to develop into more effective advocates of political reform than they have been until now.

Looking Ahead: Sources of Change and Reform Priorities

For Egypt to move toward democracy, the ruling establishment would have to share a great deal more power and open the system up to much more competition than it has to date. It would require significant further changes to the laws related to political and civic freedoms as well as the balance of powers among the executive, legislative, and judicial branches. Changes in law are important, as Egypt's political system and culture are legalistic in nature. Even authoritarian rulers in Egypt have tended to revise laws or find legalistic ways to circumvent them (for example, the state of emergency) rather than to ignore or jettison them altogether. The quality of the changes, especially the extent to which they level the playing field among political forces, would also be important. The ruling party has shown itself to be quite capable of authoring and passing constitutional amendments and new laws that are undemocratically spirited and stack the deck heavily in the NDP's favor.

Significant consensus has emerged after the constitutional amendments of 2007 among pro-reform activists from all parts of the political spectrum about the steps needed in the coming years. Limiting presidential power and setting term limits for the presidency top the list. Another strong theme is the need to ensure independent electoral supervision in the new constitutional environment. Also, the question of how to limit the deterioration in human rights protections resulting from the amendment of Article 179 and a new antiterrorism law expected to be issued in the parliamentary session 2007–2008.

Changes in law alone, however, will not be sufficient if Egypt is to move toward a sustainable process of democratization. Just as the impact of the continued confrontation between the regime and the Muslim Brotherhood needs to be addressed, the weakness of secular opposition groups and the resulting absence of a viable political center require great attention. Also, the pervasive influence of the security services in Egyptian life—and the fact that the regime often uses the security establishment and the courts against political rivals—is an important extralegal factor that cannot be ignored. Egypt would also need to move toward civilian oversight of the military, which so far remains accountable only to the president.

Limiting Presidential Power

Amending Article 76 of the constitution made the Egyptian president subject to popular elections for the first time, but other elements of the constitution—as well as political custom—still leave the president with a great deal of power and little accountability. Article 77, for example, sets the presidential term at six years but defines no term limits. Despite repeated calls from opposition groups for amending Article 77 to shorten the presidential term to four years and to establish a limit of two consecutive terms, the government refused to touch it in the two rounds of constitutional amendments in 2005 and 2007.

Just as important as setting term limits for the presidency would be a more balanced distribution of power in the political system. The constitutional amendments of 2007 empowered the legislature by giving it more budgetary oversight. They expanded the role of the prime minister by passing to his office the powers of the vice president if there is none (since he became president in 1981, Mubarak has not appointed a vice president). The most significant of these powers are those related to succession in case the office of the presidency is not occupied and in case the president cannot perform his duties. The amendments also stipulated that the prime minister must approve or be consulted with regard to the president's exercise of his vast executive and quasilegislative authorities. The problem, however, is that amendments did not fundamentally alter the distribution of power in Egypt. The president continued to enjoy sole authority over the appointment and dismissal of the prime minister and was given the right to dissolve parliament without a referendum.

Some opposition groups, notably the Muslim Brotherhood, have called for a parliamentary system with a much weaker presidency, one that would be principally symbolic and nonpartisan, as well as detached from executive authority. Given the long-established tradition of powerful presidents in Egypt, such a course would be possible only if there is a more radical shake-up of the system than currently seems likely.

Independent Electoral Supervision

The amendment replacing the constitutional requirement for comprehensive judicial supervision of elections with authorization for an independent electoral commission created a problem but also an opportunity for reform in Egypt. On one hand, judicial supervision of elections in 2000 and 2005 had markedly increased the fairness and transparency of the process, and its diminution is reason for strong concern. On the other hand, the Egyptian government's professed desire to abide by internationally recognized best practices by creating an independent electoral commission is an opening that opposition and civil society groups are poised to seize. Ensuring the organizational and financial independence of the electoral commission, as well as the strength and independence of the individual commissioners, will be key to avoid a situation in which the commission becomes a marionette of the executive.

Antiterrorism Law and Civil Liberties

The amended Article 179 and the new antiterrorism law threaten to result in significant deterioration in human rights protections. Many judges and legal scholars are saying that the constitution should be re-amended to restore human rights protections. Others are suggesting that for now it will be more practical to press the government to endorse the narrowest feasible interpretation of terrorism crimes to be covered under the new law. Considering the track record of the Egyptian regime, which has long claimed that only terrorism and drug crimes were prosecuted under the emergency laws but in fact systematically used them to tackle political and religious cases, this less ambitious approach might prove highly relevant in the short term.

In addition to the antiterrorism law, a series of deliberalizing laws passed in the 1990s would need significant revision to restore damaged civil liberties. As a general rule, the Egyptian government has tended to overregulate nongovernmental entities such as professional and civil society associations partly because they emerged in the 1980s and 1990s as alternate forums for political activity by opposition groups, including the Muslim Brotherhood. The 1993 Syndicates Law would need amendment to remove provisions requiring unrealistically high quorums for elections. Provisions in the 1995 Press Law allowing incarceration of journalists convicted of libel should be removed. The 2002 NGO law would need thorough revision to lift excessively intrusive licensing and regulatory powers of the ministry of social affairs, as well as the minister's ability to dissolve any NGO by decree. A transparent process, in which interested parties in civil society have the opportunity for real input into new legislation, would be critical to a meaningful revision of such laws.

Opposition Parties and Movements

The relative strength that the Muslim Brotherhood demonstrated versus political parties, including the NDP, in the 2005 parliamentary elections suggests that steps to rectify a distorted political landscape are sorely needed. Currently, politics are polarized between a ruling party that employs a combination of patronage and intimidation to organize support and a Muslim Brotherhood that is barred by law from becoming a party. In between are a collection of licensed leftist and liberal parties that are mostly stagnant or harassed by the regime and a few newer groups that have been denied licensing so far.

Empowering secular opposition is therefore crucial to broaden the political spectrum and move political competition beyond the current NDP–Brotherhood polarization. The expected return to a predominately party list system of parliamentary elections could significantly strengthen the role of parties. However, as long as the government continues to impose legal and political restrictions to prevent the licensing of new secular parties and hinder the activities of existing ones the positive impacts of the new electoral system are bound to remain negligible. Specifically, the Political Parties Law that was amended in 2005 would require further changes to remove the ruling party's stranglehold and allow new parties to emerge more naturally.

Yet, secular parties and groups have also contributed to their own weaknesses. Even with all its limitations, Egypt's politics offers some space for action and chances to compete that they have not been capable of exploiting. Decaying structures and aging leadership have long undermined the efforts of some secular parties to reach out to constituencies, whereas others have systematically failed in capitalizing on the shortcomings of the NDP and the Muslim Brotherhood to garner popular support and get out convincing electoral messages. To become more viable, secular parties and groups need to undergo internal transformation as well.

The considerable gains of the Muslim Brotherhood in the 2005 parliamentary elections led the regime to stage a major crackdown on the movement. Throughout 2006 and most of 2007, the security services systematically arrested Brotherhood leaders and activists and detained some of them for long periods. Most significantly, in February 2007 President Mubarak used his powers under the state of emergency to transfer a group of forty-one detainees, among them the second deputy of the supreme guide and influential businessmen associated with the Brotherhood, to the military tribunal under allegations of money laundering and terrorism in addition to the usual charge of belonging to a banned organization. The regime also carefully designed the 2007 constitutional amendments to limit the power of the emboldened Brotherhood by enshrining the ban on religious-based political activity in the constitution and by permitting the return to a predominately party list electoral system to downscale its participation in parliamentary politics.

Notwithstanding the potential success of the current crackdown at taming the Muslim Brotherhood in the short term, the regime risks its own stability by slamming the political door in the face of a popular opposition movement that has grown increasingly committed to peaceful participation. The recent constitutional amendment declaring that not only can there be no political party based on religion, but no political activity drawing on any religious reference point removes any incentive for the Brotherhood to further moderate its positions. Disaffected members may find an outlet in militant activism against the government as they did in the 1980s and 1990s following similar blows. The political system would continue to be skewed unless some way is found for Islamists to be included legally and openly. Egypt can maintain the ban on overtly religious parties but needs to undergo a process akin to that which has taken place in Jordan, Morocco, Turkey, Yemen, and other countries that have found formulas for Islamist participation within their systems.

Role of the Security Services and the Military

The internal security services and the armed forces represent distinct challenges to the prospects for democratization in Egypt. Security services pose the more difficult near-term problem because they permeate and distort everyday life and political activity to an extent inconsistent with a democratic system. Egyptians are regularly required to inform security officers about political activities and discussions in which they have participated, leading to a climate of mutual suspicion. Security officers work with certain journalists to plant stories in the media, which are often directed at smearing the reputations of or creating divisions among opposition activists. The security services have also fanned the flames of differences inside opposition groups, contributing, for example, to a leadership crisis that brought down the Labor Party in 2000 and another inside the new Ghad Party in 2005. Furthermore, security services intimidate and abuse political prisoners to obtain information from them or punish them.

Especially after the 2005 elections and in the face of the continued weakness of the NDP, the role of police and intelligence services in managing the political scene has expanded dramatically. In today's Egyptian politics the security establishment dominates the executive. Its members are overrepresented in key government positions when compared to other groups that make up the ruling elite such as technocrats and business communities.

Security services and security courts are deniable weapons used selectively by senior Egyptian officials to punish and humiliate political rivals and deprive them of public support. If Egypt is to democratize, the role of the security services would have to be redefined as protecting the country and the state only from violent challenges such as those posed by terrorists rather than political challenges posed by nonviolent dissidents. Existing laws against torture also would need to be enforced in a serious way.

In contrast to the security forces, the armed forces have generally withdrawn from the political realm over the past twenty years, and the recent constitutional amendment makes another military president less likely. The last military leader with an independent political base was Field Marshal Abdel Halim Abu Ghazala, whom Mubarak removed from his position after a corruption scandal in 1989. Since then, senior military leaders have shown unwavering loyalty to Mubarak. They are likely to support any president legitimately chosen and are unlikely to take a position against further political reforms as they will not touch the military's extensive prerogatives in the near term. The armed forces represent a challenge to democratization, however, in that they belong directly to the president and are not subject to real parliamentary or judicial oversight. In the longer term, if Egypt is to democratize, the military and security forces would need to become subject to civilian authority through transparent budgets, parliamentary oversight, and a civilian president as commander-in-chief.

How Outsiders Can Support Reform

Although calls for change from within Egypt have strengthened in recent years, they are still weak and could be easily ignored or suppressed by the regime if they do not enjoy the support of major outside powers. The United States and European Union are important to Egypt in terms of military and economic assistance, strategic cooperation, and trade; the government, therefore, cannot afford to alienate them.

The single most important thing for the United States and Europe to do is to sustain an active interest in democratization in Egypt in the coming years. The United States started to do this in 2004–2005, but then backed off in 2006 when it became preoccupied with regional crises and concerned about Islamist electoral victories. Mubarak's last years in office, when he should be concerned about his legacy, and particularly the early years of his successor's term offer special opportunities that should not be squandered. Although U.S. and European interest in reform would have little effect if Egyptians themselves were not pressing the issue, the United States and Europe have played important roles in draw-ing the Egyptian government's attention to internal demands for reform. Support by the United States and Europe for these internal demands can influ-ence how quickly Mubarak follows up on his promises, how substantive his reform proposals are, and to what degree he accommodates opposing demands.

Yet Europe and the United States face difficult choices about how strongly and by which methods to encourage democratization, particularly as it has become clear that the Muslim Brotherhood is presently the only significant opposition group. On the one hand, if the United States and Europe press too aggressively for change, there is a real possibility of alienating the Egyptian government or even of forcing Egypt into a chaotic political opening in which illiberal or undemocratic forces, whether Islamists or perhaps from the mili-tary, might emerge triumphant. On the other hand, if Europe and the United States are too patient, Egyptian advocates of reform might well go down in defeat while the country settles in for many more years of autocratic rule, human rights abuses, and stagnation.

The United States and Europe should maintain active support for democ-ratization in Egypt despite the evident strength of Islamists and weakness of the secular opposition. For all their flaws, the 2005 parliamentary elections were a more authentic reflection of the state of political life in Egypt than pre-vious elections. Long-standing impediments to democratization—overwhelming voter apathy, the extreme weakness of political parties, the need to work out some legitimate political role for Islamists, the role of the security forces—are now acknowledged openly and can be addressed. The proper role for outside powers is not to impose or even suggest solutions to these problems but to promote the openness and provide resources that will enable Egyptians to address these problems themselves.

The nature of Islamist participation, for example, is a problem that does not lend itself to direct involvement by outsiders because of the widespread suspicion of U.S. and also European intentions. U.S. and other Western diplo-mats should be free to meet with elected members of parliament or other figures from the Muslim Brotherhood as is deemed useful to understand the movement's positions. At the same time, the principal role of foreign gov-ernments is not to negotiate with oppositionists but to deal with the Egyptian government. Thus, what the United States and Europe can and should do is press the Egyptian government to keep open the political space needed for productive dialogue between Islamists and secularists. Such a dialogue among Egyptians themselves is where solutions to the problem of Islamist inclusion in the political sphere can emerge.

If U.S. engagement with Egypt on democratization is to be effective, it needs two components: a strong connection to the issues Egyptian reformers are raising and integration into the overall U.S.–Egyptian bilateral relationship. It makes no sense for the United States to invent its own agenda for democratization in Egypt. Egyptians will easily see through occasional public statements or isolated programs on democracy that the United States jettisons the moment it has other interests to pursue. The issues the United States should pursue now are those identified above: limiting presidential power, promoting independent electoral supervision, safeguarding civil liberties and human rights against the background of the new antiterrorism law, empowering secular opposition, pushing the Egyptian regime to move beyond the head-on confrontation with Islamists, and introducing accountability and transparency as benchmarks with regard to the role of the security establishment.

Public Statements and Private Diplomacy

But how can the United States pursue those issues within the overall relationship with Egypt? In commenting publicly on political reform in Egypt, the United States and Europe would be wise to focus on bolstering the calls of Egyptian reformers for the development of a democratic system. Keeping comments relevant to the current debate but also general in nature—for example, commenting on the importance of the principle of judicial independence rather than on the contents of a draft law of the judiciary—shows that outside powers are in touch with what is going on while dampening claims of interference in internal affairs. In addition, it is important that senior U.S. and European officials object publicly to violence against or harassment of nonviolent dissidents; they must raise the cost of such methods to the Egyptian regime.

In constructing public statements, the United States and Europe will need to become increasingly sophisticated in distinguishing real from cosmetic reforms. Authoritarian and semiauthoritarian regimes are well known for taking steps that change the forms of political life but do not fundamentally alter the ways in which power is acquired and practiced; in fact, such reforms often effectively consolidate the ruling elite's hold on power. The United States found itself in such an awkward position in spring 2005, when senior U.S. officials at first praised Mubarak's initiative to open the presidency to elections as "bold" and then later found themselves on the wrong side of the issue as reformers criticized the actual constitutional amendment as anticompetitive and undemocratic. Although there is nothing wrong with commenting positively on government initiatives, such remarks should be calibrated carefully to reserve judgment until the initiative is translated into real steps and to contain clear expectations of further movement. If praise is unqualified, the message might be understood to mean that the government need go no further.

However important public statements may be, there is no substitute for direct, private engagement with Egyptian government officials, especially at the highest levels. As with public statements, the content of private messages should be relevant to current debates and should draw attention to the demands of Egyptians pressing for reform. While conversations between presidents and foreign ministers often remain general in nature, working-level officials should carry on the conversation with greater specificity and link the general goals with specific incentives related to assistance and other forms of cooperation, including trade.

Assistance, Cooperation, and Trade

Economic and military assistance, as well as trade relationships, are among the tools the United States and Europe can and should use to promote democratization in Egypt. As a general principle, the United States and Europe should make clear that the amount and types of assistance they are willing to provide will depend in part on Egypt's progress toward democracy. Specific decisions on conditioning assistance or trade benefits should be made on a rolling basis, depending on which reform measures are urgent and where donors have the most leverage. In most cases political conditionality should be kept private between the donor state and Egypt, as making it public can back the Egyptian government into a corner. In a few cases—when an important issue is at stake and there appears to be no chance of reaching an understanding with the Egyptian government—it may be productive to expose differences publicly to show Egyptians that the United States and Europe are standing up for democratic principles.

Between 2003 and 2006, the United States took several steps to increase its ability to use assistance programs as leverage for democratization. As part of the Middle East Partnership Initiative launched in 2002, the U.S. Department of State reviewed economic assistance to Egypt (approximately $600 million annually at that time) for effectiveness in promoting democracy. In 2004, Congress took on the issue as well, eventually passing an amendment to the Foreign Operations Appropriations bill that specified that the United States could give democracy assistance to NGOs without the approval of the Egyptian government. As a result, the United States changed its democracy assistance programs to focus more explicitly on political areas than it had previously done and began to choose at least some programs and partners without seeking approval from the Egyptian government. These were constructive changes and allowed the United States, as well as Europe, to promote transparency in the 2005 parliamentary elections by funding the training of thousands of monitors by civil society organizations.

In democracy assistance programs in Egypt, the United States (which has spent about $50 million annually on such programs in recent years) and Europe should maintain flexibility and keep goals to the short term for as long as the situation remains fluid and it is not yet clear whether Egypt is in a real transition. Areas that deserve immediate attention include general voter apathy and lack of political mobilization, political party weakness, outdated and incomplete voter lists, and the need to develop a competent, truly independent electoral commission. Potential programs might include large-scale civic education programs, training for political parties and groups in how to build and mobilize constituencies, further training for electoral monitoring and watchdog groups, and cooperation with the electoral commission. The United States and Europe often can support reformists most effectively not by providing funds but by pressing the Egyptian government to undertake policy changes that will open up the system to a greater degree.

Economic assistance to Egypt is likely to continue to decline over the coming years and thus will no longer be a potential tool for conditionality; soon all that will be left are democracy, education, and economic reform programs that the United States does not want to sacrifice. The larger target for potential conditionality is military assistance, and the U.S. Congress started down this avenue in June 2007 by withholding $200 million of a total $1.3 billion in military assistance until it could be certified that Egypt had made specified improvements in human rights and Gaza security. This move reflects understandable frustration in Congress about how to get a message through to the Egyptian government, but it remains to be seen whether Egyptians interpret it as a wake-up call or merely a signal that the military partnership with the United States is drawing to a close. There are also more constructive ways to leverage the close military relationship to help build support in the Egyptian military and civilian bureaucracy for political reform. Programs such as International Military Education and Training, currently funded at only $1.2 million annually, could be expanded to help expose senior and mid-level military officers to critical concepts such as civilian control of the military in democratic systems.

Trade is the most important dimension of Europe's relationship with Egypt and is becoming an increasingly important aspect of Egyptian–U.S. relations as well. Egypt and the United States have had the Trade and Investment Framework Agreement since 1999, and trade has increased significantly since the establishment of Qualifying Industrial Zones (incorporating Israeli inputs into Egyptian goods, which then enter the United States duty free) in 2004. The United States and Egypt were planning to open negotiations for a full free trade agreement in early 2006, but the United States cancelled after an Egyptian court sentenced opposition politician Ayman Nour to seven years in prison on politically motivated charges. In the long run, the United States and Egypt should get back to free trade talks, but that will have to wait until Egypt is on a clearer trajectory toward reform—and also until the U.S. president regains Trade Promotion Authority.

The Nour episode demonstrates the many difficult choices the U.S. government will have to make in pursuing several strategic objectives—regional peace, military cooperation, counterterrorism cooperation, economic development, and democratization—with Egypt concurrently. The Bush administration was right to cancel the talks, because opening them at that time would have been seen as a reward to an Egyptian government that was taking unnecessarily harsh steps against peaceful dissidents. In any case the administration could not have obtained congressional approval for a free trade agreement in view of growing anger in congress over political repression in Egypt. The United States will need to articulate again and again that the quality and pace of political reform in Egypt will be a key element determining how the U.S.–Egyptian relationship—political, military, economic, and trade—will develop in the coming years.

Appendix: 2005 and 2007 Political Reforms

2005:

- Article 76 of the constitution, amended to allow direct popular election of the president, stipulate how parties and independents could get on the ballot and establish an electoral commission.
- Presidential Election Law 174 of 2005, specifying campaign regulations.
- Political Rights Law 73 of 1956, establishing an electoral commission for parliamentary elections.
- Political Parties Law 177 of 2005, changing procedures for forming parties.[5]

2007:

- Article 1 of the constitution, amended to specify that the Arab Republic of Egypt is a "state with a democratic system that is based on citizenship."

- Article 5 of the constitution, amended to forbid any political activity or the establishment of any political party with any religious frame of reference or on the basis of religion, gender, or origin.
- Article 62 of the constitution, amended to allow change to a mixed system of proportional and individual districts in parliamentary elections.
- Article 76 of the constitution, amended to allow registered political parties that hold at least 3 percent of the seats in the People's Assembly and Shura Council to nominate a candidate in presidential elections. The amendment also specifies that in any election taking place in the decade following May 2007, any party with a single elected seat in either house of parliament may nominate a candidate.
- Article 82 of the constitution, amended to specify that if the president becomes unable to perform his duties, they will be performed by the vice president—or if there is no vice president—by the prime minister. The interim president may not request constitutional amendments, dissolve parliament, or dismiss the cabinet.
- Article 88 of the constitution, amended to require that elections take place nationwide on a single day and be supervised by a supreme electoral commission (replacing the role previously played by judges).
- Article 115 of the constitution, amended to specify that the government must submit its budget to the People's Assembly at least three months before the beginning of the fiscal year, that the parliament will vote article by article, and that it may amend the budget.
- Article 127 of the constitution, amended to allow the People's Assembly to vote no confidence in the prime minister and to dismiss him without the need for a popular referendum.
- Article 136 of the constitution, amended to allow the president to dissolve parliament without a popular referendum. He is required to call new elections within sixty days of the dissolution.
- Article 173 of the constitution, amended to create a council to manage judicial affairs headed by the president.
- Article 179 of the constitution, amended to allow the president to refer civilians in terrorism cases to trial in military courts and to allow the government to bypass human rights protections afforded in Articles 41, 44, and 45 of the constitution to facilitate counterterrorism efforts.
- Political Rights Law 73 of 1956, amended to establish a single electoral commission and to specify its authority over campaign regulations, voter lists, balloting, counting, and election monitoring.

Notes

1. For more on political deliberalization during the 1990s, see Eberhard Kienle, *A Grand Delusion: Democracy and Economic Reform in Egypt* (London: I. B. Tauris, 2001), pp. 52–64.

2. For a more detailed discussion of the evolution of the Muslim Brotherhood from the 1980s onward, see Mona El-Ghobashy, "The Metamorphosis of the Egyptian Muslim Brothers," *International Journal of Middle East Studies*, vol. 37 (2005), pp. 373–95.

3. For a full discussion of the 2007 constitutional amendments, see Nathan Brown, Michele Dunne, and Amr Hamzawy, "Egypt's Constitutional Amendments," Carnegie Endowment for International Peace Web Commentary, March 23, 2007, available at <www.carnegieendowment.org/publications/index.cfm?fa=view&id=19075&prog=zgp&proj=zdrl,zme>.

4. Since the establishment of party politics, there has typically been one dominant party. Before the 1952 coup, the Wafd Party (founded by Saad Zaghloul during the 1919 revolt against British control) dominated political life, albeit within the context of a continuous triangular power struggle with the monarchy and the British. After 1952 the Revolutionary Command Council abolished all political parties and the monarchy. Eventually Nasser established a single party (first called the Liberation Rally, later the Arab Socialist Union) that is the forebear of today's National Democratic Party. Although Sadat reintroduced party pluralism in 1977, allowing the Wafd to reemerge and engineering the creation of loyal parties to the right and left, the NDP continued to dominate the system through its connection to the president and monopoly on patronage.

5. In addition, the parliament made minor adjustments to the People's Assembly Law (Law 175 of 2005, amending Law 38 of 1972) and Shura Council Law (Law 176 of 2005, amending Law 120 of 1980), to bring them into conformity with campaign and other regulations in the laws listed here.

ILLUSIVE REFORM:
JORDAN'S STUBBORN STABILITY

Julia Choucair-Vizoso

Since independence in 1947, Jordan has shown a remarkable ability to survive as a political entity. Surrounded by regional conflict and starved of resources, it has endured a massive influx of Palestinian refugees and numerous coup attempts. For decades, the Hashemite monarchy has overcome these political and economic storms by weakening institutionalized opposition to its rule and relying on the distribution of benefits and privileges to create a cohesive support base and a security establishment loyal to the existing political order. The regime has been able to sustain this situation by capitalizing on Jordan's geographic centrality. Benefiting from Jordan's image as an oasis of stability in a deeply troubled region, the monarchy has been able to secure a flow of external assistance that has helped counteract the lack of natural resources and maintain domestic political stability. But the balance has always been precarious. The contemporary process of political reform in Jordan must be understood in this context.

Launched by King Hussein in the late 1980s and continuing under his son Abdullah II after he took power in 1999, Jordan's reform process has brought about positive changes. Political parties are now legal, parliamentary elections have become more regular, and significant economic reforms have been introduced. The process, however, has not resulted in democratic change. Rather, it has been a halfhearted and hesitant top-down reform effort, driven by the monarchy's desire to build its support base and maintain domestic political stability in the face of significant external challenges. As a result, the changes have been limited. Many initiatives have been launched and committees created, but substantive change has not matched the rhetoric. Although there is now open debate about the fundamental problems in the Jordanian political system, real structural reforms are not on the agenda. The monarchy retains its monopoly on power in the country, and institutions that are not accountable to the electorate, such as the royal court and the intelligence services, still make major decisions.

In the past several years, Jordan has witnessed a significant setback in political freedom. King Abdullah II has responded to pressures created by a deteriorating regional situation and continuing economic troubles by clamping down on political and civil liberties and increasing the pervasive role of the security services. The question about Jordan's political future is not whether the political reform process will continue, but whether there will be one at all. The answer depends on whether the regime will be convinced that Jordan's stability is best maintained through a political opening rather than through repression.

The regime's decision will be affected by whether and how it can resist pressures for change arising from regional and domestic challenges. Can the monarchy continue to walk a tightrope and keep the opposition in check despite widespread dissatisfaction with the country's foreign policy? Will economic policy alienate the monarchy's support base? What role can the United States and Europe play in these changing dynamics? Unlike the situation a few decades ago, today the survival of Jordan as a state is not threatened. The Hashemite monarchy has succeeded in creating enough interests (both domestic and foreign) in the survival of the state to assure Jordan's place in a changing regional order. However, while Jordan's existence is not at stake, the shape of its political future is unclear.

Jordan's Dilemmas

Jordan's political reform process cannot be understood without an appreciation of the external and domestic threats the modern Jordanian political system has faced. The Hashemite Jordanian kingdom has long seemed precarious. Established by Great Britain in 1921, it was a resource-scarce land with a population lacking a cohesive ethnic or religious identity or a strong loyalty to the installed Hashemite ruler from Mecca. Moreover, its geographic location has often made it susceptible to the push and pull of regional geopolitics. The Arab–Israeli conflict in particular has had a profound effect on Jordan's domestic balance of power and interests. Political reform must thus be viewed against the backdrop of the monarchy's continuous struggle to maintain the existing political order and stabilize the country in light of perceived and real threats to its authority.

Ever since its establishment, the Hashemite monarchy has relied on a strategy of seeking aid from abroad to create a domestic support base. Initially dependent on subsidies from Great Britain, the monarchy was later able to convince the United States and conservative Arab states of its vital role in maintaining regional security. The resulting flow of external assistance from these states permitted payoffs that allowed the monarchy to build a support base.[1]

The monarchy rallied support by offering government jobs and special privileges to certain population groups, a practice that began when Transjordan was still a British mandate. Abdullah I (1921–1951), son of Hashemite King Hussein of Mecca, consolidated his rule by forming a coalition composed of tribal leaders (descendants of Bedouins who had migrated from Arabia), Christians, Circassians, and Chechens (who came to Jordan in the early twentieth century, fleeing Russia's southward expansion into the Caucasus). Abdullah I also shifted the electoral balance from rapidly growing urban population centers to rural areas, where he cultivated a loyal constituency. This practice continued under King Talal (1951–52) and King Hussein (1952–1999). As a result, members of these communities came to occupy most public jobs, and electoral laws guaranteed their overrepresentation in parliament.

Capitalizing on this support, the monarchy was able to unilaterally control political life. The 1952 constitution declared Jordan a constitutional monarchy, but it allowed the king to appoint and dismiss the prime minister, the cabinet, and the upper house of parliament at his discretion. It also allowed the monarch to dissolve parliament, veto legislation, and decree "provisional laws," which have the full effect of law when the parliament is dissolved.[2] It gave institutions outside the monarchy, such as the cabinet and parliament, limited powers: Legislation passed by the elected lower house has to be approved by the senate, whose members are appointed directly by the king. These institutions were also prevented from functioning efficiently. Real power rested not in constitutional institutions like the cabinet and the parliament, but in the royal court and the security services, which were not regulated by the constitution and not accountable to parliament.

This political arrangement, however, has continuously faced tremendous pressure due to changing internal and regional conditions. In the past 80 years, Jordan has found itself at the heart of ideological and political struggles in the Middle East. The emergence of Arab nationalist and leftist groups in

Jordan and in powerful neighboring countries, such as Syria and Iraq, in the 1950s and 1960s clashed with the conservative, pro-Western stance of the Hashemite monarchy. In 1957, rising demands for Jordan's transformation into a republic or for its union with Syria and Egypt threatened not only the authority but the existence of the monarchy. The state was also in danger of being pulled apart by Cold War rivalries. In the 1950s, the Hashemite monarchy witnessed various attempted coups by antiroyalist movements (supported in many cases by other Arab states).

The most significant challenge to Hashemite authority, however, has been the Arab–Israeli conflict. Although it has affected most Arab states to some extent, in Jordan the conflict has such a profound impact that many consider it a domestic issue. Successive waves of Palestinian refugees since 1948 and the 1950 decision of King Abdullah I to incorporate the West Bank into Jordan's territory brought into the already weak state an urbanized, educated, and politicized element with no strong affinity for or allegiance to the Hashemite monarchy. The reality of a large population of Palestinian origin has been a defining element of Jordan's internal dynamics.

The history of Palestinian–Jordanian relations is a traumatic one for both Jordanians of East Bank and West Bank origin. In the late 1960s, the presence in Jordan of many Palestinian political groups, such as the Palestinian Liberation Organization (PLO) and the Popular Front for the Liberation of Palestine, threatened the authority of the king. These groups acted as autonomous movements outside the authority of the king, and some even called openly for the overthrow of the monarchy. The situation eventually led to open warfare between the regime and leftist guerrilla groups in the Palestinian refugee camps in 1970–71. By July 1971, the regime had forced most Palestinian movements, including the PLO, to relocate to other countries. The monarchy had survived one of the greatest challenges to its authority and asserted its control over the country.

Although the security threat was neutralized, the Palestinian issue has continued to threaten the Jordanian state. The greatest threat is the claim by many Israeli right-wing groups that the Palestinians do not have the right to establish an independent state in the West Bank and Gaza, because a Palestinian state—Jordan—already exists on the East Bank of the Jordan River. Ariel Sharon espoused this so-called Jordan option when he entered politics in 1974, and he repeatedly advocated removal of the "artificial kingdom of Jordan" and transformation of the country into a Palestinian state.

The presence of a large number of Jordanians of Palestinian origin also threatens the monarchy's system of governance, which favors traditional East

Bank elites. The exact composition of Jordan's population is a sensitive and contested issue. According to a September 2002 official statement, Palestinians constitute 43 percent of the Jordanian population, but the more commonly cited estimate is 60 percent. The overall balance of political and economic power between Jordanians of Palestinian origin and Jordanians of East Bank origin is highly complex, and a detailed discussion falls outside the scope of this chapter.[3] Suffice to say that although Jordan hosted successive waves of Palestinian refugees and offered them citizenship, many of those who arrived after the 1948 war and after the Israeli occupation of the West Bank in 1967 felt that they were treated unfairly and remained estranged from the Jordanian system. In contrast, wealthier Palestinians who migrated to the country from Kuwait during the 1990 Iraqi invasion were able to integrate and are now part of the economic elite.

Palestinian Jordanians, however, remain largely underrepresented in the public sector and in the political power structure. Only seven of the 55 senators—all appointed by the king—are of Palestinian origin, and the electoral laws for the lower house of parliament are designed to overrepresent segments of the population allied with the regime. Rural, promonarchy districts are favored, while urban areas that are bastions of Palestinian or Islamist support are underrepresented. Palestinians rarely hold more than seventeen of 110 lower house seats. As a result, turnout in rural areas tends to be very high, whereas urban Palestinian-majority districts register the lowest turnouts in the kingdom.

Careful manipulation of the political system has not always sufficed to maintain stability in the kingdom, however, and Jordan has experienced repeated crises. Historically, the monarchy responded to open challenges by cracking down on all political activity. Following attempted coups in the 1950s, Arab nationalist and leftist opponents of the Hashemites were severely repressed. Political parties were legal only between 1955 and 1957, and martial law was declared after the 1967 Arab–Israeli war. Although the constitution recognized the basic freedoms of expression and assembly, press and penal laws were enacted to prohibit criticism of the royal family and the armed forces or any statement considered harmful to national unity or Jordan's foreign relations. Parliament was dissolved numerous times—most notably for two decades between 1968 and 1989—whenever the monarchy sought to avoid potential opposition to controversial policies and legislation. Successive kings also relied on the powerful General Intelligence Department (GID), or *mukhabarat*, to suppress political activity.

Hussein's Abortive Political Opening

Beginning in 1980, Jordan's strategy of depending on external revenue as a way of preserving its internal political balance was severely undermined by a decline in U.S. support and remittances from its citizens working in the Persian Gulf. In response to significant revenue loss, in 1989 King Hussein introduced limited openings in the political system. The political liberalization process was designed to generate support for economic policies rather than to introduce real political change.

In 1980, the United States terminated its economic package to Jordan after King Hussein refused to join Egypt in signing a peace treaty with Israel. At the same time, the Gulf states diverted assistance from Jordan to Iraq to support its war against Iran. As the price of oil fell during the 1980s and the demand for foreign workers decreased, Jordan also lost some of the funds it had been accruing from its citizens' remittances. By 1989, the kingdom was forced to default on its foreign debt and resort to a loan by the International Monetary Fund (IMF) with strict conditions. The mandated decreases of subsidies on fuel and food led to civil disturbances in the southern city of Ma'an, a traditional heartland of Hashemite support, which eventually spread to other towns and cities also viewed as bastions of support for the regime. Although the rioters did not criticize the king or make explicit demands for democracy and civil liberties, they did call for the revocation of austerity measures, the resignation of the government, new parliamentary elections, and the punishment of corrupt officials. Ultimately, the riots prompted a shaken regime to respond with promises of political reforms. Between 1989 and 1993, the Jordanian political system witnessed significant liberalization.

The reforms were designed to reward regime supporters and to redefine the relationship between the regime and the opposition. A major step was allowing parliamentary elections in 1989, the first such elections since 1967. Although political parties were still illegal, independent candidates were allowed, and the elections were considered honest. Islamist candidates achieved a major victory, gaining almost 40 percent of the seats in parliament. Twenty of the twenty-six Muslim Brotherhood candidates as well as twelve independent Islamists won seats (in total, thirty-two of eighty-six contested seats).

Another landmark event was the issuance of the 1991 National Charter, which laid the foundation for political pluralism in Jordan. In the wake of the riots and the resumption of parliamentary life, King Hussein appointed a sixty-member commission—which included well-known government supporters as well as leading members of leftist parties and the Muslim

Brotherhood—to draft a charter to define the goals and parameters of Jordan's liberalization process. During the drafting of the charter, the government offered the opposition a basic proposition: If the opposition recognized the legitimacy of the Hashemite monarchy, the regime would allow a reemergence of political party pluralism in Jordan under the power of the king. As a result of the charter, martial law was lifted, and parliament authorized the formation of political parties in 1992. Political exiles were permitted to return and the government relaxed restrictions on demonstrations.

Finally, a new Press and Publications Law in 1993 lifted some restrictions on Jordan's print media, and several new weekly newspapers were licensed. Journalists at the time criticized the law for not being liberal enough (particularly the stipulation that journalists must be members of the Jordan Press Club to work legally), but it is now lauded as the most liberal that Jordan has known.

Never truly committed to democratization, King Hussein started undermining the reforms as soon as he saw an opportunity to win back U.S. financial and political support. The opening of talks between the PLO and Israel at the 1991 Madrid Peace Conference (in which Palestinians were included in a joint Jordanian–Palestinian delegation) provided Hussein with an opportunity to play a role in the process. This, Hussein hoped, would confirm Jordan's political role in the region, neutralize the Israeli threat of turning Jordan into a Palestinian state, restore good relations with the United States, and secure renewed U.S. assistance. The Jordanian regime publicly sought debt reduction, foreign aid, and foreign investments for Jordan as a reward for signing a peace treaty with Israel, but this official position ran into considerable opposition by a public deeply distrustful of Israel and the United States. In an attempt to undermine internal opposition to the peace treaty, the regime orchestrated a series of measures designed to decrease the influence and voice of opponents, particularly Islamists.

The most important measure was the amendment to the electoral law. Under the old law, voters could choose as many candidates as there were seats in their district. In August 1993, presumably to curb the electoral success of Islamists in the 1989 elections, the law was amended, restricting each voter to choosing only one candidate, no matter how many seats were to be filled in the district. The controversial "one-person one-vote" law, as it became known, bolstered tribal candidates and undermined large parties: Forced to make only one choice, voters tended to pick the candidate they knew personally. As a result, the 1993 elections heavily reduced the influence of the Islamic Action Front (the political party of the Muslim Brotherhood) in parliament. In

November 1994, the peace treaty with Israel signed on October 26, 1994, was ratified by a comfortable margin.

The regime also rolled back reforms in other areas. A 1997 decree amending the press law raised the minimum capital requirements for newspapers, increased penalties for violations of the law, and increased prohibitions on content. The amendments were annulled by the High Court of Justice, which found them unconstitutional, but most restrictions were reinstated by a 1998 law. In response to domestic and international criticism, a more liberal law was passed in 1999. It halved the capitalization requirement for weeklies, reduced fines for violations, transferred the power to revoke a publication's license from the minister of information to the court system, and withdrew the courts' authority to suspend a publication.

By the time of Hussein's death in February 1999, it was clear that the liberalization experiment had been a temporary tactic by the king to reduce opposition to unpopular economic policies. The changes had never been intended to open to public choice the basic structures of the political system. Opponents of regime policies concluded that they could only express their dissent outside the system. Many boycotted the November 1997 parliamentary elections and demanded the revocation of the one-person one-vote law and the amendments to the press law as well as an end to normalization with Israel.

Despite the opposition it generated, the peace treaty brought significant rewards to the regime. The United States declared Jordan a major non-NATO strategic ally, wrote off its debt, and raised aid levels progressively, making Jordan in less than a decade the fourth largest recipient of U.S. economic and military assistance.[4] Jordan also became one of the first countries in the region to sign a partnership agreement with the European Union.

Reforms Under Abdullah

As in other Arab countries where a son succeeded the father in the late 1990s (Bahrain, Morocco, and Syria), the accession of King Abdullah to the throne in February 1999 brought with it expectations that Jordan would move forward with reform. Indeed, at the opening of the parliamentary session on November 1, 1999, the new king proclaimed that Jordan's democratic course would remain a "national and unwavering choice." It was soon clear, however, that economic reform and regime stability would take priority over political reform. Abdullah's approach to political reform in his first years in office was similar to his father's. It was designed to temper the effects of significant regional challenges by strengthening the political base of the monarchy, promoting national unity, and shifting public attention from the crises brewing on Jordan's frontiers. It was not designed to transfer political power from the monarchy to elected institutions.

Abdullah made economic reform his primary concern, with a particular focus on attracting foreign investment and increasing exports. In a departure from his father, Abdullah surrounded himself with economic specialists. In his first two years in office, he renewed Jordan's program with the IMF and launched reforms that would lead to Jordan's entry into the World Trade Organization in 2000. The showpiece achievement of this effort was the free trade agreement with the United States in 2001 and the qualified industrial zone (QIZ) program, under which manufacturers could export tariff free to the U.S. market by meeting precise rules of origin.[5] Furthermore, the government privatized part of Jordan's telecommunication system and railways and passed news laws concerning intellectual property and antitrust regulations. The king also gave special attention to administrative reform and the need to fight corruption in the public sector.

As regional pressure mounted following the collapse of the Palestinian–Israeli peace process, and as U.S. plans for an Iraq war materialized, security concerns brought about restrictions on political activity. The clearest example of this was the delay of parliamentary elections originally scheduled for 2001. Elections were first postponed to allow for the implementation of a new electoral law and then on the grounds that the regional climate was "difficult." Having decided to quietly support the United States in the war in Iraq, the regime was concerned with criticism and political activity from a public opposed to the war.

While parliament was suspended (between June 2001 and June 2003), King Abdullah issued 211 provisional laws and amendments, many of which marked a significant reversal in civil liberties. The public gatherings law of August 2001 banned rallies and public meetings without the government's prior written consent. In practice, few permits were granted, and when they were, the government dictated the locale and the number of protesters. Amendments to the penal code in October 2001 imposed fines and prison sentences on publications that carried "false or libelous information that can undermine national unity or the country's reputation." Another decree allowed the prime minister to refer any case to the state security court and denied the right of appeal to people convicted of misdemeanors. More recently, there have been several attempts to limit the activities of professional associations, which had become the main opponents to normalization with

Israel after the 1994 peace treaty. The government has proposed a draft law that would require associations to adopt a new, indirect method of leadership selection, obtain advance written approval from the interior ministry to hold a gathering or meeting, and cover only topics that the government specifically designates "professional matters." These include "cultivating scientific research," "publishing specialized scientific publications," and "providing advice to official bodies in relation to the practice of a profession and its development."

Beginning in 2002, King Abdullah took a series of steps to refocus attention away from the Palestinian problem and onto domestic issues—economic development, modernization, and gradual political reform. These measures include the "Jordan First" initiative launched in October 2002, the creation of the ministry of political development in December 2003, and the 2006 National Agenda. Although these documents contain some fairly explicit recommendations about economic transformation and modernization, they are vague about political change. For example, the National Agenda, which outlines a ten-year plan for comprehensive reform, including "political development," only makes general statements about the need to "enact a law to guarantee the freedom of political activity and ensure the protection of individuals and groups engaging in such activity" and to make sure that "legislative amendments shall aim to achieve increased protection and greater respect for human rights."

King Abdullah has often stressed the need to amend the political party and electoral laws. Although changes have been made in the realm of political party legislation, no serious talk on the much more important issue of electoral reform has occurred.

The government has emphasized the need to produce "powerful political parties" and eradicate the "culture of fear" that prevents Jordanians from joining political parties. The Jordan First initiative suggested merging the present numerous, fragmented political parties into three main currents (Islamist, leftist, and nationalist). The launching of the ministry of political development also aimed to "create strong parties that endorse King Abdullah's vision of 'Jordan First'; to increase the political participation of women and youth; to advance democratic dialogue and respect for the opinion of others; and to promote a responsible press which serves the objectives of the Jordanian state and its people." Following years of debate, a new political parties law was approved by the Jordanian parliament in March 2007. The law introduced government funding to political parties in accordance with the number of seats a given party wins in parliamentary or local elections. It also raised from

50 to 500 the number of members necessary for registering or maintaining party status and raised the minimum number of districts from which parties must draw their members. Political parties, many of which are unable to meet the new requirements, unanimously rejected the new law and threatened to appeal its constitutionality.

Political party legislation is unlikely to strengthen the parties unless the electoral law is also changed, most Jordanian analysts believe, because the electoral system is the real cause of party weakness. Opposition parties and democracy activists have called on the government to change the one-vote law used in parliamentary elections since 1993 and have suggested replacing the one vote system with a mixed system. Under this proposal, half of the parliamentary seats would be allocated to national party lists through proportional representation, and the other half to single-member geographic districts. Each voter could cast two votes, one for a national list and the other for a district candidate. While the National Agenda outlines aims and principles for electoral law reform, including a mixed electoral system, even the biggest proponents of the agenda admit that serious electoral reform is not on the table because it is too contentious.[6] The most optimistic reformists expect only superficial modifications to the law.

Looking Ahead: Prospects for Political Reform

Reforms in Jordan under King Hussein and King Abdullah have aimed to stabilize the regime in the face of regional and economic challenges rather than to significantly open the political system. In the last fifteen years, martial law has been lifted, political parties have been legalized, there have been significant efforts to improve the socioeconomic situation, and media freedom has increased. But none of the reforms have targeted the distribution of political power. The fundamental power relationship between the monarchy and the citizenry remains unchanged. Political liberalization has allowed the expression of some public grievances, but all substantive decisions are still made by the palace. Real power remains not with the cabinet or the parliament, but with the royal court and the intelligence services. Although there are clear and vocal demands for structural reform, such as addressing the shortcomings of the election law, fundamental issues have never really been on the table. Successive amendments to the Electoral Law have changed the number of seats and electoral constituencies and have somewhat improved the transparency of the electoral process, but they have not addressed the underrepresentation of opposition voices and the predominance of the traditional elites—on the contrary, they have reinforced them. In summary, there is little substance to show for the various initiatives and dialogues launched by the regime.

Furthermore, the process of political reform has come to a complete halt or even been reversed whenever the regime calculated that cracking down on civil and political liberties would maintain stability. Even prominent political figures have been arrested for stepping over certain redlines. In the most famous recent case, Toujan Feisal, a prominent feminist activist and former member of parliament, was arrested in 2002 and convicted of "defaming" the prime minister and the government. Although Feisal was later pardoned and released, she was barred from running in the 2003 elections. Suspects continue to be routinely detained without a warrant, and there is evidence of torture and other mistreatment of political detainees.[7] Editors and journalists continue to receive official warnings not to publish certain articles, and security officials still pressure printers to hold publication until editors agree to remove sensitive stories.

Given this history of oscillation between liberalization and repression, it is clear that Jordan has not yet embarked on a process of democratization. For Jordan to actually democratize, the monarchy would have to move toward becoming a constitutional monarchy not just in name but also in practice.

To date, deep reform has been hindered by three main factors: an unstable regional situation that has placed security considerations above political reform; an opposition that has been unable and often unwilling to push for such change; and a regime support base that believes that a central and uncontested role for the monarchy is in their best interest. The possibility of democratization in Jordan depends on whether changes in these three fronts will force the regime to significantly open the political space.

Regional Conflict

Since its establishment, the monarchy has faced real threats to its survival as a political institution, and it has chosen to deal with the threats by restricting political freedom in the kingdom. Regional political instability has long exerted pressure on the monarchy that has led it to delay the path toward greater political freedom. Today, the monarchy finds itself once again surrounded by regional conflict. The Israeli–Palestinian conflict and the Iraq war have served to put political reform in Jordan on the back burner.

As long as the Palestinian–Israeli conflict is unresolved, the monarchy will not be forced to reform the electoral law and settle the question of Palestinian Jordanian representation in the kingdom. The Hashemite monarchy has delayed reforming the electoral system by trying to forge an identity consensus between Transjordanians and Palestinians, one that depends on maintaining the notion that Palestinians might someday have the choice to return to their homes in what is now Israel. As such, government officials repeatedly argue that fundamental changes to the electoral law (amending the district boundaries and sizes) cannot be made until a final peace settlement is reached between Israelis and Palestinians.

Although this argument may serve as a convenient excuse to maintain a system that favors regime supporters, it is also based on a real concern among some pillars of the political establishment that an increase in the representation of Jordanians of Palestinian origin will confirm the stance of Israeli right-wingers who argue that a Palestinian state already exists in Jordan. This fear is exacerbated by the deterioration of Israeli–Palestinian relations and Israel's unilateral withdrawal from Gaza. The regime fears that the lack of options for a viable Palestinian state will encourage Palestinians to leave the territories, further altering Jordan's demographic balance. Thus, King Abdullah has repeatedly urged Washington not to endorse the Israeli unilateral withdrawal plan from the West Bank, which would hurt the chances for an independent and geographically connected Palestinian state.

The worsening conflict has also hindered political reform by strengthening conservative elements around the monarchy, especially the security establishment, and undermining the more reformist elements in the regime. Recurrent episodes of violence, especially since the 2000 intifada, strengthen the security elite and make the regime respond to criticisms of its policies from opposition movements as a security threat. In recent years, the unrest in Palestine has resulted in violent clashes between protesters and security forces. The relationship between the monarchy and the main opposition movement, the Islamic Action Front (IAF), has also become more confrontational because the regime is concerned about ties between the IAF and Hamas, particularly since Hamas's victory in the Palestinian legislative elections in January 2006. In addition, the government has stepped up its efforts to clamp down on "antinormalization" activism in the professional associations.

The conflict in Iraq has exacerbated the regime's feeling of insecurity. Given Jordan's proximity to Iraq, its reliance on Iraqi oil, and Jordanian popular opposition to the war, the monarchy has, since the start of the war, feared a popular backlash. The suicide attacks on hotels in Amman on November 9, 2005, which killed 60 people, revealed how vulnerable Jordan is to the situation across its border. Masterminded by Abu Musab al-Zarqawi, a Jordanian jihadi commander fighting in Iraq, the attacks were carried out by Iraqis who were angered by events in their country and chose a close U.S. ally as a target. A new counterterrorism law passed in September 2006 expanded the power of the secret police and the intelligence services. It gives the security services carte blanche to take measures against those the authorities believe support terrorist ideas, incite attacks, or express sympathy for suicide bombings. Since the Iraq war began, Human Rights Watch has issued a series of reports detailing the rising power of an unchecked GID.

As long as the regime feels threatened by the situation in Palestine and Iraq, it is unlikely to open up the system. Jordan's history shows that threatening regional scenarios undermine the reform agenda by increasing the influence of security-oriented figures in the elite and undermining reformist voices. If the regime will not willingly open up amid the current regional conflicts, the question is whether pressure from below can force it to open up.

The Jordanian regime's response to both the Palestinian–Israeli conflict and the war in Iraq is a source of deep popular discontent. King Abdullah II has placed the highest priority on maintaining close security relations with the United States. Having long been aligned with U.S. policy in the Middle East, since September 11, 2001, Jordan has taken a more active role in supporting the U.S. regional agenda and has adopted a key role in the U.S.-led war on terror. Jordan's General Intelligence Department has been described as the United States' most effective allied counterterrorism agency in the Middle East.

U.S. policy toward the Palestinian–Israeli conflict and the war in Iraq has created unprecedented anti-U.S. sentiment in Jordan. Analysts of Jordanian politics unanimously point to the widespread discontent beneath the surface in Jordan and to a public that is increasingly alienated from its leaders. While this sentiment may trigger sporadic outbursts of fury, it is unlikely that pressure from below will make the regime introduce reforms, unless it comes from a strongly organized opposition movement capable of sustained action.

How Far Can the Opposition Go?

There is consensus among opposition groups in Jordan—which include independent civic actors as well as secular and religious political parties—about necessary political changes: a democratically elected government in which the prime minister would be elected by the parliament rather than appointed by the king; a strong parliament and longer parliamentary sessions; a new press and publications law with more lenient licensing and censorship practices; new legislation that prevents the government from controlling the internal functioning and financing of nongovernmental organizations (NGOs); a reduced role for the security services in politics and public affairs;

the establishment of a Constitutional Court to help resolve disputes over the constitutionality of laws and decrees; and electoral reform that would make elected bodies, particularly the parliament, more reflective of the country's demographic makeup.

Despite the consensus, individuals and organizations calling for these changes lack the ability to push them through. Civic associations lack the power to pressure for change. By law, they cannot engage in any political activities and must abide by tedious and complicated administrative and oversight requirements.[8] The government directly interferes with their leadership to remove members it deems threatening to state interests. Trade unions have limited power and independence: They are required by the government to be members of the General Federation of Jordanian Unions (the sole trade union federation), whose salaries and activities are subsidized and audited by the government. Furthermore, the Public Assemblies Law limits worker rights to freedom of association and collective bargaining.

The most independent and openly critical civic groups are the professional associations. Given the relative weakness of the party system, the professional associations have become a potent alternative force and an institutional base for opposition within Jordanian politics. Factions of the various opposition groups generally led the professional associations during the mid-1990s. Currently, most of them are controlled by members of the Muslim Brotherhood. The associations challenge the government's political decisions—especially those on foreign policy—as out of step with majority opinion in the kingdom and too close to U.S. policy in the region. After the 1994 peace treaty with Israel, opposition to normalization with Israel became one of the central concerns of the professional associations. In recent years, they have called for new press and association laws and have led a campaign against counterterrorism legislation. These bodies, however, are very limited in their ability to serve as instruments of political change because they do not have formal institutionalized venues in which to pursue their policies. While they may oppose certain policies and voice their concerns in meetings with government officials and personalities close to the regime, they cannot actively alter the course of policy. Furthermore, the government consistently invokes the law to punish professional associations for political activism. In November 2002, for example, it dissolved the Council of Engineers Association, the most powerful of Jordan's professional associations.

Political parties, which were banned for thirty-six years, are extremely weak. Most of the thirty-one registered parties have no more than several hundred members, lack clear agendas, and do not influence decision making.

They are viewed by the general public as being ineffective and unable to field winning candidates or influence government. The majority of parties, in fact, do not even declare their candidates, who stand as independents for fear that voters from tribal and rural areas will refrain from voting for them if they are seen as affiliated with a political party.

The Jordanian Muslim Brotherhood—and its political party, the IAF—is the only truly organized opposition movement. The Muslim Brotherhood has been prominent on Jordan's political scene since its establishment in 1945. Unlike leftist and Palestinian movements that clashed with the regime during the turbulent 1950s and 1960s, the Muslim Brotherhood did not threaten the monarchy but asked instead to be allowed to pursue its Islamic path in Jordan. It has been argued that the Muslim Brotherhood provided the monarchy with a reliable ally and a counterweight to the influence of communists, Baathists, and pan-Arabists. The Muslim Brotherhood remained legal during the thirty-six-year ban on political parties, because it was considered a social organization, not a political group.

Many of its members served in government, and after the 1989 elections, the movement controlled the education and health portfolios. Participating unofficially in elections since the 1950s, it has used parliament as a forum to call for the implementation of Islamic law. When parties were legalized in 1992, the Muslim Brotherhood founded the IAF under the conditions set in the political parties law. The relation between the Muslim Brotherhood and the IAF has been defined as a strategic division of power, allowing the former to continue to function as an Islamic charity organization unhindered by the political parties law.

Despite its close relationship with the monarchy, the Jordanian Muslim Brotherhood was never fully co-opted. It has always maintained a somewhat critical stance, but only toward policies, not the regime itself. A central focus of the criticism has been the regime's foreign policy, particularly Jordan's peace treaty with Israel. In May 1994, before the treaty was signed, the IAF and seven leftist and Arab nationalist parties formed the Committee for Resisting Submission and Normalization. The Muslim Brotherhood has also been very critical of the U.S.-led war on Iraq. IAF members in parliament have increasingly called for political reforms, such as greater public liberties, press freedom, and greater respect for human rights. Criticisms of corruption and of deteriorating socioeconomic conditions have also figured among its main initiatives in parliament. In recent years, the IAF has led a campaign against the government's attempts to amend laws on professional associations, political parties, and counterterrorism legislation.

Despite this critical stance, the Muslim Brotherhood's capacity to be a catalyst for reform is limited. First, there are deep divisions within the movement about reform priorities and also about the relationship with the regime. More important, there are severe institutional constraints on the IAF's power, since it is hemmed in by an election law designed to weaken its influence. The 1993 one-person one-vote electoral law was enacted after the IAF's strong showing in the 1989 election to prevent a repeat.

The Muslim Brotherhood has called for a repeal of this law as well as for new rules on electoral districts that would give urban areas fair representation—at present, for example, one seat represents 19,691 people in Tafila and 85,728 in Amman. The regime has responded to criticism of the electoral system by simplifying voter registration procedures, counting votes in a more transparent manner, and so forth. But it has not been responsive to the call for a fundamental review of districting.

There is very little the IAF can do to push for more fundamental change. Outraged by the 1993 election results, the IAF led other opposition parties, associations, and prominent independent political figures in a boycott of the November 1997 parliamentary elections, demanding annulment of the one-person one-vote system, abolition of the changes to the press law, and an end to normalization with Israel. But the leadership of the IAF eventually realized that by operating outside parliament it lost rather than gained leverage and decided to participate in the 2003 elections, in which it won 17 of 110 seats. The experience of 1997 clearly demonstrated the limits to the IAF's options for influencing policy making in Jordan. By agreeing to play by the rules of the Jordanian political game, the furthest it can go is a boycott of elections, and many members believe that is not in their best interest. Unless the Islamists want to push harder on the system, which they have so far shown no inclination to do, their ability to press for change in Jordan is limited.

Cracks in the Regime's Support Base

The greatest pressure for political reform is thus likely to come not from the opposition but from economic changes and conditions that affect the regime's support base. To date, the Jordanian system has been sustained in large part by groups that believe that a central and uncontested role for the monarchy is in their best interest. The economic and political challenges the country faces, however, are beginning to erode some of this support.

Jordan's economic reforms have produced mixed results. Through generous assistance from the United States and through the IMF structural adjustment program, Jordan has been able to liberalize the private investment regime and establish modern regulations and institutions for the development of the private sector. There has been a steady growth in the economy in recent years, but this growth has yet to improve the living standards of many Jordanians. Opponents criticize the regime's emphasis on export-oriented growth, foreign aid, and foreign investment as opposed to social welfare and income distribution. Unemployment remains high (the official rate is 13.5 percent, but the real rate is over 20 percent), and there is an expanding and very visible gap between rich and poor. The QIZs, established to increase foreign direct investment and to help alleviate chronic unemployment, so far have not contributed to productive development or employment growth. Most jobs have gone to South Asian immigrants (who cannot legally unionize or engage in collective action). In 2003, only half of 50,000 workers in the QIZs were Jordanian nationals. More than 80 percent of the firms located in Jordan's QIZ are South Asian textile manufacturers.

Jordan's mixed record in improving economic conditions has led to widespread dissatisfaction in traditional areas of Hashemite support, straining relations between the monarchy and the rural tribes and ethnic minorities who historically had been its most loyal constituencies. As mentioned earlier, removal of subsidies on some food and fuel in 1989 led to riots in the southern town of Ma'an, considered a bastion of Transjordanian support for the regime. Since then, there have been four additional incidents of political violence in Ma'an, the most recent in November 2002. Although the Jordanian government insists that the violence in 2002 was caused by armed thugs and smugglers, many analysts believe that it was primarily a consequence of the government's failed socioeconomic, security, and political policies.[9]

The Jordanian regime is thus caught in a quandary. The policies it must adopt to face the challenge of economic development—particularly administrative reform and privatization—threaten the monarchy's support base. Privatization and civil service reform are crucial to making Jordan more competitive and to attracting foreign investment, but in the short run they would result in a significant number of dismissals from the bureaucracy and state-owned enterprises, weakening the social contract that has maintained regime stability. The monarchy has long relied on a strategy of placing Transjordanians in the public sector. Given the Palestinian private sector/Transjordanian public sector divide, it is not surprising that Transjordanians feel threatened by economic restructuring.

So far, the monarchy has handled this problem by remaining in control of partially privatized entities so it can supervise the economy. Partial privatization aims to reduce the government's budget deficit by offering public enterprises for sale to "strategic investors" (that is, investors with strong ties to the palace). For example, in June 2005, King Abdullah II ordered shares of privatized companies to be set aside and offered at reduced prices to past and present members of the security forces. This policy avoids the political consequences of unemployment, maintains certain privileged positions, and ensures that alternative power bases do not emerge. The monarchy is thus able to avoid alienating the Transjordanian base.

Jordan's economic liberalization measures to date have attempted to maintain the monarchy's relationship with both its Transjordanian support base and the local business community. The monarchy has rewarded both groups with public jobs, subsidies, regulatory protection, and state contracts. In recent years, however, the powerful private business elite, who had long supported Hashemite rule because it furthered its economic interests, has become more influential. It may push for more privatization.

The monarchy's traditional support base has also expressed concern that King Abdullah II, unlike his father, is too westernized and insensitive to their demands. This discontent has already led the parliament to block some of the king's choices. The most prominent example was the decision of "loyalist" members to prevent a confidence vote in support of the nomination of the liberal Adnan Badran as prime minister in early 2005.

Balance Sheet

Since independence, Jordan's political system has survived severe challenges to its legitimacy through a delicate balancing act. Today, Jordan faces another critical moment. Deteriorating conditions on its borders, a lack of tangible economic success, and an extremely unpopular foreign policy are emboldening an increasingly vocal Islamist opposition movement while simultaneously eroding the regime's traditional support base.

Although this mix of factors creates some pressure for change, it does not constitute a democratic push and the monarchy is unlikely to respond with democratization. First, the current regional conditions have exacerbated the monarchy's feeling of insecurity, and it is unlikely to open up the system if it feels threatened. Barring fundamental changes in Jordan's neighborhood, such as an end of violence in Iraq or the renewal of a peace process between Israelis and Palestinians, reformers in the political elite are unlikely to gain the upper hand over more security-minded figures. Second, the Jordanian opposition remains weak due to structural conditions that are unlikely to change in the near future. Impediments such as the highly fragmented structure of the opposition, the marginal role of parliament in the political process, the central role of tribal relations, and the legacy of three decades of martial law will continue to hinder the opposition's ability to promote its goals. In addition, opposition groups have been unable to join forces, except on rare occasions, such as protests against the politics of normalization with Israel. Even the most popular and best-organized movement, the IAF, is unable to move beyond a political battle with the regime and periodic confrontations. Finally, the discontented elements in the monarchy's traditional support base are not calling for greater political openings, but rather for maintaining their privileges in a changing economic system.

The regime's reaction to these pressures will be, at best, gradual and limited liberalization, not far-reaching political reform. From the monarchy's point of view, the choice is between maintaining political stability by a gradual, limited opening of political space or by continuing to clamp down on liberties. So far, King Abdullah has chosen to resist these pressures by increasing the pervasive role of the security services and limiting political space. At a time when public dissatisfaction with Jordan's foreign policy is increasing, such an approach merely delays dealing with problems that may worsen over time.

The Role of External Actors in Promoting Reform

The United States and Europe have the potential to play a significant role in pushing for political reform in Jordan, given the close political and economic relations they maintain with the regime. Through economic and military assistance, strategic cooperation, and trade, the United States and Europe have played a decisive role in helping Jordan maintain its stability and prosperity. Despite this potential, however, the prospects for the United States and Europe advocating democratization are not promising.

Jordan is a classic case of the United States and Europe shying away from promoting political reform because of other strategic interests. For Washington, Jordan's significance does not stem from how democratic its political system may be, but from its role as a dependable strategic ally in the region. Jordan's military and intelligence cooperation with the United States (most recently in the U.S. war on terrorism) and its proximity to and peaceful relations with Israel render its stability a primary goal of U.S. foreign policy. For Europe, Jordan plays a similar and valuable role as a "stabilizing and modernizing factor" and a "consistent force of peace in the region and a key partner in attempts to find a political solution to the conflict."[10]

It is unrealistic to expect a transformation in this relationship anytime soon. Ultimately, however, the long-term interests of both the United States and Europe are best served by an opening in Jordan's political space. Jordan's stabilizing role in the region would be best fulfilled not by the superficial appearance of stability maintained by political oppression, but rather by a process of political opening that provides legitimate channels through which concerns can be expressed.

The United States and Europe thus need to encourage a political opening in Jordan by pressing the Jordanian government to start a dialogue with opposition movements and to deepen formal and informal channels of communication and representation. This can be done in a number of ways. The most significant tools the United States and Europe can use to encourage the regime to open the political system are economic assistance and trade relationships. Given Jordan's reliance on large aid packages as well as trade agreements with these countries, making this assistance dependent on demonstrable progress toward democracy would provide great incentives for reform.

The U.S. government has rewarded Jordan for its role as a moderate, pro-U.S. Muslim country with generous economic and military aid since 1951; it is currently the fourth largest recipient of U.S. aid worldwide, after Israel, Egypt, and Colombia. Levels of aid have fluctuated. They significantly increased after Jordan signed a peace treaty with Israel in 1994—Jordan received approximately $225 million in annual U.S. assistance since the mid-1990s. After the war in Iraq began, Washington doubled its annual grants to Jordan to around $450 million ($250 million in economic aid and $200 million in military assistance), in addition to more than a $1 billion supplement to offset the effects of the war on Jordan's economy and bolster its security. Since entering the Euro-Mediterranean Partnership in 1997, Jordan has received over €570 million from the European Union (EU), making it the second largest recipient of EU assistance per capita after Palestine. None of this aid, however, has been conditional on political reform in the country.

The entry of Jordan into the Millennium Challenge Corporation's (MCC) Threshold Program in September 2006 offers an opportunity for constructive change. The MCC approved up to $25 million in assistance to Jordan to advance reforms in three of the sixteen indicators MCC measures to select countries eligible for funding—"political rights," "voice and accountability," and "trade policy." As presently envisioned, however, progress will be measured by the success of two initiatives: "strengthening municipal governance" and "modernizing customs administration." More substantive reforms—reforming the electoral system, strengthening political parties, enhancing the roles of the parliament and judiciary, increasing government transparency,

broadening freedoms of the press and assembly, and decreasing public corruption and human rights violations—are mentioned in the program as
"related reforms." Although municipal governance is worthy of attention, Jordan should not be upgraded for Millennium Challenge Account Compact
assistance unless there are signs of significant improvement in at least some
of the "related reforms."

In addition to direct economic assistance, trade is a very important element
in U.S.–Jordanian and U.S.–European relations and should also be used to
leverage political change in Jordan. Jordan is the linchpin of the Middle East
Free Trade Area (MEFTA) and became the first Arab country to sign a free
trade agreement with the United States. Political reform in Jordan was not a
determinant in the negotiations for the United States–Jordan Free Trade
Agreement, which went into effect in December 2001. However, the United
States can still use the agreement to articulate its support for political reform
and the improvement of human rights. The key is that this is the first trade
agreement concluded by the United States that, within the text of the agreement itself, conditions trade privileges upon the parties' continuing
enforcement of their respective domestic labor laws and their adherence to the
core labor standards outlined in the International Labor Organization (ILO)
Declaration on Fundamental Principles and Rights at Work.

The agreement explicitly lists the right of association, the right to organize and bargain collectively, and the prohibition on use of forced or
compulsory labor. It allows each government to take "appropriate" measures
if a dispute remains unresolved after completing all the steps in the dispute
resolution process. These measures may include a visit from an ILO delegation, a training program for workplace inspectors, a monetary fine, and/or the
withdrawal of trade benefits covered in the agreement. However, before Congress voted on the FTA, the U.S. trade representative and the Jordanian
ambassador exchanged letters in which they agreed that they would not
"expect or intend" to use trade sanctions to enforce any provisions in the
agreement. The United States should return to the spirit of the agreement and
state that the respect for human rights is a central element of the U.S.–Jordanian relationship.

The EU's Association Agreements with Jordan link free trade and political
reform, but the EU has so far avoided using its economic leverage to push the
regime to democratize. Like all association agreements, the EU–Jordan agreement includes a legally binding, nonnegotiable commitment on the part of
the Jordanian government to "human rights and democratic principles." In
principle, this clause would allow the EU to suspend parts of the aid and trade

provisions, but in practice, the conditions that would allow such a suspension are ambiguous. The EU's Neighborhood Policy has attempted to create a more direct link between the prospects of greater trade integration and political reform, good governance, democracy, and human rights. However, the new policy is still plagued by ambiguities and the lack of clearly defined benchmarks about the type of reform the EU expects. These flaws can be explained by the particular institutional and procedural constraints under which EU decision making and policy implementation in foreign affairs takes place. In the case of Jordan, there are deep differences among the union's member states on the desirability of making aid conditional on reform.

In addition to making assistance and trade relations dependent on Jordan's progress toward democracy, the United States and European countries should support reformist voices in Jordan through direct democracy assistance. To date, a very small portion of U.S. and European funds have been destined for democracy promotion. Furthermore, these funds have not been used in the most productive way.

The EU provides some democracy assistance to Jordan through the Euro–Mediterranean Partnership (EMP), but this aid is focused on a wide range of activities that are not directly related to democracy promotion. For example, the EMP Country Strategy Paper of 2002–2006 provided €7 million (of €110 million) to strengthening women rights; protecting children's rights; promoting freedom of the media, association, and assembly; strengthening civil society; promoting the fight against drugs and organized crime; and managing migration and refugees. EU democracy assistance would be more effective if democracy promotion projects were separated from more generic socioeconomic goals. A constructive change was the creation of the European Initiative for Democracy and Human Rights (EIDHR) in 1999, but since Jordan was not identified as a priority country, it is only eligible for a few microprojects.

Furthermore, the EU provides assistance to NGOs, but much of the funding distribution has to be agreed to by the Jordanian government and, as a result, ends up going to NGOs headed by members of the royal family (known in Jordan as the "royal NGOs"). EU assistance would be much more effective if greater efforts were placed in funding independent civil society groups.

The U.S. government also provides limited democracy assistance. For example, of $247.5 million in economic assistance funds for FY2006, $14.9 million were destined to support initiatives aimed at "strengthening civil society to promote philanthropy and encourage civic participation; strengthening journalism; and improving the legal system."

Through the National Democratic Institute for International Affairs and the International Republican Institute, the United States also provides democracy assistance aimed at developing the political and advocacy skills of emerging community leaders to enable them to run for office, training political parties in building and mobilizing constituencies, training MPs to better cater to their constituents' needs, and advocating women's rights. These are worthy goals, but they do not get at the heart of Jordan's political problems, such as political party weakness and voter apathy. And while it is true that Jordan's political parties are disorganized and could benefit from the training, fundamentally their weakness lies in a deeply flawed electoral system that does not encourage voters to join political parties and vote. It is useless to support political parties if the legislative process does not change. In this context, the best and most effective way for the United States and Europe to support reformists is by pressing the government to adopt policy changes to open up the system.

The United States and Europe should press the Jordanian regime on the issue of political reform in public statements as well as in private meetings between officials. At the very least, they should refrain from praising Jordan's government when it is clearly cracking down on civil and political liberties. That Jordan has emerged unscathed from the Bush administration's emphasis on political reform in Arab countries robs the policy of any credibility. At a time when even longstanding U.S. allies such as Egypt and Saudi Arabia have been publicly rebuked at least occasionally by U.S. officials for their authoritarian practices, Jordan should not be hailed as "a force for reform and positive change in the region."[11] In October 2006, in the midst of a government crackdown on opposition in Jordan, U.S. Secretary of State Condoleezza Rice singled Jordan out at a press conference, affirming that "Jordan is making really great strides in its political evolution."[12] To the Jordanian government, such statements confirm that reform is irrelevant to its relations with the United States. To Jordanian democracy and human rights activists (and to activists around the Arab world), they confirm the belief that the Bush administration is not really interested in promoting reform.

Pressuring the Jordanian regime to open the political system will not undermine Jordan's role as an ally in the region. This pressure is highly unlikely to lead the regime to stop cooperating in military and counterterrorism efforts. The Jordanian regime cooperates on these issues based on its own calculations, not as a favor to the United States or Europe and, therefore, will continue to do so even if pressured to reform. To avoid alienating the regime, the United States and Europe should negotiate with the Jordanian government over the expected improvements. A good start would be to focus on the demands already put forth by Jordanian activists, such as expanding legislative powers, adopting new press legislation, decreasing regulations on NGOs, and undertaking electoral system reform. In this manner, the United States and Europe could play a constructive role in promoting an environment in which Jordanians can address these issues and begin to find long-term solutions to Jordan's dilemmas.

Notes

1. Laurie A. Brand, *Jordan's Inter-Arab Relations: The Political Economy of Alliance Making* (New York: Columbia University Press, 1994).

2. The Jordanian constitution allows provisional laws to be issued when there are necessitating circumstances. As specified by the High Court of Justice in January 1998, these circumstances arise only in times of war, catastrophe, or internal strife. Provisional laws can also cover matters that "admit no delay or which necessitate expenditures incapable of postponement." The parliament can nullify or amend them.

3. For details, see Adnan Abu Odeh, *Jordanians, Palestinians, and the Hashemite Kingdom in the Middle East Peace Process* (Washington, DC: United States Institute for Peace, 1999); see also Laurie Brand, "Palestine and Jordan: A Crisis of Identity," *Journal of Palestine Studies*, vol. 24, no. 4 (Summer 1996).

4. Jordan was designated as a major non-NATO ally of the United States on November 13, 1996. This status "makes Jordan eligible for priority consideration for transfer of excess defense articles, the use of already appropriated military assistance funds for procurement through commercial leases, the stockpiling of U.S. military material, and the purchase of depleted uranium munitions." See Alfred B. Prados and Jeremy M. Sharp, "Jordan: U.S. Relations and Bilateral Issues," *CRS Issue Brief for Congress* (Washington, DC: Congressional Research Service, May 19, 2005), p. 14, available at <http://fpc.state.gov/documents/organization/48595.pdf>.

5. The rules specify that a minimum of 11.7 percent of the exported goods must be from Jordan, 7-8 percent from Israel, and the remainder from any combination of the United States, Jordan, Israel, or the West Bank and Gaza.

6. The National Agenda proposed a mixed electoral system that combines both district and proportional (party) lists and stipulates that electoral districts shall be drawn in line with the set objectives and that the "supervision of the elections shall be assigned to an independent committee comprising judges and public figures known for their integrity and impartiality." Most important, it calls for the elimination of the "current closed districts and other appropriations (quota) systems, and divides the Kingdom into electoral districts along demographic, geographic and social lines, ensuring fair representation of the country's regions."

7. Under the constitution, suspects may be detained for up to 48 hours without

a warrant, and up to ten days without formal charges being filed. Courts routinely grant prosecutors fifteen-day extensions of this deadline.

8. NGOs must obtain a permit from the ministry of social development, which has the right to reject an application for any reason, and there is no mechanism for judicial review of the decision. The ministry can order the dissolution of any NGO at whim—without judicial oversight and an appeals process—and can send representatives to observe any meeting or election and to inspect any records at any time. Many NGOs register under the ministry of trade as nonprofits to avoid these problems.

9. For more detail, see International Crisis Group, "Red Alert in Jordan: Recurrent Unrest in Maan," International Crisis Group Briefing (Brussels: February 19, 2003). Also see "Ma'an: An Open-ended Crisis" (Amman: Center for Strategic Studies, University of Jordan, September 2003).

10. "Jordan: Country Strategy Paper 2002–2006," available at <http://ec.europa.eu/comm/external_relations/jordan/csp/index.htm>.

11. Remarks by President George W. Bush at a White House press conference with King Abdullah on May 6, 2004, available at <www.whitehouse.gov/news/releases/2004/05/20040506-9.html>.

12. Secretary of State Condoleezza Rice press briefing on October 1, 2006; available at <www.state.gov/secretary/rm/2006/73397.htm>.

REFORM IN SYRIA:
STEERING BETWEEN THE CHINESE
MODEL AND REGIME CHANGE

Ellen Lust-Okar

The issue of political reform in Syria straddles the line between reform of political institutions and removal from power of a particular regime and entails both domestic and external actors. The regime of Bashar al-Assad is under pressure from its own citizens who want a different political system and different leadership and from the United States, which wants Syria to change its regional policy—specifically, stop intruding in Lebanese affairs, reduce support of Palestinian groups, and make a bigger effort to prevent infiltration of radical Islamists into Iraq. It is impossible to separate the domestic process of political reform from the external reform pressures. Indeed, the two are entangled to a much greater extent in Syria than in any other country in the region except Iraq. The analysis that follows in this chapter reflects this entanglement.

The issue of political reform has been on Syria's domestic agenda since July 2000, when Bashar al-Assad succeeded his father Hafez as president. Bashar sought to use reforms to consolidate his political power in the face of economic stagnation, high unemployment, poverty, and social tensions. After 2003 the regime also experienced internal power struggles as well as quickly deteriorating relations with the United States. Calling on Syria to fall in line with U.S. regional interests, the United States first enacted the Syria Accountability and Lebanese Sovereignty Act of 2003 (SALSA) and then fostered UN Security Council Resolution 1559, calling for the withdrawal of Syrian troops from Lebanon and the end to support of Hizbollah. This external pressure in turn further encouraged Syrian opposition forces to intensify their demands for political reform and to work together to obtain it. Reforms have been limited, however. The regime has responded to the external pressures by fostering nationalist and anti-Western sentiments, convincing most Syrians that the United States and its allies are interested in control over the Middle East, not in Syrian political evolution. Bashar al-Assad has also slowed the program of political reform and has increasingly focused on economic reform, arguing that he seeks "Chinese style" reforms, which he defines as slow, gradual economic change implemented while maintaining political stability. The regime has strengthened its stance by narrowing the ruling coalition and repressing the opposition; it also has gained some popular support through its anti-Western rhetoric.

The United States and the European Union (EU) can help reverse this bleak picture of political stagnation, but doing so will require a significant change in existing policies. The West must shift its emphasis from demands for changes in Syria's regional policies to demands for domestic reform. It must focus also on providing direct support for social and economic development programs that help the population. A Western policy that supports domestic political reform and economic development would help reduce the commonly held view in the country that the United States and the EU disregard Syrians' interests and are simply concerned with defending their own, even if it means supporting a repressive regime. To avoid exacerbating the widespread frustration and cynicism that Syrians feel toward the West, the United States and the EU should concentrate their efforts on small and achievable steps—improving human rights, the rule of law, and social development—not establishing democracy all at once.

The Syrian Political System

The current regime in Syria finds its institutional origins in the Baathist coup of 1963 and in the 1973 constitution, which confirmed the leading role of the Baath party. But Hafez al-Assad, who rose to power in an internal coup in 1970, soon established a parallel power base for his regime. He first sought to broaden his support by providing space for old business elites and allowing small, weak parties a minor role in the Baath-dominated National Progressive Front (al-Jabhat al-Taquddumiyya al-Watanniyya). By the end of his regime, however, he came to rely increasingly on the Alawite minority and a personal network of supporters, which undermined state institutions and the Baath party.

The conflict between formal institutions and the regime's personalistic power base was clearly evident when Bashar al-Assad assumed the presidency after his father's death in June 2000. The parliament and Baath party gave him their support, revising the constitution to allow him to assume the office despite his young age, nominating him for the presidency, granting him the highest military rank, and appointing him head of the Baath party. Yet, the most important factor in his rise to power was that he was the former president's son. As one high-ranking member of the Baath Regional Command noted: "Comrade Dr. Bashar Hafiz al-Asad ... was born and brought up in the home of the late leader, educated in his school and drank from his overflowing fountain of wisdom, knowledge, morals, faith in the issues of the homeland and people and commitment to the objectives of the nation."[1] In a regime where personal relations and informal power structures were far more important than formal governmental structures or Baath party institutions, Bashar was seen as the person most likely to continue the legacy of his father. The young president's own inexperience and underdeveloped political base were arguably an advantage for an old guard anxious to retain its influence.

Bashar al-Assad and the External–Internal Tangle

Bashar al-Assad started his presidency under a modicum of goodwill both domestically and internationally. Within a few years, however, he lost much of the internal support and became entangled in an increasingly hostile relationship with the United States, France, and to a lesser extent other European countries. Syria's descent into international pariah status and domestic stagnation was the result of a mixture of failed regime policies and rapidly changing international circumstances.

Domestically, Bashar experienced an initial grace period, while enjoying the backing of the party and many of his father's old guard. Syrians outside the corridors of power also offered cautious support in return for the anticipated political liberalization.

And indeed Syria enjoyed a brief political opening, with a flourishing of opposition-led political forums discussing both political and economic reform. The political fervor of the Damascus Spring inspired hope that the president could garner sufficient support and enthusiasm to stand up to hard-line, antireform figures within the regime. By August 2001, the stirrings of the opposition made the old guard within the regime increasingly nervous; at the same time it was becoming clear that the opposition was ultimately too weak to offer a real counterweight to hard-line forces. Prudently, Bashar moved closer to the positions of the old guard and cut short the Damascus Spring.

The international community also initially welcomed Bashar al-Assad's presidency. The United States sought a chance to improve U.S.–Syrian relations, which had soured during the 1990s as the fitful and unsuccessful

Syrian–Israeli negotiations under U.S. tutelage undermined trust between the Syrian and U.S. administrations. The United States' optimism about the young president appeared vindicated in the initial months after September 11, 2001, when Syria proved ready to cooperate with counterterrorism initiatives. The Europeans, too, demonstrated support for the new president and sought to move forward with the Syrian track of the EU-Mediterranean agreement. The French gave especially strong support to the new government, even sending a team of consultants to provide advice on administrative reforms in 2003.

Changing regional and domestic circumstances eroded the goodwill toward the Syrian regime. Facing domestic tensions and regional crises, Bashar al-Assad assumed a regional leadership position against the West, issuing strident calls opposing the "aggression" of coalition forces against Iraq. U.S.–Syrian relations deteriorated in response. Some congressional leaders had long sought to put pressure on Syria, but the U.S. administration had refused to follow suit, convincing them to shelve the draft Syrian Accountability Act before bringing it to a vote in 2002. Yet, as regional conditions worsened with increasing trouble in Iraq and a continued intifada in the West Bank and Gaza Strip, the George W. Bush administration changed its stance. On March 3, 2003, Secretary of State Colin Powell broke with earlier positions to refer to the Syrian troops in Lebanon as an "occupation army," and later that month he declared that Syria must end "direct support for terrorist groups and the dying regime of Saddam Hussein."

By fall 2003, the Bush administration supported SALSA, which condemned Syria's support for terrorism, its occupation of Lebanon, and its development of a weapons of mass destruction program. It also gave President Bush a menu of economic and diplomatic sanctions that he could implement until Syria complied. Three points of this act are significant. First, the pressure leading up to the passage of the act, the text of the law itself, which focused on Syria's external relations, and the authorization for the U.S. president to provide Syria with assistance requires not only that progress be made on these fronts, but also progress in "negotiations aimed at achieving a peace agreement between Israel and Syria."[2] Despite the heightened U.S. rhetoric about promoting democracy in the Middle East, the act made no mention of democracy or human rights in Syria.

Second, the economic and diplomatic sanctions on Syria were of limited real effect. Syria has long been listed as a state sponsor of terrorism, and both economic and political relations with the United States are minimal.

Third, the act was nevertheless extremely painful to the regime, which saw SALSA as signaling Syria's isolation from the broader international community and believed that the act could provide the basis for more serious measures in the future.

And it did provide such a basis. The United States continued to garner international support in its efforts to pressure the Syrian regime, most notably from France. By September 2, 2004, the United States and France joined forces to endorse UN Security Council Resolution 1559, which called for Syria's withdrawal from Lebanon, the disarmament of all Lebanese and non-Lebanese militias in Lebanon, and free and fair presidential elections, devoid of foreign (that is, Syrian) interference. Damascus responded to the resolution by supporting the extension in office of the Syrian-backed Lebanese president Emile Lahoud, effectively thumbing its nose at UN (and U.S.) demands.

The tensions escalated further after the assassination of former Lebanese prime minister Rafiq Hariri on February 14, 2005, which Syria was suspected of ordering. The United States and France took advantage of the situation to call on Syria to withdraw its forces from Lebanon and encouraged anti-Syrian forces in Lebanon to mobilize. Syria withdrew its troops in the shadow of the Cedar Revolution (the civil unrest that followed Hariri's assassination), with its massive anti-Syrian demonstrations in Beirut. Led by Detlev Mehlis, the UN investigation into Hariri's assassination and the Syrian government's potential involvement in it put additional pressure on the regime. On October 20, 2005, the first Mehlis report blamed high-level Syrian officials for the assassination, and the October 31, 2005, UN Security Council Resolution 1636 established targeted sanctions against individuals suspected in the assassination. The Syrians feared that sanctions and further retribution would be forthcoming. Tensions subsided only slightly when questions emerged about the reliability of the witnesses cited by the commission, and the second UN report released on December 10, 2005, failed to be conclusive about Syrian involvement.

The international pressure on Syria exerted by the United States, France, and the United Nations had substantial repercussions on socioeconomic conditions in Syria as well as on domestic politics. Domestic conditions deteriorated significantly following the U.S. invasion of Iraq, which ended favorable economic arrangements between Syria and Iraq. Popular discontent resulting from economic deterioration led the government to curb domestic debates and to restrict the focus of those that were allowed to continue from broad issues of political reforms to narrower ones of economic policy.

The ultimate outcome of this tangle of foreign and domestic developments has been a narrowing of Bashar's power base. Bashar has removed many individuals who had been prominent during his father's administration. Among the members of the old guard sidelined by Bashar and his closest associates were those in the security and intelligence apparatus. Even major players such as the head of intelligence Bahjat Suleiman, head of military intelligence Hassan Khalil, head of political security Adnan Badr Hassan, and Vice President Abdel-Halim Kaddam lost their positions. Old Baath party leaders have also lost ground in recent years. As a result of these and other changes, power has become increasingly concentrated in the hands of the so-called triumvirate: Bashar al-Assad, his brother Maher (head of the Republican Guard), and his brother-in-law Asef Shawkat (head of military security). The narrower the coalition has become, however, the wider the base of the opposition.

Assessing Reforms Under Bashar al-Assad

Although attention has been focused on the most dramatic recent developments in Syria, particularly its role in Lebanon and the growing tensions with the United States and the international community, both the regime and the opposition have been engaged in a less apparent attempt to bring about some domestic changes. In particular, the regime has increasingly emphasized economic and administrative reforms over political change. Opposition forces have tried to reshape themselves to respond better to the new circumstances.

Neither the steps taken by the regime nor the efforts of the opposition have so far been significant in terms of altering the distribution of power in Syria and making the regime subject to a popular mandate. In general, the reforms introduced by the government in the economic and, to a lesser extent, political spheres have been more cosmetic than consequential. Particularly given the social tensions within Syria, the minority basis of the regime, and the example of sectarian violence in neighboring Iraq, regime elites—as well as many average Syrians—are reluctant to see reforms move too quickly for fear of destabilization. The sluggish reforms implemented to date are thus not likely to promote a gradual process of democratization from the top, although they might have the unintended consequence of increasing the likelihood of a full breakdown of the Baathist regime. In contrast, the steps taken by the opposition are more likely to strengthen pro-democracy forces. Even these changes, however, should not be overstated, nor should the possibility that a breakdown of the regime would usher in a democratic, pro-Western regime.

Regime Efforts

ECONOMIC AND ADMINISTRATIVE REFORMS. Like many other Arab governments at this time, the Syrian regime is not averse to change, particularly concerning the economy and the administrative systems, but it wants these reforms to take place in a slow, steady manner, without loss of political control. Government officials explicitly seek to emulate the Chinese model of reform, in which the government promoted economic reform and modernization in many sectors while retaining complete political control. The Syrians are determined to avoid the experiences of Eastern Europe and the former Soviet Union, where modest political openings quickly mushroomed into regime collapse. Syria, they argue, needs to promote economic growth without sacrificing political stability.

The process of economic and administrative reform has been real, even dramatic to some extent. In the last five years, Syria has seen the establishment of private banks and universities, major reductions in customs duties, and the expansion of foreign investment opportunities. Indeed, more than 134 laws and presidential decrees to reform the economic and administrative system were signed in 2005 alone. The president's emphasis on economic reform is illustrated by his personal choice of Abdallah Dardari, first as the head of the independent Syrian Planning Commission and subsequently in the newly created position of vice prime minister for economic affairs. Dardari has promoted the private sector over the state sector, a striking change for the socialist-oriented Baathist system. Indeed, the June 2005 Baath Party Congress confirmed that Syria would develop a "Socialist Market Economy," and serious discussions have taken place about the future shrinking of the public sector and the resulting potential for increased unemployment.

These reforms have been somewhat significant in loosening government control over the economy and providing more space for private sector growth. There is no indication, however, that the growth of the private sector has changed the balance of political power in the country, creating new political forces autonomous of the government or stimulating a greater degree of political pluralism. On the contrary, as is often the case in countries seeking to reform socialist economic systems, the revitalized private sector is creating new monopolies controlled by members of the governing elite rather than avenues through which new players can gain wealth and political influence. Furthermore, the economic reforms likely to have the largest effect, such as a significant reduction in the public sector, have not yet been implemented.

POLITICAL REFORMS. The government has announced numerous political reforms during the last five years, but to the extent to which they have been implemented, such steps have served to reinforce, not undermine, the regime's power. Among the announced reforms were calls to differentiate more clearly the government from the Baath party, and the decision to allow private print media. The government also promised to enact a new law governing political parties but has not yet done so. Nor has it responded to a fundamental demand of the opposition, the lifting of the state of emergency that has been in force since 1963.

The June 2005 Baath Party Congress provides an excellent example of the narrow limits of political reform under Bashar al-Assad. The congress was held immediately after the withdrawal of Syrian troops from Lebanon and was preceded by an extraordinary debate between hard-liners and reformers. Many party members objected to the way in which the delegates were elected by the party branches, forcing the Baath's leading organ, the Regional Command, to allow more than one hundred unelected delegates to participate in the congress. Nevertheless, the results of the congress were largely disappointing for those seeking reform. President Bashar al-Assad openly stated that major political change would not be forthcoming: There would be no major constitutional reform, no relinquishment of the Baath's leading role in the state, and no real opening to the opposition parties, particularly to the Muslim Brotherhood. As if to emphasize the latter point, the last real remnant of the political opening of the Damascus Spring, the Jamal Atassi forum, saw members of its board arrested for reading a letter from the Muslim Brotherhood shortly before the congress.

The congress did promise that work would move forward on a long-expected law governing political parties, but the new draft law has been disappointing. It requires that new parties be "allied to, created by, or friends of the Ba'ath."[3] Party founders must be over thirty-five years old, have no criminal record, and be proven supporters of the Baathist March 8 Revolution. This effectively precludes opposition figures from forming new parties. The parties themselves cannot be based on religious, sectarian, or tribal identities and cannot have operated before 1963 (only the Baath Party, the Syrian Social Nationalist Party, and the Communist Party are exempted from the last restriction). This prohibits the legalization of the Muslim Brotherhood or the Kurdish nationalist parties. Party formation is further hindered by the need to have ten founding members, and at least 500 members present at a founding conference. According to the draft law, the decision whether to grant a new party a license will be made by a committee that includes the head of the Shura Council, the ministers of justice and interior, and the minister of state for people's assembly affairs—all of whom are Baathists—and three independent judges. Finally, even legalized parties will be severely disadvantaged vis-à-vis the ruling Baath party: They cannot obtain foreign funds or mobilize support outside the country, even among the Syrian diaspora; they cannot be active in religious places or use the government-owned media for propaganda (although they can publish their own newspapers); and they cannot enlist government employees as members.

Most of the restrictions, of course, do not apply to the Baath party: Civil servants will continue to constitute a large percentage of the 2 million Baath party members, the party will continue using the government media for propaganda, and it will continue drawing on government revenue for resources and on government institutions to mobilize support. It is important to note that the government has not shown any intention to amend Article 8 of the constitution, which states that the Baath party is "the ruling party of state and society." Rather than weakening the Baath party's role, the new political parties law will reinforce it by making it virtually impossible for opposition parties to register. As the Baathist Speaker of Parliament Mahmoud al-Abrash explained, "rotation of power is unlikely."[4]

A Divided Opposition

Opposition forces have also seen important changes in the last five years, above all making a concerted effort to find common ground to increase their effectiveness. Even a modicum of coordination—if only for tactical purposes—would be critical in allowing the Syrian opposition to take advantage of the pressures on the Syrian regime to push for change and potentially for democracy. However, despite some progress in achieving coordination, the Syrian opposition remains essentially weak and divided.

THE NATURE OF SYRIAN OPPOSITION. The Syrian opposition spans a broad and diverse range of socioeconomic and ideological positions. There are three main categories of present or potential opposition forces in Syria. The most moderate opposition consists of the recent defectors (and potential defectors) from the regime: former regime members who had been sidelined, young lower level Baathists who seek to revitalize the system through strengthening the party, and potentially old business elites, who have found themselves losing ground to "sons of the regime." They generally hope to see the Baath party remain in power but seek greater competition within the regime. Other opposition forces seek the Baathist regime's demise, and they have a longer history of opposition: secularist intellectuals inside Syria; the Muslim Brotherhood, whose leadership is based in London; and secularist opponents living in Europe (primarily in France) and the United States. These have been weakened by years of repression and have weak ties to the population. A final and less-well-understood potential source of opposition is local leaders within Syria, likely of an Islamist bent. Such local elites may arguably be the most powerful forces of mobilization should the regime start losing control, yet they remain largely unknown.

The opposition is divided along a number of dimensions. They differ over the extent to which they are willing to rely on external actors, particularly the United States, in changing the regime. Similarly, they differ in the extent to which they are willing to accept gradual reforms rather than a more dramatic and risky regime overthrow. They seek a range of ultimate outcomes—from expressly secularist, democratic regimes to Islamist caliphates. Finally, opponents are fragmented by regional divisions, sectarian splits, and personal animosities.

BOLDER CHALLENGES. The opposition has become increasingly bold since 2000. Initially, the non-Islamist opposition within Syria sought limited reforms, signing the Charter of the 99 and the Statement of the 1000, both of which emphasized political liberalization—calling for lifting the 1963 state of emergency, releasing political prisoners, and expanding the freedom of the press and public gathering. The president reportedly encouraged these moves, both by emphasizing democratization in his inaugural speech of July 2000 and by allowing close associates to sign the declarations. Indeed, opposition leaders repeatedly claimed in the early years of Bashar's presidency that they did not seek the overthrow of the regime but a degree of political liberalization that would make the Syrian regime resemble Mubarak's Egypt.

In contrast, the Damascus Declaration of October 2005 took a much harsher tone and was signed by a wider range of opposition forces. The declaration blamed the "authorities" for the

> rending of the national social fabric of the Syrian people, an economic collapse that poses a threat to the country, and exacerbating crises of every kind, in addition to the stifling isolation which the regime has brought upon the country as a result of its destructive, adventurous, and short-sighted policies on the Arab and regional levels, and especially in Lebanon.

Although stating that change needed to be gradual and based on national dialogue, the document clearly demanded democratization. Unlike the earlier statements, the declaration was not encouraged by the regime.

WEAK COALITIONS. Syria's divided opposition forces also attempted to build bridges with one another, but with limited success. The Muslim Brotherhood has had a steep hill to climb in regaining the trust of the Syrian people, particularly the secularist opposition forces. A violent conflict with the regime in the early 1980s not only left the Brotherhood largely decimated within

Syria, but it also undermined trust between secularist opponents and the Brothers. The Brotherhood has subsequently reached out to secularists and emphasized its desire to build a democratic Syria. The most notable effort was the convening of a conference in August 2002 to discuss a National Charter for Syria, which included respect for human rights and the rejection of violence, and the unveiling of a political program in 2004 that supports a democratic transition. Their efforts have had mixed results, however. Many secularist opponents are eager to work with the Brotherhood, believing that they are an important and powerful part of the Syrian political spectrum. The Brotherhood has reached out to liberal groups and to former members of the regime. For instance, it gained public cooperation from a leader in the opposition-oriented Jamal Atassi forum, who read a statement from the Brotherhood in 2005 and was subsequently arrested for this action. The Brotherhood also coordinated with former vice president Abdel-Halim Kaddam after he left Syria and denounced the regime on December 31, 2005. However, other opposition forces were less enthusiastic about cooperating with the Brotherhood, including Riad Turk, arguably one of the most legitimate secularist opposition leaders inside Syria.

Reformists within the Baath party have also sought to establish links with opposition figures. The frustration within the Baath party is in some ways not new; it was the voicing of Baathists' concerns in summer 2001 that most worried hard-liners within the regime and contributed to the end of the Damascus Spring. Ayman Abdel Nour, a Baathist reformist, has also long attempted to promote discussions among various factions through his daily bulletin, All4Syria. More formal efforts have also been made since April 2004, when party reformers reached out to legal opposition parties. In December 2005, efforts were made to bring a somewhat broader spectrum of forces (yet excluding the Muslim Brotherhood) together to sign a statement calling for reform. However, while signatories came from various parties, they signed as individuals, not party representatives. Despite these efforts, bridging the gap between the Baath party reformers and opposition forces is a difficult task. Opposition forces are often skeptical of the intentions of the Baathist reformers and of their effectiveness, and Baathist reformers have legitimate fears of losing their relative privileges should change move too quickly.

Finally, many opposition forces have attempted to build bridges with the United States, but this seems to have limited effect. U.S.-based opponents of the regime such as Farid Ghadhry face problems of legitimacy among Syrians. Others incur both the ire of the regime and the suspicion of other opponents. For example, Kamal Lebwani, a rising opposition leader, was arrested as he returned to Syria after a visit with U.S. officials in 2005. The arrest, and questions among the public about his ties to the Bush administration, quickly faded his fast-rising star.

Priorities for Reform

There is no mystery about the reforms Syria would need to undertake to start a process of democratic transformation in earnest. Like most other Arab countries, Syria needs to lift the state of emergency, promote rule of law and the independence of the judiciary, amend the elections and party laws, and increase the power of the parliament vis-à-vis the executive. Promoting social and economic development would also be crucial to facilitate a transition. None of these reforms is particularly difficult to envisage. However, all these reforms would entail a loss of power for the regime and thus are unlikely to be implemented unless the regime comes under a great deal of pressure.

Eliminating Martial Law

Perhaps the single most important step toward democracy would be eliminating the martial law in place since 1963. This allows the ruling regime to supersede all constitutional guarantees of basic human rights and to use martial courts, which deny due process. Not surprisingly, an end to the state of emergency has been a long-standing demand of opposition forces.

Promoting the Judiciary and Rule of Law

Judicial reform and promoting the rule of law would also be a critical step toward democracy. The government has taken some steps in this direction, such as the decision to increase oversight of the judiciary and to raise the salary and benefits of judges in an attempt to reduce their incentives to engage in corrupt practices. These reforms may reduce petty corruption, but they will not check major abuse by the regime. As long as judges serve at the will of the executive, they cannot effectively enforce the rule of law.

Eliminating the Baath Party Monopoly

Reforms should also focus on eliminating the primacy of the Baath party. The first step is to remove Article 8 of the constitution, which ensures that the Baath party is the leading party of government and society. The Baath party may remain dominant for the foreseeable future, but changes in the constitution, electoral regulations, and party laws can create an open playing field.

Promoting Competitive Elections

Eliminating the Baath party's monopoly on power will also allow for democratic elections. For the legislature, this requires eliminating the requirements that reserve two-thirds of seats for the Baathist-dominated parties of the National Progressive Front, with the majority going to the Baath party. For the presidency, it entails replacing the present system in which the Baath party proposes a candidate, the parliament nominates him, and the populace confirms the choice in a referendum. Bashar al-Assad has reportedly favored such reform. Bolstered by the nationalist reaction to U.S. pressure and the war in Iraq, coupled with weak opposition, he should be able to win handily a competitive election and gain increasing legitimacy as a "reformer." A democratic election is not likely to undermine the regime, but it would set a precedent, move Syria toward democracy, and help to provide an exit option for current regime elites.

Changing Party Laws

The proposed political party law should provide for an inclusive system that could, in the long run, transform into democracy. The draft Political Parties Law should be revised to eliminate advantages granted the Baath party, to allow for a wider range of political parties, and to reduce the restrictions placed on party founders. In conjunction, Law 49, which stipulates that membership in the Muslim Brotherhood is a capital offense, should be repealed. The Brotherhood must be allowed to operate as a legal political force if Syria is to include all relevant political forces.

Changing Executive–Legislative Balance of Power

Changes in the Political Parties Law will have limited effect, however, if the legislature is not given effective power. The legislature must be given the ability to censure members of government, to approve judicial appointments, to pass legislation in critical areas, and to influence government formation. Until the legislature has power, the parliament will remain heavily dependent on the executive, and individuals will vote for candidates who simply kowtow to the regime.

Moreover, as long as parliamentarians' legislative powers are limited primarily to acting as a rubber stamp, political parties will remain weak. Political entrepreneurs have little incentive to work within political parties, to develop political platforms, or to join in coalitions. Constituents also have little incentive to join or support political parties. The result is a system of weak parties, unstable legislatures, and a failure to develop alternative centers of power.

Promoting Social and Economic Development

Social and economic development is also critical for the promotion of democracy. Syria's low per capita income would make it hard for Syria to establish and sustain a democratic regime—research has proven conclusively that democratic reform in low income countries tends to be short-lived. In addition, well-designed development projects that seek to incorporate and advantage Syrians without regard to sectarian or regional bases could help to reduce social tensions. Implementing programs so that they do not advantage the "sons of the regime" is a difficult task. Development programs in Syria often bribe regime supporters—only helping to exacerbate conflicts between Syrians from different sects, families, or regions. This is counterproductive. Only if the current Syrian regime can slowly reduce the sharp inequalities in access to state resources and diminish the salience of social identities in the distribution process can it sustain a gradual, democratic transition.

Obstacles to Democratic Reform

Although the necessary reforms are clear, the obstacles to their implementation are formidable and rest in both the regime and the opposition. The major difficulty facing the ruling coalition is that its basis of support is narrow, which makes reform extremely risky. For the opposition, the problem is its overall weakness: lack of strong leadership; weak ties to the population and above all to organized constituencies; internal divisions based on regionalism, sectarianism, and personal animosities; and scarcity of financial resources, particularly in the absence of strong and sustained support from the business community.

The regime faces a catch-22: It desperately needs to reform to stay in power, and yet any move in that direction threatens its collapse. It is not lost on elites in power that Syria faces severe crises at home and abroad. The deteriorating economic situation, combined with a burgeoning young population, has led to unemployment rates exceeding 22 percent. Official poverty rates stand at 11.4 percent, and a 2005 UNDP study found that more than 30.1 percent of Syrians, or almost 5.3 million individuals, live below the poverty line. As Syrian analyst Samir Aita noted in an April 2006 Arab Reform Brief, the "economic situation has deteriorated to levels dangerous for social stability."[5]

Indeed, social tensions are high. Although explicitly secular and nonsectarian, the regime has exploited communal ties to shore up its power. Alawites constitute only an estimated 10–15 percent of the Syrian population, but they dominate the regime and provide support for it. This has reinforced the salience of sectarian identities, exacerbating tensions between the various social groups. At present, small altercations quickly take on ethnic and sectarian tones, with emerging strife most notably in Kurdish areas and in a more limited form between Ismailis and Alawites.

Perhaps the greatest barrier to reform lies in the widespread fear of social violence if the regime loses control. Most Alawites seem to fear that heads would indeed roll if the regime falls, and the exploding civil war in Iraq only reinforces these fears. Facing the possibility of costly retribution, regime elites fear reforms that promote democracy, thus giving the majority the upper hand, and seek to foster the fear of sectarian violence among the general population. For instance, a posting on the All4Syria forum in February 2006 reported that the Syrian population is as fragmented as that of Lebanon: 45 percent Sunni, 20 percent Alawite, 15 percent Kurdish, and 12 percent Christian, with a number of smaller minorities. The message was clear: The destruction of the Syrian regime would plunge Syria into a Lebanese-style civil war.

In response, opposition leaders consistently claim that they will not discriminate among Syrians on a sectarian basis, but it is not clear that they are capable of delivering on such promises. The opposition lacks strong leadership, both inside and outside the country, with the internal forces decimated by years of harsh repression and external groups lacking widespread grassroots support. They also have limited organizational resources. The regime controlled most organizations, including trade unions, professional associations, and public mosques, since the late 1970s. Of course, the opposition has more space to organize outside of Syria, with the Muslim Brotherhood being the most important organization; however, distance makes it more difficult to foster local ties and support. Ties to the population are further weakened by significant sectarian, regional, and personal divisions in the ranks of the opposition and among the general population.

Finally, Syrians across the political and social spectrum mistrust the opposition, concerned that it may be no more democratic than the current regime. Some voice skepticism about the ultimate goals of the secular, Damascus-based, Sunni bourgeoisie, who they believe exploited the Syrian population in the 1940s and 1950s. Many also wonder about the Muslim Brotherhood's commitment to democracy, despite the Brotherhood's consistent attempts to allay these fears. The regime benefits from the belief that Islamist organizations will dominate if the current regime fails, and they encourage the idea. For example, in February 2006 the Syrian authorities were slow in stopping protests against the Danish cartoons caricaturing the prophet Muhammad, allegedly to suggest to both domestic and international audiences that

Islamists are strong and most likely to succeed should the regime fall. Whether justified or not, the belief that opposition leaders are not committed to democracy undermines support.

Future Scenarios

Quite simply, the high stakes for regime elites combined with the weak opposition make an orderly, peaceful process of democratic transition in Syria unlikely at present. Given the dire prospects that regime elites face if they lose power, they are unlikely to step down without assurances of protection. The opposition may commit to this, but they cannot guarantee that they can deliver on it. Consequently, the most likely scenario is survival of the regime, as it is or in a modified form. It is also possible that pent-up frustration will lead to a popular upheaval with an unpredictable outcome. Before examining how the United States and Europe may promote and respond to these possible outcomes, it is important to consider the three most likely scenarios.

Scenario 1: The Regime Digs In

The first and most likely scenario is the survival of the regime. President Bashar al-Assad may not remain the most powerful member of the triumvirate that also includes Maher al-Assad and Asef Shawkat, but the existing power structure will prevail.

The regime may survive the many pressures, particularly if the investigation into the Hariri assassination cannot find conclusive proof of Syria's involvement. To date, Bashar has been able to capitalize on the regional and international pressures to foster support on the street. Syrians are widely skeptical of U.S. intentions, and they generally believe that the United States and Europe are not serious about promoting democracy and human rights in Syria. Thus, many see international pressure on the Syrian regime as a manifestation of hostility toward all Syrians, and indeed, the Arab world more generally. This perception, combined with the humiliation of the forced withdrawal from Lebanon, the international investigation into Syria's role in the assassination of Rafiq Hariri, and the resentment of U.S. intervention in Iraq and its policy toward Israel, has reinforced Syrian nationalism and increased support for the regime. Bashar has also been able to take advantage of the widespread anti-U.S. sentiment in the Arab world to boost his regional standing.

The regime may thus survive. Domestically, it will continue to circle the wagons, maintaining a narrow base of support, and justifying repression in the name of external threats. Regionally, it will continue developing its role as the anti-Western, regional leader, strengthening the Iranian–Syrian–Hizbollah axis. As Bashar noted in his recent speech to the Arab Parties Congress, Syria will find friends elsewhere than in the West (that is, the Gulf, China, Russia), rejecting both the support and the opposition from the West.

Scenario 2: An Alawite Regime Remade

A second possibility is that increased popular and international pressure will weaken the regime and leave it vulnerable to an internal coup carried out by Alawites in the military. Alawite elites are largely convinced that they cannot afford to lose control over the reins of power. As long as the Assad family appears best-placed to maintain control, it is unlikely to face an Alawite opposition. If its grip should start slipping, Alawite military forces may attempt to take matters into their own hands.

The obstacles to an internal coup are significant, however. Since the mid-1980s, the Syrian military has been deliberately fragmented. Real military and security powers have increasingly been concentrated in the Republican Guard, under the control of the president's brother, Maher al-Assad. Finally, the death of Interior Minister General Ghazi Kanaan, the former Syrian intelligence commander in Lebanon who was perhaps the most likely to succeed in such an attempt, both removed an important potential coup leader and demonstrated the difficulties that such an operation would face.

If such a coup were to succeed, it would not represent a paradigm shift toward democracy. Any Alawite-based regime is bound to fear real democratic reforms, because Alawites are too few to win a popular election. Small improvements in human rights and political freedoms might take place, particularly in the early honeymoon period of the regime. The major change is more likely to be in foreign policy, with a shift toward better U.S.–Syrian relations. The regime would try to make itself indispensable to the United States, but in doing so, it would probably also reduce U.S. interest in promoting Syrian democracy.

Scenario 3: Regime Collapse

A complete collapse of the regime brought about by a popular uprising appears even more remote, but nevertheless should be considered. The old adage, that revolutions appear impossible before they take place and inevitable afterward, is apt. Beneath the heightened Syrian nationalist sentiment are widespread grievances caused by high unemployment and underemployment, increasing poverty, economic stagnation, and limited political and social freedoms.

The major military and security forces appear to be firmly in the regime's hand, but it is difficult to know what would happen if the regime were confronted with widespread disorder and mass demonstrations, for example. A collapse would become more likely if business elites and the reformists within the party—who would prefer regime change but largely sit on the fence, fearing that such changes would not be successful—became convinced that the regime's days were limited. The critical question is what factors would lead to such a change in expectations. One triggering element might be a growing perception among Syrians that the regime had lost its capacity to repress the opposition, or if they became convinced that a revolt against the regime would gain international support.

The consequences of regime collapse would be far reaching but not necessarily positive. The change would likely restore a Sunni-based regime, but it would not necessarily be either pro-Western or democratic. The opposition forces that stand at the forefront of the public movement are largely divided themselves over the degree of democracy and the nature of the regime they want. Even pro-Western, prodemocracy forces tend to favor limited democracy, fearing the potential for Islamist victories or sectarian conflict. Regime collapse is not a sure path to democracy.

Options for the International Community

None of these scenarios suggest that pro-Western, liberal democracy is likely to emerge in Syria in the short run. The prospects for a significant paradigm shift are virtually nil if the present regime remains in power. They would remain very low even if a new military-based Alawite regime were to take power, although such a scenario would probably lead to improved relations with the United States. Regime collapse would of course represent a definite paradigm shift, although not necessarily one toward democracy. If regime collapse were followed by long-term instability and domestic conflict, the cause of democracy would not advance. If stability were quickly reestablished, the new government, if majority-based, might not be initially democratic, but it might ultimately find democratic reforms less threatening than the present, minority-dominated regime does.

The international community is thus faced with two possible challenges: If the regime survives, can it take steps to encourage reforms that would improve conditions for Syrians, regardless of the regime in power? And if the regime collapses, could it help to steer the country away from civil conflict and make the aftermath more conducive to democracy?

Promoting Domestic Reform

The United States and European countries can promote some reforms that, while falling far short of democracy, would improve the daily lives of Syrians, help to stabilize the country, and even eventually evolve toward democracy. To succeed, however, any outside force must emphasize steps that do not directly threaten the regime. For example, it should advocate reforms that improve respect for human rights or help broaden press freedom, rather than call for free and fair elections and support opposition groups.

Measures currently adopted by the United States are the most likely to prove counterproductive in promoting democratization. As we have seen, the forceful positions Washington has taken vis-à-vis Syria—imposing sanctions through SALSA, steering Resolution 1559 through the UN Security Council, and expressing strong disapproval of the regime in every possible forum—have caused a nationalist backlash that plays into the hands of the Syrian government. Washington's efforts to support the prodemocratic opposition have instead undermined the opposition's legitimacy and further split these forces. The United States has little leverage to affect democratic regime change in Syria: Economic ties have always been minimal, and U.S. influence has been further undermined by SALSA and popular hostility to U.S. policy in the region. The United States would have a greater effect on reform if it deescalated its criticism of Syria's policies in the region, stopped calls for regime change, and relied instead on conditional aid and diplomatic pressure to convince the Syrian government to improve human rights.

European countries are better placed to influence change. The EU has stronger economic relations with Syria and thus has more economic carrots and sticks. So far, however, the EU has steered away from demanding significant political change as a condition for stronger economic ties. This stance has led many Syrians to conclude that European countries are only interested in economic benefits and do not care about reforms that affect Syrians. Moreover, socioeconomic development programs such as those supported by the EU can have the unintended consequence of reinforcing the regime, pouring large sums of money into the hands of individuals and groups closely associated with the ruling elite. For the EU to tie economic and social development programs to political reform, and to ensure that development programs are implemented in ways that reduce social disparity, will require a great deal of political will and attention to implementation.

Even more carefully designed development programs, however, would not immediately bring democracy. Nevertheless, the West must avoid the temptation to seek more dramatic results. Attempts to support specific opposition groups in the hope of enabling them to challenge the regime more effectively are not likely to succeed. Financial support of Syrian opposition forces (such as that provided for by the current Middle East Partnership Initiative) will only taint groups that accept it and make it more difficult for them to build constituencies.

An attempt to overthrow the Syrian regime by force is even less likely to serve U.S. or European interests. There is little question that the Syrian regime could be relatively easily removed from power, much as the Iraqi regime was. As in Iraq, however, regime overthrow would result in a long, costly period of instability and conflict, heightening resentment of the United States and leading even further away from the establishment of a pro-Western, democratic regime.

Putting pressure on the regime to improve human rights and providing development assistance, in contrast, will demonstrate to skeptical Syrians that the West is concerned with their problems, not just its own interests. Although anti-U.S. sentiments will not disappear completely without major changes in U.S. policies toward Israel and Iraq, a clear commitment to improving conditions for Syrians will help to undermine the anti-Western sentiment that reinforces the regime.

Avoiding Conflict and Instability

Even modest efforts such as those outlined above may nevertheless provide a catalyst for more radical regime change, as set forth in regime change scenario 3. As seen in Iran during the 1970s, opposition leaders may increase their pressure if they perceive the regime to be weakening. Even modest domestic reform may thus stimulate regime collapse.

But regime collapse would not necessarily be a positive development. Syria suffers from long-standing sectarian and regional divisions, as seen in its early, tumultuous history. Social trust among different groups has been further undermined by the past forty years of Baathist rule, which played on social divisions to strengthen the regime. Regime weakness or change could provide a catalyst for sectarian violence and even secessionist movements in areas such as Jebel Druze and the Kurdish northeast. The weakness of cohesive, national opposition groups, discussed earlier, would compound the problem, increasing the influence of locally based, fragmented opposition forces that, given the prevalence of weapons in Syria, would probably be armed.

The West must thus prepare for the possibility that the regime will collapse, even if it follows a cautious policy of promoting domestic reform. The most important challenge for the United States and the EU will be to minimize civil conflict. This means making sure that the military and security forces remain intact at the lower level even as the top officer ranks are removed and that the state apparatus continues to function, in other words, avoiding massive purges of people previously associated with the Baath party. The United States and EU would also need to avoid the tendency to pick winners and losers, looking for allies they can trust while excluding others from the political process. Doing so is likely only to support the introduction of a nondemocratic regime and to prolong the process of consolidating a new regime.

There is no easy, safe policy to encourage political reform in Syria that the United States and Europe could embrace. An aggressive policy of supporting the opposition and putting strong pressure on the government is likely to backfire, discrediting opposition groups and increasing popular support for the regime. A cautious policy of encouraging economic development and improvement in human rights is an unsatisfying response to a difficult, hostile regime. Even modest changes could destabilize a regime with as narrow a support base as the present one, leaving a vacuum of power likely to be filled by fragmented sectarian groups with access to weapons.

Whether the regime survives or collapses, Syria is not on the verge of democracy, and Western policymakers must keep this in mind. Current leaders and their supporters see the regime's survival as a matter of life-and-death and will not give up power easily. The Syrian opposition is too weak and fragmented to either force the regime from power or to create an orderly, democratic new system if the regime collapses. The specter of civil conflict and nondemocratic successors—whether Islamist or secularist—leaves many Syrians wondering if they may not be better off with the devil they know. In this difficult terrain, democracy promotion by outsiders must be a cautious endeavor with a long-term horizon.

Notes

1. "Syria: Ba'ath Party Deputy Pledges Continuation of Al-Asad's Policies, Ideals," Syrian Arab TV (Damascus), in BBC Monitoring International Reports, June 17, 2000.

2. Section C(2) of SALSA, available at <www.fas.org/asmp/resources/govern/108th/pl_108_175.pdf>.

3. Sami Moubayed, "Allied to, Created by or Friends of the Ba'ath," available at <www.mideastviews.com>.

4. Cited in Sami Moubayed, "Allied to, Created by or Friends of the Ba'ath," available at <www.mideastviews.com>.

5. Samir Aita, "What Reforms while a Storm Is Building?" in Arab Reform Initiative, Arab Reform Brief no. 60, April 2006, available at <www.arab-reform.net/IMG/pdf/Syria__word_1_-_final_-_aita.pdf>.

REQUIEM FOR PALESTINIAN REFORM: CLEAR LESSONS FROM A TROUBLED RECORD

Nathan J. Brown

Never has the cause of political reform in the Arab world received as strong verbal support—on both the international and domestic political levels—as it did in Palestine between 2002 and 2006. And while much of the Palestinian reform agenda remained unrealized, Palestinian governance changed in fundamental ways during the reform wave. But international backers of reform in particular had a remarkably short-term focus, a highly personalized view of the process, and an extremely instrumental view of reform, leading them to turn harshly against the achievements of the Palestinian reform movement when it brought unexpected results. What can this combination of success and disillusioned failure teach us about the cause of Arab political reform?

The Palestinian Reform Coalitions

A reform coalition of Palestinian parliamentarians and intellectuals began sketching its plans for a different kind of Arab political system in 1996. The coalition's goal was to undermine the emerging authoritarianism of the Palestinian Authority (PA), a political system governing Palestinian-administered areas of the West Bank and the Gaza Strip since 1994. The PA oversaw most civil affairs for the Palestinian population of those two areas and was also seen by most Palestinians living there as an embryonic Palestinian state. From an early date, some Palestinian activists insisted that their state be born reformed, avoiding the authoritarian features common to Arab regimes in the Middle East.

But not until 2002 did the coalition's efforts receive a hearty international endorsement. That year, the United States and the European Union intervened in a remarkably frank and direct manner to support the cause of Palestinian political reform. With international backing, the reform movement began to effect some significant changes, most notably in constitutional structure and fiscal transparency. Ten years after the effort began, it achieved its greatest success: In 2006, a professionalized body (the Central Elections Commission), operating with international technical assistance and political protection, oversaw a national election in which, for the first time in Arab history, voters repudiated a deeply entrenched party. And the victor was a reform-oriented party called Change and Reform that had made corruption and abuse of power the focus of its campaign. Never before had a reforming opposition party won power at an Arab ballot box. Sitting alongside the reform party was a popularly elected president who, though affiliated with the erstwhile (and now discredited) governing party, was often seen as a friend of the Palestinian reform movement.

No Arab political system had ever showed such an ability to reform itself—albeit with a significant measure of international assistance. But many of the friends of Palestinian reform, especially but not exclusively its international allies, quickly concluded that their efforts had given birth to a monster. The problem, of course, was that the victorious reform party had goals that went beyond good governance: Change and Reform was the creation of the Movement of Islamic Resistance. Known by its Arabic acronym, Hamas, this Islamist party bitterly opposed the internationally sponsored peace process and rejected all but technical negotiations with Israel. Its decision to downplay its international agenda (and even part of its Islamist agenda) for the election campaign hardly reassured its critics.

Some supporters of Palestinian reform merely abandoned the effort, but others went further, actively seeking to destroy what they had once so enthusiastically supported. For instance, in December 2006 the Palestinian president moved in blatant violation of the critical constitutional reforms of 2003 (reforms that had at the time resulted in his appointment as prime minister) by threatening to dismiss the elected parliament. In response, the United States, which had provided critical support for the constitutional reforms, not only encouraged him but also offered material support to the armed forces he would need to impose his will.

Indeed, for a solid year after the January 2006 elections, the international actors who had sponsored and helped fund the PA not only watched but facilitated its decay by cutting aid, boycotting its government, and blocking any private or public party from providing financial assistance. In the aftermath of the elections, Palestine's two major political parties, Hamas and Fatah, lurched between violent rivalry and attempts to form a national unity government—finding international thumbs very much on the scale tilting the balance against unity. No international actor endorsed the slide toward civil war, but the most important ones made clear that they supported (with funds and even military assistance) the presidency in any conflict with the cabinet, effectively taking sides in a brewing struggle. Even the European Union—which eventually stepped in to pay salaries to many PA employees, thus averting its collapse—publicly endorsed an imaginary presidential prerogative to call early elections.

The 2006 elections had laid bare the central problem with the Palestinian reform effort: Almost all of its powerful backers viewed reform not as an end in itself but as a means to a set of ends. Not only have the ultimate ends of various members of the reform coalition sharply diverged (and often contradicted each other), but almost all backers of reform have been strongly inclined toward short-term thinking, quick to abandon support for reform when it has clashed with other immediate goals. The result threatens not simply the achievements of the reform effort but also the entire political edifice on which it was built. By early 2007, it was still unclear whether the PA—and the embryonic Palestinian state it had sought to foster—could survive the sanctions imposed by the same international actors who had helped create it.

This chapter is an effort to answer four questions: What was the Palestinian reform movement able to accomplish and why? How and why did it fail? What remains of its efforts? What are the lessons for proponents of reform in the Arab world?

Accomplishments of the Palestinian Reform Movement

From its birth in 1994, the PA emerged as an authoritarian set of institutions in a manner reminiscent of the development of similar systems elsewhere in the Arab world. But as familiar as it may have seemed, Palestinian authoritarianism showed some very different features as well: It was very highly personalized and characterized by weak institutions and ad hoc arrangements in contrast to the prevailing Arab pattern. The Egyptian and Tunisian presidents, for instance, are very strong, but each controls his country through a set of laws and institutions that reflect and follow his will. In the Palestinian case, however, authority was not merely centralized but was also personalized: There were no clear chains of command, laws were either not issued or routinely violated, and the president dominated the system more by setting up competing fiefdoms and distributing patronage and benefits (often personally) than by devising clear procedures and structures to implement the presidential will. Yasser Arafat was not merely PA president; he also headed Fatah, the largest political party, and chaired the Palestine Liberation Organization (PLO), a body responsible for representing all Palestinians throughout the world.

The PA's international patrons themselves abetted this developing pattern, both intentionally and unintentionally. They did so deliberately by privileging the PA's security obligations and apparatus over any governance concerns. As the PA's security services burgeoned in size, international supporters accepted them partly as patronage devices that would employ those loyal to the PA president, Arafat. Other parts of the security apparatus offered less gentle benefits. For example, a set of "state security courts" were constructed that vaguely and unconvincingly mimicked judicial bodies. The courts convicted those brought before them (sometimes in the middle of the night) with ruthless efficiency. These courts won public endorsement from the U.S. vice president at the time, Al Gore.

Not all the international support for Palestinian authoritarianism was by design, however. One of the most critical institutions supporting the emerging set of unaccountable political structures was the system of monopolies and border crossings that controlled the importation of many basic commodities to the Palestinian areas. These allowed the president and his allies to dominate the economy and realize tremendous profits (most of which went to Palestinian institutions, but some of which went straight into private pockets) without any oversight. These monopolies were an unintended by-product of the customs union set up as part of the Oslo Accords.[1]

Palestinian authoritarianism was notable not only for its lack of institutionalization but also for the atmosphere of intellectual openness in which it operated. This openness had ill-defined but harsh limits—vocal critics could be harassed, threatened, arrested, and abused. But the pattern of repression was so uneven—and many Palestinians so accustomed to defying governing authority—that remarkably frank and critical discussions remained a staple of Palestinian political life. Only a small portion of this discourse seeped into the print and broadcast media, but in seminars, public discussions, and parliamentary sessions, criticism of the PA and its president could be vociferous, sarcastic, and occasionally even threatening. According to Natan Sharansky's crude but often-cited "town square" test, a free society is one in which a person in the middle of the town square can express his or her views without fear of arrest or harm. According to this standard, Palestine while not fully free was far closer than almost any other Arab society. In 1999, in an interview with the author in a public restaurant within shouting distance of the main public square in Ramallah, a leading Palestinian stated: "Our problem is Yasser Arafat." He went on to explain that there was a consensus that Arafat was a failed leader in the domestic realm.[2] One deputy sarcastically suggested in the midst of a parliamentary debate in 1998 that Arafat simply be declared to be God; the next year, another deputy shouted that an uprising against the PA would be an inevitable by-product of its corruption. Marwan Barghouti, an important Fatah leader in the West Bank, gave voice to this criticism in 1998 in a public conference:

> Talk again of building democratic institutions, meaning decision mak-
> ing by an institution in a democratic way, and talk of collective
> leadership in the shadow of Yasser Arafat are hopes with no basis in
> reality: not in the Fatah movement, not in the Palestinian people, not in
> the PLO, and not in the Palestinian Authority. As long as Yasser Arafat
> exists, he is the alternative to institutions. Yasser Arafat is the institution,
> and with his existence there will be no institutions.[3]

Thus, almost from the beginning of the PA, some leading Palestinians began to criticize the emerging authoritarian patterns, and they found some successful backing for their efforts. A report of the PA's external auditor, the General Control Institute, offered extensive documentation of a pattern of petty and not-so-petty corruption and mismanagement. When the Palestinian Legislative Council (PLC), the PA's parliament elected in 1996, obtained the report, the PLC started its own investigation, which supplemented the institute's charges. The PLC also became central to reformers' attention when it took up the matter of the PA's constitutional structure. Despite Yasser Arafat's hostility, the PLC drafted a "Basic Law," taking a document prepared by the PLO's legal committee and transforming it into the most liberal constitutional document in Arab history before passing it in 1997. The PLC also sent fairly liberal laws to the president on matters ranging from public meetings to the judiciary, and it wrote a budget law giving itself serious oversight powers and skirmished annually with the cabinet before approving the budget. But in all these matters, the PLC's attention was fitful. The body was often easily intimidated or deflected by the president and unsure how to react when he refused to sign or promulgate laws it had passed. The result was an imposing paper effort to construct the rule of law and a liberal legal and constitutional order, but extremely uneven success in implementing those efforts.

Indeed, most PLC successes actually boomeranged in the short term, aggravating Palestinian authoritarian patterns instead of limiting them. As the PLC established itself as the body that initiated PA legislation, most efforts to regularize PA authoritarian practices simply came to a halt. Authoritarianism itself did not diminish but simply moved outside legal channels. When the president wanted someone arrested, the person was arrested; when a court ordered a detainee released, prison officials—claiming that they answered to the president but not the courts—simply ignored the court. Work begun by Arafat's government on a restrictive press law ground to a halt under the suspicious eyes of the PLC, but critical journalists were still harassed (and even arrested) completely outside any legal framework. In short, whenever the PLC did what it wished, the president also did as he pleased. The centerpiece of the PLC's reform efforts—the Basic Law—sat on the president's desk unsigned for five years. Other critical pieces of legislation (such as a judicial law) also stalled.

The result was the development of an impressive reform agenda and legislative framework but a failure (actually a refusal) to implement most of it. The international community that supported the construction of the PA acquiesced in—and as in the cases of the security system and import monopolies sometimes even encouraged—emerging authoritarian practices. To be fair, there were efforts—generously supported by the international community—that carved out islands where a more liberal Palestine could emerge. The PLC, for instance, developed capacities for research, legislative drafting, and budgetary analysis that were fairly impressive for a new parliament. The weak Palestinian party system (Fatah deputies, despite having a majority, almost never met as a caucus) prevented these resources from being monopolized by uncritical supporters of the executive, as happens in other Arab parliaments.

Perhaps the most striking island of reform was the professionalizing segment of Palestinian civil society. Over the years, Palestinian society in the West Bank—and to a lesser extent the Gaza Strip—had developed layers of voluntary, charitable, social service, and neighborhood organizations. Some of these dated back to the first half of the twentieth century, such as a group of charitable women's organizations; others had been founded as recently as the first intifada in the late 1980s. What these organizations lacked in funds and professionalism they compensated for in enthusiasm, sense of mission, and grassroots support. The emergence of the PA led to the transformation of some of these groups and the founding of new ones. Whether transformed or new, some civil society organizations in Palestine were now far more capable and professional in general than in the past—but also dependent on external donors. The result, as described by one Palestinian scholar, was a civil society suspended over the rest of Palestinian society, detached from its domestic roots but highly professionalized in its operations.[4] In this new form, civil society was a key supporter of the PA reform movement, documenting abuses, developing plans, lobbying the PLC (sometimes even drafting legislation), and confronting the emerging authoritarian order.

The eruption of the second intifada in September 2000 initially sidelined the reformers but ultimately led to their victory. For two years, the escalating violence rendered talk of reform seemingly irrelevant. Nationalist and militaristic rhetoric and action dominated while institutions decayed under Israeli pressure and Palestinian disinterest. International attention to Palestinian reform flagged, and donors shifted their focus to meeting basic needs.

Yet in the spring of 2002 the reform movement suddenly reemerged, and over the course of the following year it achieved nearly all of its objectives. The general weakness of Palestinian institutions, the near collapse of the PA, and the Israeli siege on the Palestinian president evidently had led many Palestinians to believe that institutional development was an immediate and critical need rather than a luxury to receive attention after nationalist goals had been met. The elements of the international community that had supported the creation of the PA also embraced the cause, though for a different set of reasons. European donors generally believed that only a capable and institutionalized PA could be an effective participant in any renewed peace process. The U.S. government was more specific in its concerns, holding Yasser Arafat personally responsible not only for domestic Palestinian problems but also for the intifada itself. Any effort against Arafat's authority was deemed reform, and reforms that might not weaken Arafat quickly lost the support of high-level U.S. officials. Thus, there was strong U.S. support for introducing the position of prime minister and increasing cabinet control over security and the budget. New elections, however, were seen by the U.S. leadership as a possible tool in Arafat's hands. In fairness, it should be noted that below the level of the senior U.S. leadership, many Americans working in development agencies and nongovernmental organizations (NGOs) supported a less personalized vision of reform.

With a powerful—if diverse—domestic and international coalition behind it, the cause of Palestinian reform suddenly received a tremendous amount of attention. Palestinian finances, legal institutions, security services, constitutional arrangements, and NGOs were thoroughly examined—not only within Palestine but at international conferences (one summoned by British Prime

Minister Tony Blair). Reform efforts received public support from the most powerful leaders in the world. The Roadmap for Peace—a plan sponsored by the European Union, the United States, the United Nations, and Russia— imposed numerous reform obligations on the Palestinians. The attention had considerable effect. By the summer of 2003, Palestine had perhaps the most transparent and efficient fiscal apparatus of any Arab state. The Basic Law was not merely dusted off and approved, but it was also amended to transfer executive authority from the office of the president to a cabinet headed by a prime minister fully accountable to the parliament. Other dormant reform projects—the judicial law, for instance—were similarly revived and approved. The constitutional reform also placed internal security under the authority of the cabinet, theoretically ending its isolation from parliamentary oversight.

Much of this success was due to an unusual partnership: Palestinian legislators, activists, and intellectuals developed an ambitious reform plan (sometimes drawing from international advice); the PA's powerful external patrons supplied the political muscle necessary to secure presidential approval of the program; and, to the reformers' horror, the Israeli move to imprison Arafat in his headquarters left him desperate for international protection. At times the partnership was imperfect: Weeks after Arafat approved the Basic Law, President George W. Bush strangely called for a new constitution, most likely out of simple ignorance of what had already been achieved. Baffled Palestinian leaders nevertheless dutifully rummaged through domestic constitutional efforts and found a sleepy committee that had been drafting a permanent constitution for a Palestinian state whenever it would be declared. They energized and expanded the committee until U.S. attention wandered elsewhere.

Sometimes the external support went beyond the ill informed to the inconsistent, subordinate as it was to the familiar pressures of security concerns and power politics. For instance, when Israel demanded that some individuals besieged with President Arafat be surrendered and threatened to assassinate or apprehend them if they were not, Arafat hastily convened a court-like body to convict them so that they could be held by Palestinians. The wholly illegal proceedings were, of course, overturned by a Palestinian court. The cabinet, with the quiet support of Western governments, acted in direct violation of a clear constitutional text requiring them to honor court judgments and ordered the verdict ignored.

Despite this uneven pattern of accomplishments and a rather eclectic mix of reforms, by the middle of 2003 the emerging authoritarian order in the PA had been thoroughly undermined. And, on paper at least, the PA had been transformed into a far more coherent and democratic structure.

How and Why Did the Reform Movement Fail?

The most impressive accomplishments of Palestinian reform came at a time when the president was literally under siege and Palestinian public institutions in various stages of decay. Some critical structures—most notably the educational and health systems—limped along throughout the intifada, continuing to meet basic needs. Other structures, however, including most ministries, the security services, and the courts, simply could not operate at any level of effectiveness under the prevailing political conditions. Indeed, the security services aggravated the problem because their personnel were actively running protection rackets and party militias. They also tended to be highly personalistic in their loyalties and would defend their leader quite ruthlessly. As time went on, efforts to reform Palestinian governance set off power struggles within the PA and sometimes degenerated into physical (even murderous) attacks and violent demonstrations.

In retrospect, it could be said that the problems for Palestinian reform began as soon as politics left the realm of paper documents and legal texts. The various reform plans that had been produced by internal and external actors often contained detailed, ambitious agendas but almost never identified priorities or showed much attention to sequencing. Thus, when it came to implementation of the paper accomplishments, the record was haphazard, reflecting no coherent strategy but merely short-term political alliances and opportunities. For instance, Palestine had the most professional and autonomous election commission in the Arab world, as well as the most impressive domestic election-monitoring effort—all built with international assistance—at a time when the parliament met in rare sessions only by videoconference (because Israel barred travel between the Gaza Strip and the West Bank) and factions of the governing party continued to employ thuggery to jockey for positions on the electoral list.

A Shaky and Rootless Coalition

The more fundamental failure of the reform effort, however, lay in the heterogeneity, cross purposes, and shallow domestic political roots of the reform coalition. Palestinian reform had many intellectual advocates, but its domestic constituency was extremely weak. Although the benefits it offered were real, they were also diffuse and contrary to the interests of very powerful groups. Two critical types of organized political actors—civil society organizations and political parties—were in no position to give reform the support it needed.

Civil society organizations could offer ideas, train personnel, report on, implement, and follow-up on an array of reform projects, but most of them could not deliver any organized political support. This was a direct (if unintended) result of the international support they received. For every step they took toward developing professionalization, they found that their grassroots support atrophied. It was theoretically possible for these groups to reach outward in the society even as they accepted external support, but only a few managed to focus on both internal and external linkages simultaneously.[5]

Political parties provided precious little support to the reform process and were often part of the problem. The authoritarian order that emerged between 1994 and 2002 was built partly on party patronage, as Fatah gradually transformed itself from a revolutionary movement into a dominant political party in a semiauthoritarian setting. Long-term party activists staffed the emerging PA bureaucracy and the security services; party factions competed with each other for access to public benefits. But because the transformation to such a party was incomplete—and because Arafat as party leader operated by playing off factions against each other rather than by constructing rigid hierarchies—the result was a confusing set of patronage networks, party militias, and competing factions rather than a well-structured party machine. Fatah was hardly a force for reform, and indeed, it was a logical actor to be reformed itself.

To be sure, some factions in Fatah, led by members of a middle generation of party activists who had emerged in the West Bank and the Gaza Strip during the first intifada, did push for democratizing reform within the party. Their initial motivation was personal because this cadre of activists had been disappointed by the positions they had obtained in the PA and also felt that they had the grassroots support to do well in a party election. Their resentment of Arafat and his generation of party leaders ultimately led them to adopt the broader reform cause. PLC members from this generation were critical in pushing the reform program into law. But even reforming leaders within the party did little to activate the party's mass base; by the time party primaries were attempted in 2005 to determine the slate of candidates in the 2006 elections, nobody was quite sure who was a member of the party or how one joined. The disorganization and opposition of senior party leaders was sufficient to scuttle some primaries and throw the credibility of the process into doubt.

Smaller parties also found themselves caught between their origins as revolutionary movements and the attraction of playing a role in the emerging PA. But the failure of the PA to hold elections before the outbreak of the second intifada—and then the air of nationalist crisis following the eruption of violence—prevented any transformation of these smaller parties into effective forces for political reform. A few small parties did emerge with a reform agenda, but none succeeded in building grassroots support. Nor was there much of an incentive to do so until local and parliamentary elections were held in 2005 and 2006. And none succeeded in organizing any sizable constituency in the short lead-up to the elections.

Enter Hamas

There was one striking exception to the pattern of civil society and party organizations losing or neglecting their grassroots support. The leading Islamist party, Hamas, along with a network of civil society organizations associated directly or indirectly with the movement, spent the years between 1994 and 2006 organizing, building structures, and emphasizing social service and constituency building.[6] Hamas and the Islamic sector of civil society were not hostile to reform, but it was not initially a primary focus for them. But as PA misgovernance provoked popular resentment, Hamas's sensitivity to public opinion, along with its opposition to the peace process that had created the PA, led the party to adopt reform themes. This gradual tendency was augmented by the PA's action at various times to repress the Islamist movement. Although the repression was not applied in a sustained and consistent manner, it was severe and even brutal when it did occur and was executed largely outside legal channels. Thus, Hamas's critique of PA mismanagement began to blend with its outrage at the PA's harsh security practices to produce an emphasis on the need for Palestinian reform. Hamas's fellow Islamist movements—most notably Egypt's Muslim Brotherhood—had begun to emphasize political reform for their own reasons at about the same time, giving Hamas some ideological and programmatic guidance.

Hamas's program for the 2006 elections contained some hints of its Islamic origins and uncompromising stance toward Israel, but the vast majority of the document resembled the reform proposals that had been generated by non-Islamist movements over the previous ten years. The primary difference between Hamas's reform agenda and that of the reform coalition was not in content but in credibility: Hamas had earned a reputation among Palestinians for seriousness of purpose and dedication to principle and the national cause that enhanced its reform reputation despite its relatively late adoption of reform themes.

Thus, in the end, the most effective Palestinian force claiming the reform mantle also pursued an international agenda so sharply at variance with that of the PA's patrons that the Islamist electoral triumph led the global community—particularly the United States—to move against many of the accomplishments of the reform movement and even to undermine most of the PA itself. Only structures that were fully independent of the cabinet and parliament escaped international hostility. Prior to 2006, U.S. support for reform may have been inconsistent, personalized, idiosyncratically selective, and shortsighted, but it was probably far more sincere than most Palestinians were willing to allow. But as was the case with the 2006 elections, the U.S. administration quickly shifted gears and undertook, without any sense of irony, to destroy some of their earlier accomplishments.

For instance, in the security sector, much of the U.S. effort to support reform had focused on placing the security services under cabinet (rather than presidential) oversight and regularizing payment of salaries through the treasury to ensure that the security services were professional bodies designed to meet national needs rather than personal or party militias. Yet after 2006, the United States moved rapidly to cut off payments to security services now under Hamas command and to offer material support to those under presidential command, despite a clear constitutional provision—inserted with strong U.S. backing in 2003—that made the cabinet responsible for internal security.

The election of a Hamas majority in the PLC in 2006 thus revealed the shallowness of the reform coalition. The Palestinian backers of reform consisted of intellectuals and NGO activists with a powerful vision but little constituency, party activists who were often outmaneuvered within their own parties, and international sponsors of the PA who focused on personalities far more than principles and were easily distracted. Hamas stood very much outside this coalition even when it raised the reform banner, and its electoral triumph led large parts of the reform coalition not simply to abandon the cause completely but to seek to turn the clock back to an era when an unfettered president (to be fair, one who won an uncompetitive but fairly clean election) dominated Palestinian politics.

What Remains of Palestinian Reform?

The frequently feckless nature of international interest in Palestinian reform prompted cynicism among its supposed beneficiaries. Many Palestinians complained that they were being required to build a reformed set of state structures at a time when international support for actual statehood never went beyond hortatory. Lacking sovereignty, freedom of movement, fiscal autonomy, and basic security, Palestinians were still supposed to forge ahead with building accountable, professional, and efficient government structures operating in accordance with the standards of first world states.

The complaint was telling, but it obscured an uncomfortable reality: Although the international situation had created many absurdities in the Palestinian political condition, it also had provided vital support for reforms that brought some tangible benefits to Palestinian society. International backers had often cherry-picked reform efforts from the array of proposals presented to them, but the original ideas for reforms—as well as responsibility for much of the implementation—generally were those of the Palestinians. The result was that when international support collapsed in 2006, odd but important pockets of its accomplishments survived.

This pattern can best be illustrated by tracing the history of the 2006 parliamentary elections, the very event that led the reform movement into provoking an international crisis of the first order. The first PLC elections had been held in 1996 in accordance with the Oslo Accords. The original idea of holding a second round of parliamentary elections was a Palestinian one. From a Palestinian perspective, the legitimacy of PA institutions was questionable after 1999, the year designated under the Oslo Accords as the deadline for reaching a permanent settlement of the Israeli–Palestinian conflict. Many Palestinians claimed that because the PLC was elected under the Oslo Accords, its legitimacy ended with the expiration of those accords. Few outside Palestine paid much attention to this argument, partly because they did not regard the Oslo Accords as having lapsed.

But as time went on, Palestinian reformers latched on to the idea of elections as a way of renewing the vitality of Palestinian institutions and forcing a measure of popular accountability. Senior Palestinian leaders, led by Arafat himself, remained ambivalent. But when it became clear that elections might offer a tool to prove their legitimacy to skeptical Israeli and U.S. officials, they began to warm to the idea. American ambivalence, however, deepened over time for the same reason. President Bush had embraced the call for Palestinian reform, but his conception of what that entailed focused primarily on the person of the Palestinian president. Only certain electoral outcomes—those weakening Arafat—would be considered reform.

Acting with a mandate from the U.S. Agency for International Development, a team of American NGOs (the National Democratic Institute, the International Republican Institute, and the International Foundation for Electoral Systems) issued a report on the feasibility of Palestinian elections, inspired by President Bush's 2002 call for Palestinian reform.[7] The report was generally favorable, although it urged extensive preparations. Mindful of the risks accompanying possible Hamas participation in the elections, the three NGOs recommended that the Palestinians develop a code of conduct for parties entering the electoral process. Arguing that parties that embraced violence did not have democratic credentials, the NGOs suggested that the code of conduct exclude such parties. Although the requirement was clearly aimed at Hamas, Hamas did in fact disavow internal violence. Its position against Israel was far bloodier in both theory and practice, of course, but barring parties favoring war against external adversaries was an odd stance to present in Washington on the eve of the Iraq war. To make a distinction between a political movement launching suicide attacks against enemy civilians and a state overthrowing an internationally recognized government would have been more than plausible on moral grounds, but few of the Palestinians responsible for implementation and administration of elections would have been persuaded that Hamas violence against Israel rendered Hamas undemocratic. In fact, the American NGOs completely ignored the weak basis under Palestinian law for excluding Hamas from electoral participation. Whatever shaky legal argument could be made was politically impracticable to apply against a political actor who most Palestinians regarded as wholly legitimate.

In the end, the idea of elections was simply shelved until Arafat's death in late 2004, at which time the United States suddenly rediscovered the attractiveness of elections as a way for the new Palestinian leadership to shore up its position. When elections were finally scheduled, the idea of the code of conduct was revived, but this time as a wholly Palestinian project. Shortly before the elections, all Palestinian political parties agreed to a set of principles on how to campaign. The principles, which focused mostly on fair play, were largely honored and led to a fairly clean campaign. But they failed to bar Hamas or to persuade it to change its position on Israel, the original international purposes behind the code of conduct.

The strange career of the electoral code of conduct was an omen for some of the other reform efforts. They survived but were isolated or transformed to varying degrees by the changed environment. Years of training programs, scholarships, and workshops had generated a cadre of highly trained personnel, sprinkled unevenly through ministries, other public bodies, and NGOs. Perhaps the most impressive of these organizations was the set of independent public agencies—the electoral commission, the human rights commission, the monetary authority—that had been especially favored because they were central elements of the international conception of Palestinian reform. And since these institutions were not under the oversight of the cabinet or the parliament, they were not cut off from international support by the draconian sanctions that were imposed after Hamas formed the new Palestinian government.

Other public institutions have been less fortunate in the wake of the international sanctions imposed on the PA after the Hamas electoral victory. Some have retained a portion of their capabilities, but even many of these have lost their role. For instance, the research unit of the PLC is still well trained and well equipped, but its employees have not been paid since the international sanctions were imposed. They are not called upon to do much research anyway, with the PLC unable to muster a quorum because of Israeli arrests of Hamas deputies and continued Fatah–Hamas rivalry. The judiciary—fairly independent but not yet well staffed with trained personnel—somehow soldiers on, although it suffered a prolonged strike until December 2006 because support personnel were not paid.

But the political basis underlying the entire reform agenda has collapsed. Large parts of the political coalition that made the reform wave of 2002–2003 possible and weakened the Palestinian presidency (especially the United States, the European Union, and some Fatah leaders—even some of those who had been converts to the reform cause) have formed an alliance to rebuild an unfettered presidency. On December 16, 2006, President Abu Mazen, who, as Palestine's first prime minister, had led the effort in 2003 to build the rule of law and democracy in support of a renewed peace process, claimed a right to dissolve the Hamas-dominated PLC. Both the United States and key European states explicitly backed his move. But Article 47 of the Basic Law—which the president and his supporters claimed was ambiguous on early elections—states directly that "the term of the Legislative Council is four years from the date of its election." Neither Abu Mazen nor his U.S. and European backers explained which part of "four years" they found unclear. The Basic Law, the centerpiece of reform efforts for many years, was again threatened with brazen violation by some of the same actors who had forced it on Arafat.

The broader reform agenda survived to the very limited extent that it did in the hopes of a few remaining independent intellectuals and in the platform of Hamas. Indeed, with its election victory, Hamas became the only ruling party in the Arab world to call for observance of democratic procedures, the rule of law, and faithfulness to constitutional text with any consistency and sincerity. But Hamas in power—reduced to obtaining aid from abroad in cash transported in suitcases, unable to pursue any legislative agenda because many of its parliamentary deputies were imprisoned, and unable even to ensure that salaries were paid to government officials (most though not all salaries were paid as "social allowance" directly by the EU in a manner that completely bypassed the Hamas government)—proved utterly unable to pursue any reform vision.

The reformers could claim credit for building the few structures and drafting the few laws and procedures that gave Palestinian politics the little coherence and stability it retained. The Basic Law remained largely in effect, the judiciary still retained some independence, and bodies such as the Central Elections Commission retained some professionalism and credibility. But these same bodies, laws, and procedures came under tremendous pressure from the battles between Hamas and Fatah, between the cabinet and the president, and between Palestine and its former patrons. Abu Mazen's call for elections was a threat to violate the Basic Law, obtain a judicial imprimatur for a coup, and have the Central Elections Commission oversee the operation.[8] The damage to the few remaining pockets of reformed politics was clear: It turned the reformed institutions into political footballs and showed how isolated and endangered they would be in case of an all-out struggle between the PA's first leaders and its new ones.

Lessons for Reform in the Arab World

For a brief but critical moment, the circumstances favoring political reform in Palestine seemed more propitious than they ever had in any Arab context. There was a well-formed reform agenda, a strong and expert group of Palestinian activists supporting the changes, a vocally supportive international community, and a Palestinian leadership who—while resistant—was so dependent on international assistance for funds, political support, and even physical protection that it scrambled desperately to demonstrate its fealty to the reform cause. And, as the present analysis has shown, the accomplishments of that reform period were substantial and real. But the success of the coalition created the political conditions for its own dissolution, leading to clean elections, the victory of Hamas, and the shattering of the reform agenda.

Arab reform advocates and their international supporters can derive five lessons from the Palestinian experience: the need to align agendas, the peril of short-term goals, the peril of personalizing reform, the long-term nature of the reform project, and the need to engage Islamists.

Lesson 1: The Need to Align Agendas

Reform can make the most progress when international and domestic agendas are in alignment. Palestinian reformers were able to develop many plans during the 1990s, but they were continuously outmaneuvered by the Palestinian political leadership, encouraged by its international backers. Thus, in 2002 and 2003, international support proved a vital, if embarrassing, source of leverage for Palestinian reformers. But when international attention wandered, or when international support showed a very different conception of what reform meant, achievements were far more limited.

Lesson 2: The Peril of Short-Term Goals

When reform is viewed as a means of achieving other short-term goals, its benefits, if any, will be equally short-lived. Political reform is only rarely an end in itself, of course, and it is unrealistic to expect many political actors to pursue it for reasons that are completely ideological or altruistic. For Palestinians, political reform was a means of obtaining a more functional government and creating a leadership that was both more capable and more effective in defending Palestinian interests internally and externally. For the international supporters of Palestinian reform, the primary (and sometimes only) purpose of reforming Palestinian institutions was to support a peace settlement with Israel. International actors supported reform when it was seen as a tool to weaken Arafat and transfer power away from those parts of the Fatah leadership seen as uncompromising and corrupt. But support would diminish, even before the Hamas triumph, whenever reform of political institutions and electoral processes strengthened those deemed hostile to the international agenda (for the United States and Israel, this came to include Arafat himself). For the international audience, reform was highly instrumental: It was designed to build a set of structures that met Palestinian needs in a way that showed the benefits of pursuing less than maximal nationalist goals and to allow the emergence of a credible Palestinian leadership that could make agreements—including critical concessions—authoritatively in the name of all Palestinians.

The domestic and international goals were different, but they were not necessarily contradictory over the long run. The problem was that at the international level there were expectations of immediate payoffs and thus a remarkable impatience with the reform effort. Worse, when reform of Palestinian institutions contradicted other short-term goals such as backing particular leaders or parties, it was immediately and totally subordinated.

The international support for reform as part of the peace process was not necessarily quixotic. Political reform most probably could aid the cause of a negotiated Palestinian–Israeli settlement, but only over the long term. Until 2006 the Palestinian leadership clearly favored a two-state solution; indeed, it constantly endorsed the idea. But the leadership pursued the goal of two states in a way that inspired little confidence among its international interlocutors as well as its domestic constituency. Reform could help produce a leadership that could negotiate authoritatively for Palestinians and deliver economic and political benefits to the population for participating in the peace process.

The main argument for supporting reform as a means of serving the cause of peace was that it was more likely to produce success over the long term than the suggested alternatives. But the journey would be difficult, circuitous, and uncertain. Of course, since the international support was led by the United States, a country that, at the time, was preparing a military invasion of Iraq and subsequently coping with the effects of that invasion, it may have been unrealistic to expect Palestinian reform to be pursued with single-minded determination and strategic vision. European dedication to the cause of reform, less encumbered by the Iraq venture, tended to be more sustained. But the deleterious effects of willful shortsightedness on the part of the United States were far reaching. It exposed Palestinian reformers to withering domestic criticism, rendered the international effort hypocritical in the eyes of many Palestinians, and led to immediate international abandonment of the cause whenever any setback occurred.

Lesson 3: The Peril of Personality Struggles

The cause of reform will be undermined to the extent that it is reduced to a personality struggle. Palestinian reformers were quite adept at pointing out the many shortcomings of Arafat's leadership from their perspective, and many did gravitate to Abu Mazen's side when he was prime minister (and, to a much lesser extent, when he was president). But for Palestinian reformers, their cause was not a plot against Arafat or a vehicle for Abu Mazen's ambitions. But the same cannot be said for the U.S. effort. For the United States, reform was a way to diminish or remove Arafat and support Abu Mazen, a man who frustrated some U.S. decision makers by his seeming lack of ambition.

Lesson 4: Reform as a Long-Term Project

Supporting non-Islamist reformers is at best a long-term project. Indeed, support for reform can easily backfire if used as a short-term device to put off choosing between the uncertainty of democracy and the backing of particular outcomes. There were many Palestinian leaders able to articulate a powerful reform vision; such figures did not simply enjoy the regard of international patrons but were often respected domestically as well. But respect did not translate into practical and organized political support. Furthermore, international responsiveness to and support for these reformist leaders often led them to neglect the difficult task of building grassroots support and political parties or other organizations with vocal and active constituencies. Immediately after Hamas's electoral victory, there was some international interest in "supporting the moderates" and recognition that such a policy must include encouraging them to provide social services and organize their popular base. But would-be international supporters show no sign whatsoever of any recognition of how difficult and long-term this task would be.

One Palestinian NGO leader, Mustafa Barghouti, provides a cautionary tale in this respect. He rose to national prominence as the leader of a volunteer effort to provide medical care to poor and remote parts of Palestinian society during the first intifada. His organization, the Union of Palestinian Medical Relief Committees (UPMRC), provided an avenue for a generation of student activists to supply medical services to significant parts of Palestinian society. After the Oslo Accords, the UPMRC's record qualified it for considerable international support, and it became one of the most successful Palestinian NGOs at attracting financial assistance. In 2005, Barghouti attempted to use this base to form an alternative political movement, first by running for president against Abu Mazen and then by launching a new political party for the 2006 parliamentary elections. In 2005, when he was Abu Mazen's only opponent, Barghouti received 19 percent of the vote. But in 2006, when Hamas entered the electoral fray, Barghouti's party received only two out of 132 seats.

There has never been a non-Islamist Palestinian political leader better poised to make the leap from civil society activist to political party leader than Mustafa Barghouti, but he could not make the transition on short notice, perhaps in part because his effort was every bit as centered on him personally as Fatah was in Arafat's day. If non-Islamist forces are to emerge, heavy-handed international efforts to support particular favorites will do little to help them. Success will only come by a long-term effort by Palestinian actors (perhaps with some international support) to build mass-based organizations. Fatah and Hamas took decades to accomplish this task, and there is no reason to expect that others will be able to move more quickly.

Lesson 5: The Need to Engage Islamists

Finally, the Palestinian reform experience should provide the strongest possible reinforcement to a lesson that is emerging from other societies in the region as well: the path of reform cannot be followed without encountering—and probably incorporating—Islamist movements. There is no absolute dichotomy between reform and some forms of political Islam, as much as some domestic reformers and their international supporters might wish. Islamist movements have sunk deep roots in their societies, and any effort that seeks to bring democracy or renegotiate the relationship between state and society will provide openings for Islamists. And Islamists will use those openings. One of the most striking developments in the Arab world over the past few years is the skill with which many Islamist movements have grasped the reform mantle. Hamas's record in this regard is actually less impressive than that of some of its fellow movements, but pushing for reform through democratic means appears to be, as activists from other movements term it, "a strategic choice." It will do no good to question the sincerity of Islamists' dedication to reform. Their conception of political reform differs, sometimes profoundly, from that of more liberal activists, to be sure, but the ideas that rulers must be accountable; that existing Arab regimes are estranged from their societies; that repression, harsh security measures, and unrestrained executive branches have served Arab societies poorly—all fit easily and naturally within the Islamist political program and appeal.

The victory of Hamas in the 2006 Palestinian parliamentary elections starkly confronted advocates of reform in the Arab world with lessons they should have already learned in a form they can no longer avoid. Those who have not given up on the cause—and there are still many in the Arab world and a few outside it who see reform as an end in itself or as a indispensable tool for achieving other ends—must learn to see political reform as a difficult and long-term challenge rather than a solution to immediate crises, no matter how pressing those crises are.

Notes

1. Under the Oslo Accords (and specifically the Protocol on Economic Relations between the Government of Israel and the PLO, known as the Paris Protocol), all commodities destined for Palestinian markets passed through Israeli ports of entry. Israel would collect the tax for Palestinian-bound goods and pass the revenues on to the PA (after deducting an administrative fee). This allowed for trade in some commodities—such as cement and gasoline—to be tightly controlled; the PA-owned monopolies were not an inevitable product of this system, but it made it easier for them to operate.

2. Azmi Shuʿaybi, personal interview, Ramallah, Palestine, November 1999.

3. Muwatin Foundation, *After the Crisis: Structural Changes in Palestinian Political Life and Work Horizons*, proceedings of the Fourth Annual Conference of the Muwatin Foundation, Ramallah, Palestine, September 22–23, 1998 (Ramallah, Palestine: Muwatin, 1999), p. 107 [in Arabic; translated by author].

4. See the comments of Ali Jarbawi in Ziad Abu Amr, *Civil Society and Democratic Transformation in Palestine* (Ramallah, Palestine: Muwatin, 1995) [in Arabic].

5. Although the phenomenon was especially marked in the Palestinian case, it is not unusual for international assistance to detach civil society organizations from their constituencies. On the issue generally, see Thomas Carothers and Marina Ottaway, eds., *Funding Virtue: Civil Society Aid and Democracy Promotion* (Washington, DC: Carnegie Endowment for International Peace, 2000).

6. See Sara Roy, "The Transformation of Islamic NGOs in Palestine," *Middle East Report* no. 214 (Spring 2000), pp. 24–6, on the Islamist movement's turn from politics to social service.

7. International Foundation for Electoral Systems (IFES), International Republican Institute, and National Democratic Institute, *Palestinian Elections: A Pre-Election Assessment* (Washington, DC: IFES, August 2002), available at <www.ifes.org/publication/52067c9fad7971f3700b09ea3bccc2c2/08_02_Palestinian_Elections.pdf>.

8. Early elections clearly violated the Basic Law, but the Central Elections Commission took the position that its purview was limited to overseeing elections, not adjudicating constitutional disputes. The commission thus implied that it would defer to the courts. The courts themselves, however, came under a cloud: Fairly or unfairly, Hamas viewed the existing judiciary as too close to Fatah. To make matters worse, a law creating a constitutional court had been rushed through the PLC by the outgoing Fatah majority after the January 2006 elections but before the new deputies were seated. The law placed the court under presidential domination. When this law was challenged in the courts, Palestine's most senior judges upheld it. Thus, the various bodies were either too timid or too suspect to resolve the dispute over early elections in a manner likely to be acceptable to all parties.

LEBANON:
THE CHALLENGE OF
REFORM IN A WEAK STATE

Julia Choucair-Vizoso

L ebanon is arguably the most democratic Arab state. Under parliamentary rule since becoming independent in 1943, it has regular elections, numerous political parties, and a relatively free and lively news media. Lebanon also has one of the most complex political systems in the Middle East, based on the premise that a careful balance in all aspects of political life must be maintained among the seventeen recognized religious communities. Although this confessional system has spared Lebanon the authoritarianism experienced by many Arab regimes in the twentieth century, paradoxically it has also prevented the transition to a truly democratic state. Nor has the confessional system eliminated the factional strife it was designed to avoid.

Unlike most Arab regimes, which are characterized by powerful national governments, Lebanon lacks a central authority. The manner in which power is distributed among various sects results in a collection of de facto ministates responsible for all the needs of their respective constituents. Citizens have no opportunity for representation outside the confines of their sect; thus, there is no institutionalized citizen–state relationship. When the leaders of the major communities agree on specific issues, they can get things accomplished even in the absence of effective government institutions. But when they disagree, the whole system is paralyzed. The lack of a central authority with institutionalized decision-making capabilities poses significant challenges to progress toward a more complete democracy. The problem of persistent weak authority was exacerbated in 2005 by the withdrawal of troops from neighboring Syria.

Lebanon's highly segmented political landscape also creates serious problems for maintaining peace. Systemic instability has haunted the country since independence, surfacing in episodes of violence, the most significant of which was the 1975–1990 civil war. Lebanon's confessional system perhaps can best be characterized as a chronic disease that periodically relapses into a crisis. Even low levels of internal dissatisfaction or external pressure can upset the delicate balance and cause the government to disintegrate.

The assassination of former prime minister Rafiq al-Hariri on February 14, 2005, and the subsequent Syrian withdrawal have brought the intrinsic weaknesses of the Lebanese system to the surface. With the end of Syrian tutelage over its political life, Lebanon has to find a new political balance among the factions, handle a precarious security situation, redefine its relations with Syria and with the international community, and launch immediate economic reforms. More than ever, these challenges demand a unified and coherent vision for political and economic development, yet the upsetting of the old equilibrium has deepened the vacuum of authority.

As Lebanon confronts its various political, economic, and security challenges, it is once again at the center of the Middle East's political and ideological battles, as it has been for the past fifty years. Lebanon finds itself today caught in the middle of a showdown between the region's main players: Lebanon is vital to Iran's ambitions, Syria's interests, Israel's security, and U.S. strategy in the region. This configuration of interests is not entirely new, but recent developments have exacerbated the consequences of the Lebanese political system. Since 2000, the collapse of Israeli–Syrian negotiations, Israel's withdrawal from South Lebanon, the U.S. war in Iraq, and the ascendant power of Iran in the region have shattered an international consensus—present since 1990—that stability was the first priority in Lebanon. The 2006 war between Israel and Lebanon laid bare the extent to which Lebanon has once again become an arena for proxy struggles.

The domestic and international pressures on Lebanon in the immediate aftermath of Hariri's assassination provided an opportunity for change. For a brief moment, there seemed to be real determination to resolve some of Lebanon's economic and political crises. The shocks Lebanon has experienced since—numerous political assassinations and a devastating war with Israel—have polarized the political scene and renewed sectarian anxiety, undermining progress toward much-needed political and economic reform. Today, the reform agenda is eclipsed by immediate threats to the stability and viability of Lebanon as a state. The case of Lebanon provides an example of the difficulty—and near impossibility—of democratization in a weak state.

The Lebanese Political System

The Flaws of Confessional Politics

The Lebanese political system is defined primarily by confessionalism, which mandates that a careful balance be maintained between confessional communities in government, parliament, and civil administration. Different forms of confessional rule have existed since 1843, but the system became fully developed after Lebanon gained independence from France in 1943. The National Covenant (al-Mithaq al-Watani)—a 1943 verbal agreement between Lebanon's first president and its first prime minister—was a pragmatic attempt to alleviate tensions among Lebanon's religious sects. In the hope that it would build a sense of overarching Lebanese national identity that would pacify both Muslims and Christians, the covenant stipulated that Christians would forgo European protection, while Muslims agreed to set aside pan-Arab aspirations and accept Lebanon's existing geographical boundaries. The National Covenant was accompanied by an informal agreement that the president must always be a Maronite Christian, the prime minister a Sunni Muslim, and the speaker of parliament a Shi'i Muslim, and that Christians and Muslims must be represented in parliament and the civil service according to a 6:5 ratio (based on the 1932 census).

The system survived for three decades despite bouts of instability, but changing demographic trends compounded by the involvement of external actors in Lebanon resulted in the outbreak of civil war in 1975. The Arab–Israeli conflict brought the inherent conflicts of the Lebanese system to a head as groups inside Lebanon split over the domestic presence of armed Palestinian forces. The 1989 Ta'if Accord, an agreement brokered by several Arab states (particularly Saudi Arabia), ended the Lebanese civil war and codified many of the provisions of the National Covenant, thus perpetuating the principle of confessional distribution of power. To establish a more balanced distribution of power, however, the Ta'if Accord endorsed the transfer of some of the Maronite president's powers to the Sunni prime minister and the Shi'i speaker of parliament. It also gave equal parliamentary representation to Muslims and Christians, subdivided proportionally among the two groups' various denominations. The legislature today has 128 seats, with 64 Christian representatives and 64 Muslim representatives. The Ta'if Accord also reaffirmed that all positions in the state bureaucracy must be allocated along confessional lines.

While in theory a confessional representation system seems appealing in a country as religiously diverse as Lebanon, in reality it has proven problematic.

The Lebanese confessional system contains intrinsic dilemmas that are almost inevitable in all confessional systems. Rigid allocations among religious factions for the purpose of power-sharing crystallize divisions and set battle lines. They are particularly dangerous in a society such as Lebanon, where the power-sharing groups have significantly different birthrates and emigration rates. The distribution of power is still based on the 1932 census, which no longer reflects the religious makeup of the population. Thus, over time the system has become inherently unfair.

The Lebanese system also impedes the creation of a modern state with a central authority that has decision-making and decision-implementing capabilities. The Ta'if Accord created a system whereby the president, the prime minister, and the speaker of parliament all rule with almost equal power, though in different capacities. The relationship among the members of this troika overshadows the role of any institution. Since there is no central authority to arbitrate, political actors view any compromise as a threat to their very existence. Every reshuffling of top administrators since 1990 has been marred by conflict among the troika members over their respective sectarian shares. The success or failure of each leader's maneuvers to legislate or to implement policies is measured in terms of "losses" or "gains" for his respective community. The fact that every single bureaucratic post is allotted on a confessional basis further complicates an already extremely complex political landscape in which different sects are continuously vying for power without an arbiter to enforce laws. Disagreements among the members of the troika are not settled in the Council of Ministers or in parliament but outside these institutions, often with a foreign power playing the role of arbiter. The existing system also exacerbates the crisis of authority by making it very difficult for any political party or group to gain a majority of seats in parliament. Electoral tickets are often formed on a constituency-by-constituency basis by negotiation among local sect leaders. These loose coalitions generally exist only for the sake of the latest election and rarely form cohesive blocs in parliament.

The authority crisis and the sectarian-based patronage system are responsible for the disarray of the Lebanese security apparatus. The various security services are politicized and divided into disparate elements that do not respond to a common higher civilian authority. The political system is also responsible in large part for Lebanon's economic woes. Lebanon's governance structure has proved unable to promote sustained economic and social development. Overlapping policy-making powers and responsibilities and widespread corruption have obstructed the emergence of coherent economic policies and efficient institutional structures in the public and private sectors. The absence of coherent policies is obvious in all aspects of Lebanese life, from inadequate implementation of rules and regulations, to the illegal exploitation of natural resources, to chaotic urban and rural development. At the same time, the nature of the Lebanese system renders it difficult to hold government officials accountable for ultimate executive responsibility.

Thus, while the semblance of a modern state exists, there are no modern institutions. In short, Lebanon has a confessional oligarchy. The result is perpetual political and administrative paralysis; the existing institutions cannot introduce needed reforms for fear that these changes would alter the status quo and the balance of interests among the communities. This makes it almost impossible to devise a national agenda for political and economic reform.

The Consequences of Syrian Intervention

The fragmentation of the Lebanese system invites the disproportionate influence of outside actors. Because it is virtually impossible to generate sufficient power to govern from within this highly fractured system, foreign powers become crucial to providing governments with a degree of authority. Syria's role in Lebanon must be understood not only against the background of Syria's ambitions but also in light of the weakness of the Lebanese system that provided the opening to intervention.

Syrian military forces first entered Lebanon as a peacekeeping force in 1976, invited mainly by Christian Lebanese and endorsed by the Arab League. During and after the civil war, Syria—like many foreign powers before it—used the Lebanese confessional divides to its advantage, shifting alliances with various communities as they successively called on it for help. Thus, Syria became the main power broker, controlling the presidency, the judiciary, and the intelligence and security apparatus, as well as many Lebanese politicians who owed their power and survival to the Syrian authorities. Syrian control over Lebanese political life silenced sectarian tensions and swept the weaknesses of the Lebanese system under the rug. It also curtailed the political and civil rights Lebanese had long enjoyed.

Lebanese society was sharply divided about Syria's presence. In the 1990s, opposition to Syria and to the Syrian-aligned Lebanese government was concentrated among Christians. In particular, it coalesced around the Qornet Shahwan Gathering, a mainly Maronite group supported by the powerful head of the Maronite Church, Patriarch Cardinal Nasrallah Butros Sfeir. The group reflected a widespread sentiment of postwar disenfranchisement among the Christian community. With the two most prominent Christian leaders excluded from political competition—General Michel Aoun was in exile and Samir Jaja was in prison—most Christians (particularly Maronites) felt that they were no longer adequately represented.

Opposition to Syria escalated after September 2004, when the Syrian government pushed Lebanon's parliament to amend the constitution and extend the presidential term of General Emile Lahoud, who was widely seen as a Syrian puppet and whose term was due to expire in November 2004. Prime Minister Rafiq al-Hariri, who had played by Syria's rules since 1992, resigned. Political activists and parties from across the political spectrum met at Beirut's Bristol Hotel in December 2004 and February 2005 to demand a "total withdrawal" of Syrian troops from Lebanon. In addition to representatives of the Qornet Shahwan Gathering, those attending included members of Druze leader Walid Jumblat's Progressive Socialist Party, the Democratic Forum, the Democratic Leftist Parties (a conglomeration led by former members of the Lebanese Communist Party), the banned Lebanese Forces (a right-wing phalangist Christian party), and the exiled General Aoun's Free Patriotic Movement. Some members of Hariri's parliamentary bloc also attended. Notably absent were representatives of the major Shi'i parties: the Amal Movement, led by Speaker of Parliament Nabih Berri, and the Shi'i Islamist party Hizbollah.

The Syrian brazen interference with the Lebanese political system to keep President Lahoud in office exacerbated rising U.S. and French concerns about Syria's role in Lebanon. Since the end of the civil war, Syrian presence had been seen by the international community as a stabilizing factor and was tolerated. As Syrian relations with the United States soured over insurgents crossing into Iraq through the Syrian border and over Syria's stance in the Arab–Israeli conflict, the Syrian regime was increasingly isolated both regionally and internationally. Syria's control of Lebanon eventually became intolerable to the international community and culminated in September 2004 with United Nations Security Council Resolution 1559 calling for the withdrawal of "all foreign forces," understood to mean Syria, from Lebanon.

The assassination of Rafiq al-Hariri in a bomb blast in Beirut on February 14, 2005, created a clear political demarcation between anti-Syrian forces and Syrian allies. The opposition movement, which at this point included prominent Christian, Druze, and Sunni figures, immediately blamed Syria and formed an unprecedented unified front. The Lebanese public was mobilized, with hundreds of thousands of Lebanese calling for "Syria Out" and "Freedom, Sovereignty, Independence," as well as demanding the "truth" behind the assassination. In the midst of this popular upheaval and the increasing regional and international pressure, the Lebanese government resigned, and on April 26, 2005, Syria withdrew all its troops. In June, Lebanon held its first elections free of direct Syrian intervention in three decades and formed a new government.

The Aftermath of Syrian Withdrawal: A Missed Opportunity

The Syrian withdrawal and the Lebanese parliamentary elections were presented abroad, particularly in the United States, as a turning point for Lebanese democratization. In reality, the impact of Syria's withdrawal was less benign: It did restore the sovereignty of Lebanon but has also left a power vacuum that threatens the stability of the country. Instead of aiding the resolution of old problems of Lebanese politics, the upsetting of the old equilibrium has led to chaos and deeper divisions, preventing real progress toward structural change in the Lebanese political system.

Window of Opportunity

In the aftermath of Hariri's assassination, politicians and citizens mobilized in an unprecedented show of unity to demand Lebanese sovereignty and the restoration of political freedoms curtailed by Syria. The wall of fear that had prevented the Lebanese from criticizing the Syrian presence was destroyed. The withdrawal of Syrian troops shattered many postwar taboos. Issues that had been barred from discussion since the close of the civil war, from sectarian relations and the distribution of power to the question of Hizbollah's arms and the status of armed Palestinian refugees, were being debated openly again.

The parliamentary elections in June 2005 were characterized by a level of genuine competition that had not been seen in thirty years. Freed of Syria's direct interference in the elections, Lebanese had much greater freedom to discuss issues and choose their representatives. One of the issues that immediately came to the fore was that of security reform. Until 2005, the Syrian military intelligence services exercised direct control over the Lebanese security services, making sure that no coordination existed among them. The 2005 wave of assassinations and car bombings targeting politicians and journalists and the suspected involvement of the heads of the security services brought to the fore the need for an overhaul of the entire security system. There was also much discussion of economic reform.

Enduring Hurdles

Despite these positive signs, the momentum for change created by the Syrian withdrawal rapidly dissipated, and the old divides in Lebanese politics and society resurfaced. Within a year of the "Intifada for Independence," Lebanon had slid into a dangerous political confrontation that bore striking similarities to the situation that existed on the eve of the 1975 civil war.

The decision to hold elections under an old Syrian-engineered law rather than enacting a new one heightened confessional rifts. Running on the legacy of his father, Saad al-Hariri became the effective leader of the Sunni community and gained control over 72 of 128 parliamentary seats. Two parties, Hizbollah and Amal, continued to share the allegiance of the Shia community. All Druze seats belonged to Druze leader Walid Jumblat. Most of the Christian seats were divided among Michel Aoun's Free Patriotic Movement, the Lebanese Forces, and members of the Qornet Shahwan Gathering, with Aoun quickly emerging as the leader of the powerful Maronite community upon his return from exile. His role as a confessional leader with presidential ambitions has undermined his party's potential as a strong voice for reform.

Within a year of the Syrian withdrawal, these disparate parties and confessional groupings had coalesced into two rival camps. The March 14 group (named for the largest of the anti-Syrian protests in 2005) composed primarily of Sunni, Druze, and Christian politicians, controlled the majority of seats in the parliament and portfolios in the cabinet. It also received diplomatic and financial support from the United States, Europe, and key Arab states such as Saudi Arabia, Jordan, and Egypt. Its main goal was to contain Syrian ambitions and, more specifically, to ensure the implementation of a UN resolution to establish a tribunal to try suspects in the Hariri assassination. The March 8 group (named for the largest Hizbollah-led protest in 2005) brought together the two Shi'i parties (Hizbollah and Amal) with the Maronite Free Patriotic Movement led by Michel Aoun. The March 8 Group denies the legitimacy of March 14 coalition as the governing majority, claiming its actions have been unconstitutional, and accuses it of working for U.S. and Israeli interests. The March 8 group's international patrons are Iran and Syria, with Damascus providing political and material assistance and, in Hizbollah's case, military supplies.

There was an initial attempt to find compromise solutions to the major issues that divided the two camps through negotiations. The leaders of fourteen political groups launched a series of meetings—known as the National Dialogue—on March 2, 2006, and initially made some progress. They tasked the government with the setting up of the tribunal to try the suspects in Hariri's assassination; disarming Palestinian factions outside refugee camps within six months; and establishing full diplomatic ties with Syria. They also agreed that the Shebaa Farms—an Israeli-occupied area on the Lebanese–Syrian border—is Lebanese, not Syrian territory. But two of the most controversial issues remained unresolved: the UN call for the disarmament of Hizbollah and the fate of President Emile Lahoud.

The National Dialogue collapsed during the devastating 34-day war launched by Israel on Lebanon in summer 2006, after Hizbollah kidnapped two Israeli soldiers and killed three others. The war's devastating humanitarian and economic costs to Lebanon exacerbated the political divide, reversed the progress that had been made at the National Dialogue meetings, and changed the relation between the two blocs from the National Dialogue to confrontation in the streets. The March 8 group withdrew its members from cabinet in November 2006 and staged month-long sit-ins in downtown Beirut in an effort to topple the government. Amid this escalation, violent clashes erupted in January 2007, primarily between Sunni and Shi'i youth, highlighting the dangerous sectarian character the conflict was developing.

The confrontation between the two blocs was also exacerbated by a wave of assassinations of politicians and journalists belonging to the March 14 group that began even before the summer war. In 2007, a series of car bombs also began targeting civilians and commercial neighborhoods in and around Beirut. In May 2007, a radical Islamist group based in a Palestinian refugee camp in north Lebanon Fatah al-Islam attacked Lebanese army posts launching a fierce battle in the camps that was the worst internal fighting since the civil war. The outbreak of violence was symptomatic of the emergence of numerous battlefronts in Lebanon.

The standoff between the political groups paralyzed the institutions of the Lebanese state and created a political and security vacuum that is the greatest threat to stability in Lebanon since the end of the civil war in 1990.

Looking Ahead: Opportunities for Limited Reform?

The Lebanese confessional system, initially designed to provide stability to a divided society, has failed. The country has been unstable ever since it became independent. And the system had prevented the emergence of a real state, let alone a truly democratic one. Lebanon's promise as a model of confessional coexistence between Christians and Muslims, Sunna and Shi'a, has not been fulfilled. Only if the basis of this confessional system is challenged will

Lebanon have an opportunity to break out of the never-ending cycle of political gridlock and conflict.

In an ideal scenario, Lebanon would tackle the confessional problem by creating institutions and processes that would allow multiple socioeconomic interests to begin cutting across sectarian ones. Important steps would include developing a national civic program to start replacing confessional affinities with a new national consciousness, establishing integrated educational institutions, and changing the educational curriculum to include a comprehensive history of the civil war.

Politicians have paid lip service to deconfessionalizing the system. The Ta'if Accord calls on parliament to form a national council—headed by the president and composed of the prime minister, the speaker of parliament, and prominent political figures and intellectuals—to propose ways to abolish confessional representation. It also suggests that merit and capability replace confessional quotas as the basis for filling public positions (excluding top-level posts). No action has been taken in that vein because there is no political willingness to embark on this process, and these proposals are not part of a serious national political debate.

The Lebanese confessional system is deeply entrenched in politics and society and is not going to change overnight. Politicians are not questioning the rules of the sectarian game. A corrupt patronage system has created vested interests in perpetuating the status quo. The confessional system has also prevented the emergence of a powerful demand from the bottom to change the system. Thus, there are no short-term prospects for a secular, nonconfessional Lebanon.

Not only is deconfessionalization off the table, but there are also no prospects for a redistribution of power among the sects in the near future. Many politicians acknowledge that the current system is inefficient and unrepresentative, but they are not willing to challenge the idea that the Ta'if Accord continues to be the best frame of reference for discussion. Christian politicians believe that Ta'if withdrew significant power from their community, but they fear that they have more to lose than to win if the system is reformed. Maronite leader Michel Aoun rejected the Ta'if Accord from the outset and as a consequence was forced into a fifteen-year exile in France. His return to Lebanon in 2005 implied his acceptance of the agreement, although his official position remains vague. Hizbollah and Amal have at different times hinted at the need of a renegotiation of Ta'if, which gives them a parliamentary representation equal to that of Sunna but less than Maronites despite their relative demographic superiority. So far, however, they have used this discourse as a bargaining chip for short-term concessions rather than as a real demand for a change in the accord.

Thus, neither deconfessionalization nor a fundamental redistribution of power within the confines of the confessional system is on Lebanon's political agenda, and this is unlikely to change in the foreseeable future. In the long term, Lebanon's solutions depend on strengthening the state and its institutions, particularly the security and justice systems. The most that can be hoped for in Lebanon in the near future, however, is that sectarian representation be made fairer and less of a zero-sum game. Reform of the election system is an area where some progress toward the eventual deconfessionalization of the system could be made. Reforming the electoral law will not be easy. Given the precarious security situation, it can only occur at a slow pace, if it occurs at all. The various groups in government will be engaged in a tense and drawn out balancing act. However, unlike other much-needed reforms, electoral reform is already a major part of the political debate.

Electoral Reform

The problems of Lebanon's election law are widely acknowledged, and there is a growing consensus that the electoral law needs immediate revision. But there is great discord over what would constitute a fair electoral law that would not break the country apart. There are two major flaws in electoral legislation: the list system and the method for creating legislative districts. There are also other serious concerns about procedures that cannot be addressed through legislation.

Parliamentary seats in Lebanon are allocated on a sectarian basis, but the list system does not reflect the current Lebanese demographic reality and thus aggravates the confessional problem. The constitution requires that the 128 seats in parliament be equally divided between Christian and Muslim candidates. The seats granted to each community are further subdivided among various sects based on their supposed shares of the population. The distribution by individual sect is provided in table 1. But each district has its own allocation of seats, and the party lists must follow the specific sectarian distribution for that district. For example, in Beirut's first district, each party list must have two Sunni candidates, one Maronite, one Greek Orthodox, one Greek Catholic, and one Protestant. Each voter can thus vote for two Sunna, one Maronite, one Greek Orthodox, and so forth. The distribution is different in each of Beirut's other two districts (see table 2). The confessional allocations in each district are based on the 1932 census—the last conducted in Lebanon.

Table 1. Division of Lebanese Parliament by Confession

Confession	Seats
Christians	
Maronite	34
Greek Orthodox	14
Greek Catholic	8
Armenian Orthodox	5
Armenian Catholic	1
Protestant	1
Other Christian minorities	1
Subtotal	64
Muslims	
Sunni	27
Shi'i	27
Druze	8
Alawite	2
Subtotal	64
TOTAL	128

Table 2. Electoral Districts of Beirut

Beirut Electoral District	Seats	Distribution
Beirut 1	6	2 Sunna
		1 Maronite
		1 Greek Catholic
		1 Greek Orthodox
		1 Protestant
Beirut 2	6	2 Sunna
		1 Shi'i
		1 Greek Orthodox
		1 Armenian Orthodox
		1 minority
Beirut 3	7	2 Sunna
		1 Shi'i
		1 Druze
		1 Armenian Catholic
		2 Armenian Orthodox

Although the electoral system is based on faulty data, carrying out a new census is politically unthinkable. As previously mentioned, a confessional redistribution of power is not currently on the table in Lebanon. Thus, all discussion about electoral reform occurs within the parameters established in the National Pact and modified by the Ta'if Accord. In short, the seats granted to each community will not be modified. It is possible, however, to work within those parameters to reform the election law, which at present compounds the problems of confessionalism because of how the law is modified and manipulated before every election.

In a simple plurality electoral system like Lebanon's, the decisive factor in influencing the outcome of elections is the size of the electoral district. Lebanon has never had a fixed, stable electoral law; a new law is drafted before most elections, changing the number and size of electoral districts. This was the case before the outbreak of civil war in 1975 and remains the case now. With the 1989 Ta'if Accord, an effort was made to solve the problem by declaring that elections should be organized on the basis of large electoral districts known as *muhafazat*, after the redrawing of the "administrative map." At the time of the Ta'if Accord, there were six *muhafazat*, but the accord left the door open as to exactly how many *muhafazat* there should be in the future and along which lines they would be drawn. The purpose of the large electoral districts was simple: Candidates in each district would have to appeal to a broader, multisectarian constituency to win. However, Syrian officials grew concerned that some of their most important allies might lose the elections if they were forced to compete outside their narrow tribal and sectarian communities. Christian politicians also favor small electoral districts (*qadaa*) because they are a minority in many regions but the majority in a number of small districts. A districting system based on the larger *muhafazat* would thus force them to broker alliances with candidates from other communities. In a majority Sunni district, for example, Christians would have to join a Sunni-dominated list. Christian politicians argue that this situation results in Muslims deciding the Christian vote so that the elected Christian leadership often did not represent the view of a majority of Christians.

Thus, in every election since the Ta'if Accord, parliament has passed a law changing the number of districts and gerrymandering their borders. The result is a districting system that follows neither the *muhafazat* nor the *qadaa*; rather, the divisions are ad hoc, aimed at undermining potential opponents to Syria and weakening coalitions of independent candidates. The continuous manipulation of electoral districts has further distorted representation. The number of votes needed to win a parliamentary seat according to the 2000 electoral law varies from approximately 12,000 to 47,000. In some districts, constituencies of fewer than 4,000 voters are entitled to a representative from their own sect, while in others, groups of more than 10,000 voters go without sectarian representation.

Other important issues in any reform of the electoral law are voting age and expatriate voting. These issues are politically charged because different proposed solutions favor different communities. On the one hand, lowering the voting age from the present twenty-one years to eighteen would favor Muslims, who have a higher birthrate and thus a younger population. Permitting expatriates to vote, on the other hand, could shift the balance of power in favor of Christians. The expatriate community is very large and made up predominantly of Christians, many of whom left the country before 1975.

The electoral law has other deficiencies. First, there is no structured, comprehensive system for legal redress. Various institutions have ill-defined and sometimes overlapping competencies for adjudicating complaints, and procedures are not defined in detail by legislation. Second, there is no regulation of campaign spending. Candidates are not required to present any details about the sources and the amount of their campaign financing. Powerful candidates, who often own TV channels, monopolize airtime. Third, the system does not prevent extensive abuse of state resources and power by candidates during elections. Candidates who are already in office often use government facilities and staff in their campaigns and pressure civil servants to vote in their favor.

Elections in Lebanon are also marred by technical problems that cannot be addressed by legislation alone. First, in practice Lebanon does not have mandatory secret balloting. Security forces and representatives of the candidates themselves—who are legally permitted inside polling stations—watch voters cast their ballots. The absence of preprinted uniform ballots creates opportunities for manipulation and can further compromise the secrecy of the vote. This facilitates rampant vote buying, which is done by everyone. Second, voter lists are not updated, which also leads to fraud. And while soldiers are not allowed to vote, their names are kept on voting lists, and some are invited to vote illicitly by powerful candidates. Third, while the law also stipulates that election day be the same in all districts, parliamentary elections are usually staggered. Thus, as the results in the first districts are known, vote buying and electoral manipulation get more intense in the remaining districts.

There is no shortage of proposals and ideas regarding a new electoral law in Lebanon. The problem is to devise a law that would be accepted by most people as fair and that would reduce sectarian tension. One proposal is that

Lebanon move to a system of proportional representation. Proportional representation would be in line with the Ta'if Accord, which calls on parliament to enact a new election law that will allow candidates for the Chamber of Deputies to be elected "on a national rather than on a confessional basis," with the upper chamber (Majlis al-Shuyukh) structured along confessional lines. The upper chamber's powers would be confined to "crucial issues." There are numerous benefits to a proportional representation system. First, it could make Lebanese elections fairer, to the extent that it would allow equal representation among voters. Second, it would begin to undermine the sectarian character of Lebanese elections by forcing candidates to forge new alliances across the political spectrum. Proportional representation systems promote competition among political groups rather than among individual candidates. Third, it would encourage candidates to run on policy-specific platforms; if a candidate's confessional identity were no longer enough to win votes, he or she would have to speak to voters' interests beyond identity. Finally, proportional representation would also give independent candidates a better chance for at least some presence in parliament and minimize the ability of broad coalitions to dominate, as they do in the current first-past-the-post system. This would pave the way for the gradual renewal of Lebanon's political elite by allowing new blood to enter politics and create new dynamics.

It is unlikely that the idea of a full proportional representation system will gain traction in Lebanon. Most politicians are opposed to such a law as it would significantly reduce their success rate in future elections. An independent National Commission formed in August 2005 proposed a draft law—submitted to the Council of Ministers on June 1, 2006—that introduces some of the benefits of proportional representation but also maintains a majoritarian voting system. A parallel electoral system would be established in which seventy-seven seats would be elected from the *qadaa* on a majoritarian block-vote basis, and fifty-one seats would be elected from six large *muhafazat* on a proportional representation basis. The aim of the parallel system is that proportional representation would allow new groups and leaders to enter into parliament, but would also reassure the smaller confessional communities through the preservation of the familiar small voting districts.

Even though it seeks to take into account the complexities of the Lebanese political situation, however, the law is very unlikely to be endorsed in its current form by government and parliament. The strongest opposition will come from Maronite politicians, who will continue to oppose using the six *muhafazat* at all. As a result, the most probable scenario is that some of the proposal's technical recommendations will be adopted, but its fundamental systemic proposals will be amended. The new law will probably combine a mix between large and small electoral districts, but the voting system will remain majoritarian in all districts.

Even in the best case scenario, electoral reform will be difficult and will probably frustrate and disappoint reformers who want to see more fundamental changes. But it is important that electoral reform remain on the political agenda even if only slight improvements are made in the short term. For progress to be made at all, a modicum of stability will have to be maintained in the country. All political reform in Lebanon—no matter how modest—requires sustained calm. Lebanon's history has demonstrated that the country cannot be governed, let alone reformed, in an environment of widening distrust between the main political forces. In this context, the question of Hizbollah's arms will be instrumental in defining this environment.

The Hizbollah Question

Syria's withdrawal from Lebanon and international pressure have reopened the question of Hizbollah's arms and the lack of the Lebanese state's monopoly on security. The existence of an armed militia independent of the government would be cause for worry in any country, and certainly it is an obstacle to democratic reform in Lebanon. The debate over Hizbollah's status is very complex, however, because it is not limited solely to Lebanese politics but takes place against the background of the Arab–Israeli conflict and in the context of great tension in U.S.–Syrian and U.S.–Iranian relations.

Since its establishment in 1982, Hizbollah has transformed itself from a militia dedicated to fighting the Israeli invasion and occupation of Lebanon to a multifaceted organization that is a political party, a vast social welfare network, and a militia. It has participated as a legitimate political party in Lebanese elections since the first post–civil war elections of 1992. As a party, it is perceived as one of the least corrupt in Lebanon, even by those who disagree with its ideology and policies. Hizbollah is also a regional movement and militia allied with Syria and Iran to deter Israel's ambitions in the region. Its secretary-general Hassan Nasrallah has declared repeatedly that the party will remain armed "as long as Israel remains a threat to the country," even if this situation lasts "one million years."

Out of a combination of ideological conviction and pragmatism, Hizbollah has long resisted the option of disarming and becoming solely a Lebanese political movement. The party resists calls for disarmament on the grounds that the Lebanese state is weak and has repeatedly failed to defend Lebanese citizens from Israeli attacks. Hizbollah also tries to deflect calls for disarmament by periodically hinting that its arms are the great equalizer in an otherwise lopsided political system: Shi'a do not have political representation even remotely commensurate with their numbers, but they have a militia. The political ramifications of disbanding Hizbollah's militia are thus huge: Shi'a must be offered something in return, namely, the prospect of electoral reform that would guarantee them an opportunity for greater representation. This would entail launching a discussion of the deconfessionalization clauses in the Ta'if Accord, something Lebanese politicians are not ready to do.

By normalizing its status on the Lebanese scene, the movement believes it could undermine its international standing, lose its Syrian and Iranian allies, and become vulnerable to U.S. and Israeli pressure. The Ta'if Accord exempted Hizbollah from having to disband because of its status as a resistance movement against the Israeli occupation of South Lebanon, and many Lebanese supported this exemption because they viewed Hizbollah as a legitimate national resistance movement.

Since the Israeli withdrawal from South Lebanon in 2000, and particularly since the Syrian withdrawal in 2005, Hizbollah has found it increasingly difficult to cater to all of its constituencies, including Shi'a and other groups in Lebanon, Syria, and Iran. Increasingly vocal voices within Lebanon non-Shi'i communities are calling for Hizbollah's disarmament on the grounds that Israel no longer occupies Lebanese territory. The calls for disarmament increased after the Syrian withdrawal in 2005, threatening Hizbollah's image as a national movement. International pressure for disarmament has also been strong, culminating in UN Security Council Resolution 1559, which calls for the disarmament of all militias in Lebanon, in a clearly worded reference to Hizbollah. Furthermore, Hizbollah has suffered some tactical losses after the war with Israel in the summer of 2006: It had to give up control of the area south of Litani to the Lebanese army and the 15,000-troop UN Interim Force in Lebanon (UNIFIL); and it agreed to grant the Lebanese military control of Lebanese–Syrian border points.

Despite these setbacks, Hizbollah is unlikely to lose its political clout and allow itself to be disarmed any time soon. First, it continues to play the internal political game to fend off external threats of disarmament. When it organized a mass demonstration on March 8, 2005, it exclusively waved Lebanese flags, not Hizbollah banners, to present itself as a national movement that was bidding Syria farewell as opposed to urging the troops to stay. Before the elections, it formed alliances with Lebanon's most powerful political blocs—Nabih Berri's Amal Movement, Saad Hariri's Future Movement, and Walid Jumblat's Progressive Socialist Party—as a way of stalling calls for disarming. After the elections, a member of Hizbollah joined the government for the first time, but then withdrew. As it split from the governing majority, Hizbollah formed an alliance with Maronite leader Michel Aoun, as an attempt to garner a cross-confessional image for its demands—which include the formation of a government of national unity in which Hizbollah and its allies would have veto power. Hizbollah is also adept at exploiting the weakness of Lebanese institutions to enhance its own popularity. For example, in the aftermath of the summer 2006 war, it provided relief and reconstruction aid far more efficiently than the government.

Second, the movement can still claim that Israel continues to pose a grave threat to Lebanon and thus vindicate its resistance strategy. The war with Israel allowed Hizbollah to renew the credibility of its claim that it represented the resistance to the Israeli and U.S. threat. Speaking hours after the August 14 cease-fire took effect, Nasrallah argued that talking about disarming the movement at this time was "insensitive and immoral" and "totally inappropriate."

Third, barring dramatic shifts in regional dynamics, Hizbollah will continue to enjoy substantial financial and military support from Iran and Syria.

These realities indicate that the prospects of Hizbollah's disarmament remain very distant. Hizbollah's actions since 2000 prove that it is driven primarily by the goal of preserving its armed status and identity as a resistance movement. Although this goal has become more difficult in recent years, it is still an attainable one for the movement.

The Role of the United States and Europe

It is impossible to discuss reform in Lebanon without discussing international influence. External factors will in many ways decide whether the deep divisions that exist among political forces in Lebanon will continue to be managed through institutional politics or degenerate into renewed confessional anxieties and conflict. In the aftermath of the Syrian withdrawal, Lebanon can benefit from continued international support to carry out reforms. However, the wrong policies by international actors could undermine the process.

Historically, the Lebanese state's weakness has encouraged international actors to favor specific parties rather than mediate to restore a system of political compromises. Outsiders must realize that Lebanon cannot be governed without a consensus among the main political coalitions. Also, aggressive efforts to pit one party against another will not result in clear-cut victories but will only aggravate the conflict and further undermine the prospects for peaceful and democratic ways of establishing national consensus.

The United States and Europe can aid reform by continuing to protect Lebanon against undue Syrian interference, but they must also understand that Lebanon has been deeply influenced by Syria for obvious geographical and historical reasons, and that this is not going to change despite the withdrawal of Syrian troops. Syria continues to exercise vast power in Lebanon, through many allies such as Hizbollah and Amal, and through economic pressure, which it does not hesitate to use. It has also sponsored Palestinian groups with an armed presence in Lebanon and still maintains a continued intelligence presence, according to some reports. As it pursues its anti-Syrian policy, the United States should consider how its policies toward Syria will affect Lebanon.

The United States must also accept the fact that it cannot push its allies in Lebanon to take uncompromising positions, particularly on the issue of Hizbollah's disarmament. The United States must accept that the disarmament of Hizbollah can only be done in a cooperative and gradual manner, in full consultation with Hizbollah itself. The futility of attempting to forcefully disarm Hizbollah was demonstrated by the failure of Israel's attacks on Lebanon in the summer of 2006. The U.S. administration's failure to call for an immediate cease-fire damaged U.S. credibility in Lebanon and weakened its Lebanese allies. Indeed, if the United States pushes the Lebanese government too strongly on this issue, the fabric of the Lebanese state itself might disintegrate, so contentious is the issue. Most Lebanese consider Hizbollah a legitimate organization, as they credit it with pushing Israel out of Lebanon. While respecting Lebanese sensitivity on this issue, the United States must also make clear that Hizbollah is not purely a Lebanese question and that its disarmament can only occur in the context of progress toward Israeli–Lebanese and Israeli–Syrian peace agreements. The fate of Hizbollah is also tied to that of armed Palestinian groups in refugee camps and bases in Lebanon. Like Hizbollah, Palestinian groups were spared from the Ta'if Accord disarmament requirement. With the Lebanese government lacking the power to disarm these groups, the issue has to be part of a comprehensive regional peace agreement. For its part, the EU, which enjoys greater credibility than the United States in Lebanon, should continue to engage in dialogue with Hizbollah over recent proposals to merge its military wing into an auxiliary unit within the Lebanese army.

The United States and European Union (EU) can help achieve the long-term goal of a more democratic Lebanon through diplomatic and technical support aimed at strengthening the institutions of the Lebanese state through electoral, security, and economic reform. In the area of electoral law reform, both the United States and the EU should continue to encourage the opening of the debate on the electoral law to civil society activists and election law experts. Although reform must be primarily a Lebanese process, the United States and the EU should assert their support for a reform of the electoral framework, provide technical assistance when requested, and facilitate dialogue.

The EU has already been directly involved through its electoral monitoring mission. It has also issued several calls for reform of the whole electoral framework and has provided specific recommendations. It has also offered technical and financial assistance to Lebanon to reform the electoral law before the next general election, as part of its effort to revamp the Euro-Mediterranean Partnership and make a stronger commitment to supporting political reform in the region.

On the U.S. side, organizations such as the International Foundation for Electoral Systems (IFES) and the National Democratic Institute (NDI) have already involved themselves in the process by training local observers and working with members of parliament. NDI and IFES should continue to work with domestic groups such as the Lebanese Association for Democratic Elections to provide technical expertise on electoral reform and facilitate dialogue between different political forces. The benefits of such support, however, are relatively modest. It is unclear how far technical solutions such as redistricting can go toward resolving such a highly politicized issue as electoral reform. Donors can participate in two ways: provide a comparative framework of electoral reform and facilitate debate. The rest depends on the political willingness of the Lebanese themselves to invest in this process.

In security reform the international community can be crucial, as demonstrated by the UN's investigation of the Hariri assassination. The investigation marked a turning point in Lebanese history: For the first time, the security sector was sent a powerful political message that it would be held accountable. The arrest, on August 30, 2005, of the security chiefs was a dramatic move on this front. It is vital, however, that security assistance not be perceived as politicized. European organizations such as the Geneva Centre for the Democratic Control of Armed Forces are best suited for this role because, unlike the U.S. government, they can provide technical assistance on security reform issues outside the jurisdiction of foreign or defense ministries. In this context, assistance to the Lebanese army—arguably the most credible and popular state institution—can be very beneficial, as long as it is presented as assistance to a national institution rather than to a government representing a particular political bloc. In the instability that rocked Lebanon after February 2005, the Lebanese army's nonpartisanship helped guarantee stability. It maintained strict neutrality, protecting both the presidential and prime minister's headquarters, and emerged as a symbol of national unity and state authority. U.S. military assistance that is openly presented as an attempt to strengthen the incumbent government can undermine Lebanon's most popular and least divisive institution.

In the process of economic reform, the United States and Europe should continue to solicit support to help Lebanon handle the problem of its public debt. Since 1995, the rate of economic growth has been declining, and public debt has been mounting since the civil war ended in 1990. The public debt, estimated at $36 billion, is the highest in the world as a share of GDP (165 percent). The level of debt threatens domestic financial stability and has forced the government to seek external aid repeatedly, as reflected by the 2001 Paris I, 2002 Paris II, and 2007 Paris III aid conferences in which the government met with international donors to seek bilateral assistance in restructuring its debt at lower interest rates. International donors should use the most recent package to pressure the Lebanese government on the hard decisions that need to be made regarding institutional economic reforms. Economic reform has been at the center of debate since the end of the civil war, but political divisions prevented the emergence of a coherent national policy.[1] Ultimately, the hurdles to economic reform—particularly the obstacle to privatization—will remain political but external donors can put pressure on Lebanese to reach compromises on some issues.

Through the Euro-Mediterranean Partnership and Association Agreements, the EU is deeply involved in the process of economic reform in Lebanon. The Euro-Mediterranean Association Agreement signed in June 2002 (and awaiting ratification) could have a positive effect, because it advocates a greater role for the private sector and encourages the launch of legislative reforms to make possible the larger-scale economic and trade-related policy reforms required by the Euro-Mediterranean Partnership. Throughout this process, however, the EU must recognize that economic liberalization is not a substitute for policies designed to encourage democratic development. Since the 1980s, the EU has followed a policy of "economics first" that assumes that economic reform and market-related and administration-related capacity building are likely to spill over into broader political reform in the Mediterranean region. Ten years after launching the partnership, the EU is reevaluating that assumption, given that it has been discredited by the experiences of several countries in the region. For the

Euro-Mediterranean Partnership to remain relevant, it must approach economic reform as a component of a holistic approach to change that includes an emphasis on political reform.

The United States and Europe can play a crucial role in political reform in Lebanon, but their task is not easy. They should focus on stabilizing the volatile situation in Lebanon and consider how their policies toward Syria and Iran will affect this goal. While acknowledging that there are no short-term prospects for a secular nonconfessional Lebanon, they must push reforms that address the key flaws in the confessional system. They must also realize that sensitive issues such as Hizbollah's disarmament cannot be dealt with conclusively in the near future.

Notes

1. Critics of the postwar economic path blame former prime minister Hariri and his finance minister, Fouad Siniora (currently prime minister), for the mounting debt and denounce the excessive emphasis on macroeconomic and financial issues at the expense of the socioeconomic, institutional, and organizational dimensions of development. They cite increased inequities in income and asset distribution, environmental degradation, uneven development among the regions, and increasingly difficult living conditions for the majority of Lebanese. Hariri's defenders assert that he was never allowed to implement his economic vision because of sharp disputes with President Lahoud and his supporters.

DEMILITARIZING ALGERIA

Hugh Roberts

The Algerian state constituted at the end of the eight-year war of independence by the victorious Front de Libération Nationale (FLN) exhibited an impressive degree of continuity and stability during its first 26 years (from 1962 to 1988). In February 1989, however, the regime of President Chadli Bendjedid abruptly introduced a pluralist constitution and legalized parties, which, based on rival Islamist and Berberist conceptions of identity, polarized public opinion by advocating mutually exclusive Islamist and secularist conceptions of the state. In doing so, the regime set in motion a process that profoundly destabilized the state. Instead of restoring order, however, the army's eventual intervention in January 1992 precipitated a descent into armed conflict that, while greatly reduced since 1998, has still not entirely ended.

The violence that has ravaged Algeria since 1992 has expressed and confirmed the ascendancy of the military in Algerian political life and the weakness of all civilian forms of politics, both on the pro-government side and among those opposed to the regime. The civilian leaders of the Islamist movement were almost entirely outflanked by the Islamist armed movements, and within the regime the army's general staff and intelligence chiefs became the main source of decision making. In particular, successive presidents proved entirely unable to impose their authority. The deposing of President Chadli Bendjedid in January 1992 was followed by the assassination of President Mohammad Boudiaf six months later, the brief and ineffectual interim of Ali Kafi (July 1992 to January 1994), and the eventual failure also of Liamine Zeroual (1994–1999), who, despite his impressive electoral endorsement in 1995, was unable to secure a consensus within the regime in support of his efforts to resolve the crisis.

Since becoming president in April 1999, Abdelaziz Bouteflika has achieved substantial success in several key areas where his predecessors had failed. The main armed Islamist organizations that dominated the insurgency during the 1990s—the Armée Islamique du Salut (AIS) and the Groupe Islamique Armé (GIA)—either disbanded or were largely eliminated, and security was restored to most of the country. The virtual quarantine in which Algeria had been confined since 1994 was broken as Bouteflika spearheaded the country's return to the international stage, renewing relations with Paris and Washington while also recovering some of Algeria's former influence in broader African affairs. Bouteflika has also enjoyed that indispensable quality—luck. Since the events of September 11, 2001, Algeria has been seen as an especially useful and welcome ally by the U.S. government in its global war on terrorism. And financially the state's position has been transformed as a result of high oil prices; in desperate straits in the early 1990s, Algeria has recently been able to pay off its once-crippling debts and accumulate unprecedentedly ample reserves.

In terms of internal reform, however, the balance sheet is, at best, ambiguous and controversial. The system of formal political pluralism introduced in 1989 was preserved by the military-dominated regime throughout the 1990s and remains in being today. Formally contested elections have been held at regular intervals, in 1995, 1999, and 2004 for the presidency of the republic and in 1997 and 2002 for the national, regional, and municipal assemblies. Fresh assembly elections were scheduled for summer 2007. Widely perceived as authoritarian in his personal outlook, Bouteflika has chosen to live with this pluralist system while working around it. A variety of parties, some of them Islamist, remain legal and are represented in parliament, but their capacity to offer an alternative to the regime has been reduced to zero. At the same time, Bouteflika's determination to restore the authority of the presidency has entailed the curbing of press freedom—a number of outspoken journalists have been jailed as a lesson to others—and of other freedoms, notably of trade unions. And the state of emergency introduced in February 1992 has been routinely renewed and still is in force.

It would be one-sided, however, to consider these developments as a simple regression. Bouteflika's principal purpose has been to restore coherence to the executive branch of the state by reestablishing the presidency—in place of the army high command—as the supreme arbiter of policy debates and conflicts of interest. In doing this he has been taking on the vested interests of the coterie of senior generals who became a law unto themselves during the 1990s, and he has been steadily maneuvering them off the political stage.

The central issue is whether his success in this endeavor will prove permanent—and thereby open up the possibility of a progressive and eventually definitive demilitarization of the state—or whether it will be merely temporary. With Bouteflika's health now in question, his chances of securing a third term in 2009 are in doubt, and arguments over the succession have already begun to preoccupy and divide the political military elite. Moreover, the onset of a factional dispute since the summer of 2006 has coincided with a striking—and quite unexpected—recrudescence of terrorist activity. The main armed movement still active, the Salafi Group for Preaching and Combat (Groupe Salafiste pour la Prédication et le Combat, or GSPC) was previously noted for confining its attacks to the security forces and sparing civilians. Under new leaders, the GSPC has recently reverted to the indiscriminate terrorism formerly associated with the GIA while rebranding itself as a branch of al-Qaeda. With the unprecedented attack by a suicide bomber on the principal government building in central Algiers on April 11, 2007, Algerian politics has once more entered a period of uncertainty and anxiety.

The Failure of Premature Reform (1989–1999)

The generally uncritical welcome given to President Chadli's liberalizing reform by Western governments and observers at the time was predicated, among other things, on a misconception of the problems of authoritarianism and arbitrary rule in the Algerian context. It was assumed that these problems were rooted in the formal political monopoly of the Party of the FLN (PFLN) and that ending this monopoly through the introduction of political pluralism was the indispensable point of departure for political reform in the direction of democracy and the rule of law.[1] This assessment, however, ignored the facts that the PFLN was not the source of power in the Algerian state and that the problem of authoritarianism was not a function of its formal monopoly. Rather it was a function of the preponderance of the executive branch of the state over the legislative branch and the judiciary and the fact that the executive branch as a whole has been subject throughout to the hegemony of the military.

Instead of strengthening the civilian wing of the political class as the indispensable precondition of a sustainable process of political liberalization, the premature introduction of formal pluralism gravely weakened it. Prior to 1989, the PFLN had functioned as a constraint on the power of the military commanders; by licensing and even encouraging challengers to it, the regime disabled its own civilian wing and freed the army's commanders from all institutional constraints. By legalizing parties based on rival conceptions of identity, the regime simultaneously disabled public opinion, by arranging for it to be polarized between mutually exclusive and above all bitterly intolerant cultural and ideological outlooks, and ensured that political debate was fixated on alternative—and largely utopian—conceptions of the proper constitution of the state instead of alternative programs for government. And by allowing the Islamist party, the Front Islamique du Salut (FIS), to contest and win local elections in June 1990 and legislative elections in December 1991 on a platform calling for an Islamic state, the government provided the army commanders, fearful for their own prerogatives, with the pretext for finally intervening in January 1992 to depose President Chadli, abort the electoral process, violate the constitution, and suppress the FIS in the name of democracy.

The result was a conflagration that has proved extremely difficult to bring to an end. Algeria since 1992 has been a battlefield disputed not by two clear-cut sides but by a welter of distinct Islamist groups on the one hand, as inclined to fight each other and to terrorize the population as to pose a real threat to the state, and, on the other, a military-dominated regime whose internal divisions have at least partially mirrored those of the Islamists notionally opposed to it. It was only when the factional conflict within the Algerian army was provisionally resolved with the resignation of President Zeroual in September 1998 and the accession of Bouteflika to the presidency the following April that the necessary minimum of consensus was reached, and the regime at last exhibited, at least for a time, a unified approach to curbing the violence and restoring order.

This approach has involved inducing the main armed Islamist organizations to end their campaigns and dissolve themselves in return for a qualified amnesty, while at the same time refusing any rehabilitation of the banned FIS and, equally if not more controversially, any investigation into the army's conduct of its counterinsurgency campaign (notably, the resort to torture and extrajudicial executions). These measures, presented by the regime as necessary to promote "national reconciliation," seem to have enjoyed general popular approval even though they have been vigorously criticized by both human rights groups and associations representing the families of the "disappeared" (people arrested by the security forces and never seen since) as well as by the families of victims of Islamist terrorism. But they have clearly been insufficient to end the violence completely.

The most important armed movement in recent years has been the GSPC, which broke away from the GIA in 1998 in protest against the GIA's targeting of civilians. (The GIA, although now reduced to a small rump, has never disbanded.) Under its original leader, Hassan Hattab, the GSPC confined itself to attacking the security forces throughout the 1998 to 2002 period and even expressed interest in negotiating an end to its campaign. Bouteflika appears to have considered extending the amnesty formula to the GSPC in return for its dissolution, but the majority of the army commanders were opposed and Hattab's loss of control of the group to rival leaders in 2003 put paid to that possibility. Although current Western attention has focused on the GSPC's decision to rename itself "al-Qaeda in the Lands of the Islamic Maghrib," the most striking aspects of its recent mutation are its reversion to the indiscriminate terrorism that was the hallmark of the GIA and its increasing targeting of the police, that is, the civilian rather than military wing of the security forces.

The failure to end the violence completely has thus been closely connected with the persistence and resurgence of factional conflicts within the regime. This factionalism—the motor of change in the informal sector of the Algerian polity—also profoundly vitiated the introduction of formal party political pluralism from 1989 onwards. It is in fact the heart of the problem of Algerian politics and has dominated the country's political life to a degree that has always distinguished independent Algeria from the other states of the region.

The Peculiarities of the Algerian State

Algeria between 1962 and 1988 has almost invariably been described as a one-party state and accordingly placed in the same category as other authoritarian regimes based on single-party rule. However, unlike the Baath parties in Iraq and Syria and the Néo-Destour in Tunisia, the PFLN was not created on the basis of a particular program or ideology by freely acting political entrepreneurs but rather was established by government fiat.[2] It was, from the outset, a state apparatus rather than a genuine political party. It performed legitimating functions for the regime—whatever programs and policies the latter adopted—and supervised the so-called mass organizations (trade union, peasants' union, women's union, youth union, and so on) to ensure their loyalty. It was not itself a source of decision making and, in fact, during the presidency of Houari Boumediène (1965–1978), it possessed neither a central committee nor a political bureau, and not a single congress of the party was held.

On Boumediène's death in December 1978, a concerted attempt was made by senior figures in the regime to establish the PFLN as a serious institution in its own right. This attempt met with impressive initial success. A party congress at last was held in January 1979 and approved Chadli Bendjedid's candidacy to become president. The same congress finally endowed the party with a large and representative Central Committee, a seventeen-man Political Bureau containing genuine heavyweights, and a number of policy commissions. The purpose was to equip the PFLN with the formal organizational structures, powers, and capacities that would enable it to supplant the informal coterie of army commanders as the principle locus of strategic decision making in the state. In short, it was a major effort to promote the badly needed institutionalization and demilitarization of the Algerian power structure.

But its success was short-lived. In May 1980, in a climate of turmoil bordering on panic in the wake of sensational unrest in Kabylia, a resolution inspired by senior army commanders was railroaded through the Central Committee giving President Chadli, as general secretary of the party, full powers to appoint members of the Political Bureau.[3] The Central Committee, in other words, was induced to emasculate itself and the Political Bureau, from which several major figures were immediately dropped. The result was that, from that point on, President Chadli was formally accountable to nobody but informally accountable to the army commanders. The capacity of the army commanders to abuse their power was limited by their own membership of—and consequent obligation to respect the procedural rules governing—the party's leading instances.

But this curb on the arbitrary power of the military was itself limited. In line with this change of direction, Chadli dissolved most of the PFLN's new policy commissions; established a disciplinary commission to intimidate dissenting voices; reduced the size, representativeness, and role of the Political Bureau; and organized a purge of independent-minded personalities from the Central Committee. The attempt to endow the party with real functions and powers and a real inner life had clearly been defeated—to the benefit of the military, the informal sector of the polity, and the syndrome of arbitrary rule.

The Algerian state has thus more closely resembled Egypt. In both cases, the revolution that constituted the state was military in character and the nominally ruling party has in reality been little more than a façade for the executive branch of the state dominated by the officer corps of the armed forces. In both cases, the development of substantive political pluralism requires a prior reform to empower the legislative branch to curb the executive branch and replace military primacy with civilian control. Introducing formal pluralism in breach of the party's monopoly merely replaced a monolithic façade with a fragmented one. But the fact that the premature introduction of formal pluralism in Algeria had disastrous consequences owes much to the way in which the Algerian case has differed from the Egyptian prototype.

The Problem of Factionalism

The contrasts between the Algerian and Egyptian revolutions are at least as important as the formal parallels. The Egyptian revolution of 1952 was a military coup largely planned and led by one man, Gamal Abdel Nasser, such that revolutionary legitimacy was the preserve of a tiny coterie of co-conspirators (the Free Officers), and the leadership of Nasser was unchallenged. But the Algerian revolution was a protracted war, conducted in a highly decentralized manner all over the country and even outside it, and mobilized the support of the Muslim population as a whole and the active participation of scores of thousands. Thus revolutionary legitimacy has been widely diffused, with many thousands of Algerians able to claim some share in it and a corresponding share in political power for themselves and the coteries or clienteles they represent. The result has been an exceptionally intense factionalism within the power structure of the independent state.

Three developments have served to perpetuate and, if anything, aggravate the problem of factionalism since independence. The first was the emergence of hydrocarbons as the principal source of foreign earnings and state revenue. The Algerian state assumed the character of a "distributive state," and its role in allocating these resources guaranteed that the stakes in the factional competition remained high and even expanded. The second was the onset of identity conflicts and ideological divisions, a development that started in the 1980s and was exacerbated by the advent of formal pluralism. The third was the belated decision in 1993–1994 to bow to external pressure to reschedule Algeria's debt and accept its corollary, structural adjustment and the concomitant policy of privatization of state enterprises. Because all decisions concerning these matters continued to be made within the executive branch, controversies over these issues constantly galvanized factional mobilization and the rough-and-tumble of factional conflict remained the principal medium of policy making.

This factionalism has been ambiguous in its implications. On the one hand, it has contributed to the state's capacity, inherited from the wartime FLN, to co-opt a wide range of interests, viewpoints, and personalities, since it is through informal factional recruitment and alliance building that the co-optation process primarily occurs. Thus the activity of the factions has enabled the state to keep a grip on the diverse social interests and ideological trends in the country and as such has contributed to the state's own stability and capacity to survive.[4] It has also contributed to another important way in which Algeria differs from the Egyptian case: the relative weakness—or at least porousness—of the elite–mass dichotomy. But, at the same time, the role of the factions and the salience of factional allegiances have persistently prevented coherence in government policy making and the functioning of the administration. More generally, they have tended to preclude political accountability, vitiate political debate, and inhibit political institutionalization. The factions have thus been the chief guardians, as well as the chief beneficiaries, of the primacy of the informal sector of the Algerian polity over the formal sector, the corresponding backwardness of Algerian political culture, and the inadequacy of the current state framework to the requirements of a dynamic society and a modern economy.

The Problem of Presidential Authority

This exceptionally complex and intense factionalism has been all the more difficult to control because the revolution had no undisputed leader. There was no Algerian Nasser (or Ho Chi Minh or Castro or Mandela, let alone Mao Zedong). And the revolutionary elite—composed of the senior echelons of the historic FLN and above all the Armée de Libération Nationale (ALN)—has consisted of individuals who have been generally disinclined to recognize the claims to preeminent leadership of any one of their own number.

As a result, the position of president, at the apex of the pyramid of power, has usually been a relatively powerless one. The most powerful men in the FLN–ALN during the war neutralized each other's presidential ambitions and accordingly agreed on relatively weak figures (Ferhat Abbas, Benyoucef Ben Khedda) to act as civilian presidents of the Gouvernement Provisoire de la République Algérienne (GPRA) from 1958 onward. These civilians were essentially figureheads or front men for the real power holders, and they performed little more than ceremonial and public relations functions. Both of the strong-willed historic revolutionaries who briefly became president—Ahmed Ben Bella (1962–1965) and Mohamed Boudiaf (January–June 1992)—came to grief for lack of solid military support. Only Houari Boumediène was able to exercise the full powers and prerogatives of the president of the republic as defined in the constitution. But his success in establishing his authority as president was due to his unique position first as the architect of the unification of the scattered forces of the ALN in his capacity as its chief of staff and second as the organizer of the ALN's transformation into a modern regular army, the Armée Nationale Populaire (ANP), in his capacity as minister of defense after 1962. He thus brought his unrivaled authority over the armed forces with him into the presidency and made a point of retaining the defense portfolio and preserving his control over the army thereafter. Although he never wore military uniform after becoming president in 1965, his political power was in reality a function of his military power.

None of his successors has been able to emulate him in this respect. And the prospect that any one of them might eventually accumulate decisive political authority over the executive branch as a whole was profoundly damaged by Chadli Bendjedid's decision in 1984 to reestablish the ANP's General Staff.

The Problem of the General Staff

The creation of a unified General Staff of the ALN under Colonel Boumediène in 1960 was a victory for the most political wing of the ALN over the centrifugal tendencies inherent in a liberation army that had been extremely decentralized from its inception in 1954. The accumulation of authority that Boumediène's General Staff achieved through its unification of the ALN enabled it to arbitrate the power struggle within the FLN at independence in 1962 and equipped Boumediène to transform the ALN into a regular army from 1962 onward. As defense minister, Boumediène continued to act as chief of staff as well until Ben Bella appointed Colonel Tahar Zbiri to the position behind Boumediène's back—a move that spelled the end of the Ben Bella–Boumediène alliance and led to Ben Bella's eventual overthrow in 1965. As president, Boumediène retained the defense portfolio but was able to consolidate his position fully only after getting rid of Zbiri following the latter's abortive putsch in December 1967, at which point the General Staff was abolished. In other words, after 1968, Boumediène's presidential authority rested on the fact that not only was he his own defense minister, but in the absence of a General Staff, the defense ministry was the sole, unrivaled apex of the military power structure.

The reestablishment of the General Staff in 1984 changed all that. Its immediate effect was to qualify the defense ministry's control over the ANP officer corps and so dilute President Chadli's personal authority over the armed forces. That in turn diminished Chadli's ability to arbitrate and limit factional disputes within the military, especially the conflict between the coterie of former officers of the French army (the so-called Déserteurs de l'Armée Française, or DAF) and the rival coterie of officers who had emerged from the ALN's guerrilla units and then graduated from various Arab military academies (in Egypt, Iraq, and Jordan). As a result, this conflict became more intense and uninhibited. But the longer term significance of the institutional change was to establish an autonomous center of political power and decision making within the army. The implications of this became apparent only under the dramatic stresses and strains of the 1989–1992 period.

Following the ratification by referendum of the pluralist constitution in February 1989, the ANP withdrew its representatives from the Central Committee and Political Bureau of the PFLN. The move was declared—and naïvely believed—to signify the army's total withdrawal from the political stage. In fact, however, having ended its involvement with the PFLN, the army command began to engage in relations with all parties in the new pluralist dispensation. A special office to handle formal liaison with the various political parties was established under the aegis of the General Staff, and the intelligence services discreetly infiltrated all the main parties as a matter of course. Thus, the army commanders—acting independently of the defense ministry—were equipping themselves to negotiate their own, autonomous relations with the various factions of the civilian political class. The consequences for the authority of the presidency were enormous.

Immediately after the FIS's first victory in the municipal and regional elections in June 1990, Chadli was induced to surrender the defense portfolio to then chief of staff, Major General Khaled Nezzar. In June 1991, Nezzar and the General Staff forced Chadli to agree to the brutal repression of FIS demonstrations in Algiers and the eviction of the head of the government, the reformer Mouloud Hamrouche and, in addition, to give up the presidency of the PFLN. By this point, then, the army commanders had become an independent force in the political arena, dictating terms to the president and progressively stripping him of his prerogatives. Chadli's abdication of presidential authority and responsibility can thus be seen to have taken place in several stages, beginning as early as 1984, and to have been largely completed seven months before Nezzar and his colleagues finally applied the coup de grâce in January 1992.

Each of Algeria's successive presidents since 1992 has been confronted with an army commanded by officers he did not himself appoint and whom he cannot easily replace. Neither of the two presidents of the Haut Comité d'État (HCE)—Mohamed Boudiaf and Ali Kafi—was even nominally his own defense minister; both were cramped from the start by Khaled Nezzar's occupancy of the position.[5] When Nezzar was finally obliged to stand down in favor of Liamine Zeroual in July 1993, Zeroual's ability to choose his own military staff was fatally constrained, even after he assumed the presidency in

January 1994 in addition to the defense portfolio. In his last act as defense minister, Nezzar had appointed as chief of staff the ambitious and forceful General Mohammed Lamari, previously commander of the "special forces" spearheading the counterinsurgency campaign and known for his preference for "eradicating" the rebellion rather than seeking a negotiated end to it. The result was a situation of dual power, with Lamari's General Staff contesting and neutralizing Zeroual's authority over the armed forces, security policy, and, indeed, the political situation as a whole. Instead of the defense ministry tending, as under Boumediène, to enable the presidency to control the military, the army's top echelon, organized in the General Staff, was now tending to control the defense ministry. From this position, it was able to box in and hamstring the presidency, sabotage its peace initiatives, and dominate the political arena, where it possessed important civilian relays in the shape of secularist political parties enthusiastically committed to the "eradicator" policy[6] and influential daily newspapers.[7]

The power of the General Staff was such that Zeroual was even unable to dispose of the defense portfolio as he wished. When he sought to appoint his ally, General Mohamed Betchine, to the position, Lamari and the General Staff successfully blocked the move. And when, as a second-best ploy, Zeroual tried to win control of the newly formed—and state-sponsored— Rassemblement National Démocratique (RND) as a reliable party-political relay by promoting Betchine and Betchine's nominees within the RND leadership, the General Staff and the intelligence services went onto the offensive, mobilized their civilian relays, and organized a virulent press campaign against Betchine in the summer of 1998.[8] Zeroual accordingly decided that it had become impossible for him to exercise his constitutional prerogatives as president of the republic and announced his intention to call an early election so that a successor could be found.

This move apparently surprised the army power brokers, who were obliged, with audible reluctance, to agree to retired Major General Larbi Belkheir's proposal that former foreign minister Abdelaziz Bouteflika be invited to run for president with the army's tacit backing. This backing was far from total, however. Only Belkheir and his protégé, the head of counterintelligence, General Smaïl Lamari (no relation to the chief of staff), were positively committed to Bouteflika. The General Staff advertised its own lack of enthusiasm by publicly insisting that the regular armed forces were strictly neutral, and the decision makers authorized no fewer than six plausible candidates to run against Bouteflika.[9] The prospect of a genuinely contested election was destroyed at the eleventh hour, however, by the sensational collective decision of the six other candidates to withdraw from the race in protest against what they claimed was evidence of election rigging. The result was that Bouteflika became president by default through a procedure that fell far short of true election. From the army commanders' point of view, this was, of course, the ideal result. They had the man they preferred in the presidency, but so *mal élu* (badly elected) that he possessed no electoral legitimacy or popular mandate and so could be presumed to pose no threat to their domination of the political scene.

It was to take Bouteflika five years to bring the General Staff, at least provisionally and conditionally, under control. He finally achieved this when Mohamed Lamari and his supporters in the army command were forced into retirement in the summer of 2004 following Bouteflika's triumphant reelection the previous April. Lamari himself was replaced as chief of staff by the self-effacing Major General Ahmed Gaïd Salah. With the General Staff provisionally tamed, Bouteflika was able to restore the authority of the defense ministry over the armed forces as a whole by his appointment of retired Major General Abdelmalek Guennaïzia to the newly created post of minister-delegate of defense. Guennaïzia, Lamari's predecessor as chief of staff and a close associate of both former president Chadli Bendjedid and former defense minister Khaled Nezzar, carried influence with the army commanders but, having retired, was technically a civilian as well as (in principle) answerable to Bouteflika in the latter's capacity as titular minister of defense. But there is reason to doubt that this fully secured Bouteflika's authority over the defense establishment, since this authority still did not extend in practice to the intelligence services.

The Problem of the Intelligence Services

The enormous power of the intelligence services has long been the open secret of Algerian political life. Created by Colonel Abdelhafid Boussouf, the commander of wilaya V (Oranie) in the wartime FLN-ALN and subsequently minister of armaments and general liaisons in the GPRA, the intelligence services were renamed the Sécurité Militaire (SM) after independence and, while officially called the Département du Renseignement et de la Sécurité (DRS) since 1990, they are still widely referred to as "la SM."

Already a pervasive presence in Algerian political life under Presidents Boumediène and Chadli Bendjedid, the intelligence services acquired even greater influence during the 1990s. The exigencies of the counterinsurgency campaign led, in particular, to the expansion of the activities and personnel of the Direction du Contre-Espionnage et de la Sécurité Interne (DCE) within the DRS. The conduct of the DCE in combating the Islamist insurgency has long been a matter of the greatest controversy. That it actively infiltrated the Islamic armed movements is common knowledge and not in itself surprising. What has been at issue in the controversy is whether this infiltration has sought to bring the insurgency to an end or, rather, on the contrary, manipulate it for unavowed and unavowable ends.

What is certain, however, is that the political power of the services since the onset of the violence in 1992 has been greater than at any previous point in the history of independent Algeria. Since 1990, Algeria has had five heads of state (Chadli, Boudiaf, Kafi, Zeroual, and Bouteflika), eleven heads of government[10] and four defense ministers,[11] but throughout this entire period the DRS has been commanded by General Mohamed Mediène and the DCE by General Smaïl Lamari. During the protracted "dual power" impasse of 1993–1998, when the Zeroual presidency was engaged in a continuous trial of strength with the General Staff, it was Mediène who was the effective arbiter of the conflict. That the DRS eventually arbitrated in favor of Bouteflika against Chief of Staff Mohamed Lamari in 2004 is clear. But it is by no means certain that the provisional taming of the General Staff signified a reduction in General Mediène's influence to the presidency's benefit or that any real progress has been made toward holding the intelligence services accountable to anyone other than their own commanders.

Restoring the Presidency and Reining In Pluralism

The consensus that existed among the decision makers at Bouteflika's accession in April 1999 concerned two main points. The first was the pressing need to break out of the debilitating "quarantine" that Algeria had been confined in by the attitudes of its main Western partners, France above all, since January 1992 and especially since the hijacking of the French Airbus at Algiers airport in December 1994. In this respect, Bouteflika's accession to the presidency fitted precisely the tradition of the military using civilian *chargés de mission* to front for them. As a former and most effective foreign minister, Bouteflika was the ideal choice. He scored early successes with the Organization of African Unity summit held in Algiers in July 1999 and with his flamboyant state visit to Paris in May 2000. But the public relations problem was enormous. For the Algerian state to be perceived once again as a legitimate partner, it was essential to reduce the violence very appreciably.

This was the second point of consensus. It meant providing a political and juridical framework for the deal that had already been tentatively struck by the

ANP with the Armée Islamique du Salut, and a number of smaller armed groupings that had associated themselves with the AIS's cease-fire since October 1997. Thus Bouteflika was authorized by the army commanders to do the honors at home as well as abroad, by securing the passage of the Law on Civil Concord in July 1999, which encouraged members of armed groups to give themselves up in return for certain guarantees, and by promulgating a decree in January 2000 providing for a qualified amnesty for the AIS and associated armed groups in return for their dissolution.

The controversial nature of these measures worked to Bouteflika's advantage, since he was able to argue that the Algerian people as a whole should be consulted. He was accordingly able to call a referendum in September 1999 in which the electorate was invited to say whether it approved the president's "approach" or not. The resounding "yes" vote both secured approval for the Law on Civil Concord and for the subsequent amnesty decree and, by endorsing Bouteflika's policy, compensated him for his "bad election" the previous April.

Although this strengthened Bouteflika's hand, he was unable to get his own way on the composition of the new government, which was formed only in December 1999, after months of haggling. The army commanders vetoed his choice of Noureddine Zerhouni for defense minister (obliging Bouteflika to retain the portfolio himself while making Zerhouni minister of the interior) and insisted that the new government should reflect the party political composition of the National Assembly. Since the army commanders effectively controlled the leaderships of the main parties (not only the PFLN and RND but also the Berberist RCD and the Islamist MSP), they were in effect using the system of formal political pluralism to constrain the president and buttress their own power. The truth of the matter was clearly stated by Bouteflika when he declared in regard to the new cabinet: "I am forced to accept a mosaic that does not suit me."

This framework of political maneuvering endured throughout Bouteflika's first term. On the one hand, Bouteflika sought continuously to milk the "national reconciliation" agenda to bolster domestic popular support while seeking external endorsement and legitimation (especially from Paris and Washington) through his orchestration of Algeria's return to the world stage and his support for the neoliberal agenda of economic reform.[12] At the same time, he presented himself to the army as its champion and defender, the main, if not sole, guarantor that its commanders would not be held to account for the "dirty war" they had conducted against the Islamist insurgency. The persistence of international pressure on this point, fueled by a series of sensational revelations, enabled Bouteflika to bargain with the army command-ers.[13] In return for shielding the army, he sought to induce it to withdraw from the political stage and also to reshuffle the high command and push into retirement the generals responsible for the 1992 coup and its bloody aftermath.

On the other hand, the generals in question had no intention of going qui-etly and maneuvered constantly against the president, blocking the extension of the "national reconciliation" amnesty measures to those armed groups still active (especially the GSPC),[14] exploiting the U.S.-led global war on terrorism to develop their own relations with external partners and sources of support and legitimation in the Pentagon and NATO, provoking lethal riots in Kabylia in the spring and summer of 2001 and then seeking to channel the massive Kabyle protest movement that resulted into attacking the presidency,[15] quietly encouraging extraordinarily vitriolic attacks on Bouteflika in the secularist press (notably Le Matin) and, finally, encouraging the new general secretary of the PFLN, Ali Benflis, to run against Bouteflika in the presidential election of April 2004.

In behaving in this way, the army commanders (Lamari and the General Staff in particular) were acting to preserve the commanding political power they had acquired since deposing Chadli in 1992. Seeing the power rivalry with the presidency as a zero-sum game, they were determined to prevent Bouteflika from securing a second term and consolidating his position at their expense. The fact that they failed was of historic significance. Boute-flika's success in getting reelected in April 2004—the first Algerian president to complete his first term and get a second since Chadli Bendjedid achieved this in December 1983—was a crucial moment in the restoration of the pres-idency as the substantive and not merely formal apex of the Algerian power structure. It led directly to the retirement of Lamari and his closest support-ers in the army and thus the taming of the ANP General Staff, at least for the time being. But the coalition of factions and other interests that Bouteflika put together to support his reelection bid was an extremely heterogeneous one and that, too, has had implications and repercussions.

A fundamental handicap for Bouteflika throughout this relentless trial of strength was his lack of a reliable party-political relay for his position. The two state-sponsored façade parties, the PFLN and the RND, were coalitions in which all the main factions in the power structure were represented, but they were ultimately controlled by the army commanders through Major General Mohamed Medième's DRS. Of the notionally "opposition" parties, the docile Islamists of Mahfoud Nahnah's Mouvement de la Société pour la Paix (MSP) and the Berber-secularists of Saïd Sadi's RCD were, as a matter of public notoriety, inclined to take their bearings from the military décideurs. The more independent parties, Hocine Aït Ahmed's Front des Forces Socialistes (FFS), Abdallah Djaballah's Mouvement de la Réforme Nationale (MRN), and Louiza Hanoune's Parti des Travailleurs (PT), were generally supportive of Bouteflika's national reconciliation agenda. But they were among his sharpest critics on other issues and neither disposed nor able to support him in his duel with the army commanders.

To drum up electoral support, Bouteflika has accordingly been inclined to rely on organized forces outside the party system—the administration, the state-controlled television and radio, various voluntary associations, and the Sufi orders (which Bouteflika openly courted during his reelection campaign)—and to rein in rather than encourage pluralism in the formal political sphere. His national reconciliation agenda, which is popular and which he has been intent on monopolizing, has entailed a strategy of co-optation on the regime's Islamist and Berberist flanks, with the docile Islamists of the MSP kept inside successive coalition governments throughout and Thamazighth (the Berber language) at last recognized as a national language in the constitutional revision of April 2002. This strategy has been consistent with the tacit promotion of the recovery of the PFLN, which regained its old status as the country's principal party in the legislative elections of 2002. A corollary of this has been the regime's hostility to the principled opposition parties such as Aït Ahmed's FFS and Djaballah's MRN. The regime's concern to regain lost ground in Kabylia has led it to promote the PFLN there at the expense of the FFS, which is now in possibly terminal crisis. And, as part of Bouteflika's drive to co-opt the "Islamic-nationalist" trend in opinion—an ambition symbolized by the appointment of Abdelaziz Belkhadem to replace Ali Benflis as the PFLN's general secretary—the interior ministry has recently been facilitating the takeover of the MRN by an anti-Djaballah faction willing to accept co-option by the regime.[16]

This draining of vigor and combative dissent out of the party political sphere has had its counterpart in the press. With the end of the duel between the General Staff and the presidency, journalists can no longer insult the president of the republic with impunity. That was made brutally clear in June 2004 when *Le Matin* editor Mohamed Benchicou, who had been especially virulent in his attacks on Bouteflika in the run-up to the 2004 election, was jailed for two years and the newspaper was forced to close.[17] Numerous other journalists were subsequently jailed or subject to other forms of harassment (notably lawsuits), especially those with the temerity to publish articles—or even cartoons—critical of officeholders.[18] And measures taken under the "national reconciliation agenda" have gone so far as to criminalize critical discussion of the army's behavior during the "dirty war."[19]

The Uncertain Prospect

The central thrust of Bouteflika's project and impact has been the reconstruction and rationalization of authoritarian government on the basis of presidential power. A secondary, but very important, aspect has been the curbing of the ferocious identity politics of the 1989–1999 period by means of the effective assertion of a more inclusive conception of the Algerian national identity. In both respects, Bouteflika has been continuing aspects of the course charted by Liamine Zeroual, although with more success than his predecessor. In addition, with the recovery of the state's financial position, the regime has been able to resume in some degree its old developmental role, notably in the renovation and extension of the national infrastructure, a fact that has contributed to its partial recovery of popular legitimacy.

The restoration of the power of the presidency has been premised on a new balance between the military and civilian wings of the Algerian oligarchy. The excessive power of the regular army commanders has been curbed; the influence of the interior ministry has increased; the role and size of the police force have grown; and the president's personal authority over the government has been reasserted. In sum, the main trend has been for the form of government in Bouteflika's Algeria to approximate (notwithstanding certain differences) that of Hosni Mubarak's Egypt, as Boumediène's regime at least formally approximated Nasser's.

The trend may well continue if Bouteflika secures a third five-year term in 2009. But that would require a revision of the 1996 constitution, which limits presidents to two terms and is accordingly controversial. In addition, the president's health has been giving cause for concern since his nineteen-day stay in a Paris clinic for treatment of an undisclosed ailment in late 2005. Given the absence of an obvious alternative, however, a consensus within the military and administrative elites could crystallize in support of Bouteflika's continuation in power—at least for as long as his health permits.

Reasons for doubting that the Egyptianization trend will continue for long are furnished by the two most significant ways in which Algeria's social structures and political traditions have differed historically from the society of the Nile valley. The first is the size and political importance of the country's mountain-dwelling populations, who furnished the human bedrock of the national liberation struggle. The second is the comparative weakness of the central power and, in particular, the absence of anything resembling the pharaonic tradition of commanding personal rule.

The continuing vitality of the rebellious political traditions of the countryside has been evident in recent years in the propensity of ordinary Algerians to riot in protest at misgovernment and abuses of power (as in October 1988 but also, if on a smaller scale, since then).[20] It has been particularly evident in the remobilization of the tradition of the *maquis*[21] by the Islamist revolt of the 1990s and in the remarkable protest movement, rooted in the mountain villages, in Kabylia from 2001 to 2004.[22] But the vigor of insurgency and protest movement alike was matched in both cases by their political incoherence and ultimate failure. The trend of social change, above all the relentless dynamic of urbanization, is steadily eroding the traditional political weight of the countryside. This trend is reflected in the composition of successive governments over the last fifteen years as well as in the military high command, where members of both old and new urban elites now predominate, in sharp contrast to the patterns of the 1960s and 1970s.

More important is the absence of a tradition of strong personal power. The accumulation of power that Boumediène brought to the presidency was quickly dissipated under his successors. The arduous accumulation of power that Bouteflika has been able to achieve has owed a great deal to two very specific factors: his own remarkable talent for political maneuvering and the fact that circumstances—the bad odor in which the army commanders found themselves and the interest of Paris and Washington in providing external endorsement to his position—favored his enterprise. There is little reason to expect Bouteflika to be able to bequeath to his successor the authority he has built up. Indeed, there is cause to fear that the succession would be the occasion for a fresh intensification of factional conflict within the political-military elite, which only the army commanders would be able to arbitrate.

In this context, two features of the present conjuncture are especially disturbing. The first is Bouteflika's reported intention to use the planned revision of the constitution not only to authorize a third presidential term but also to reduce the already severely limited role and prerogatives of the national parliament. The danger is that his drive to consolidate his personal position as president will be at the expense of, among other things, the much-needed institutionalization of Algerian political life and the development of the civilian component of the political class. Such a turn of events could only favor the continued primacy of the informal sector of Algerian politics over the formal sector and the preeminence of factionalism and thus the absence of any serious possibility of progress toward the rule of law for the foreseeable future.

The second is the recrudescence over the last nine months of the terrorist activity of the GSPC coupled with its recent change of name. The danger in this is not only that it rules out any question of a negotiated end to the GSPC's campaign but also that it may turn out to imply the effective end of Bouteflika's "peace and national reconciliation" agenda and the crisis of his political project as a whole. For it could furnish a pretext for the army commanders to try to reassert their general hegemony over the Algerian state in the name of the global war on terrorism and at the expense of presidential authority, the improved military-civilian balance, and the relative order that Bouteflika had provisionally secured.

This point is of special salience in regard to the intelligence services. The extraordinary importance and power they have acquired over the last fifteen years has been in large part a function of their role in combating the Islamist insurgency. A clear implication of the definitive ending of the violence is the reduction of their influence to its previous, more limited, proportions. Equally clear, the resurgence of terrorism, if it continues, will have the effect of sustaining and buttressing the political power of the intelligence services indefinitely. That can only work to postpone or subvert the possibility of real political reform in the medium and longer term, insofar as it hinges for the time being on the restoration of the presidency. The complete recovery of presidential authority unquestionably requires the president of the republic to be able to exercise to the full his constitutional prerogatives as commander in chief of the armed forces, including the power to appoint the heads of the intelligence services—a power he still does not possess in practice.

Conclusion

In view of the terrible damage done to the Algerian polity by the events of the 1990s, the relative restoration of peace and order that has taken place under President Bouteflika was arguably as much as could realistically be hoped for. Given the weakness of the democratic current in Algerian political life, and especially the salience of mutually antipathetic forms of identity politics, it was inevitable that this restoration would exhibit an authoritarian aspect. Insofar as this has involved at least partial curbing of the power of the military, it has opened up the possibility of interesting political reform in the medium to longer term.

There can be no doubt that the demilitarization of the Algerian polity is a fundamental precondition of the advent of law-bound government, let alone democracy. That is something Western governments and media appear to have overlooked in the 1989–1991 period, when the precipitate introduction of formal pluralism was greeted with a degree of enthusiasm in Western capitals that it most certainly did not warrant. The pluralism in question was above all that of competing forms of identity politics, which fell far short of offering plausible programs for government but succeeded very well in splitting public opinion into sharply opposed camps and thus sowing the seeds of the subsequent violence. Although it made possible an unprecedented degree of public debate and press freedom for a while, it had no other democratic implications and throughout was subject to manipulation by the military decision makers.

At present, it would be extremely unrealistic for Western governments to suppose that they are in a position to promote progressive political reform in Algeria. The simplistic recipe of formal party-political pluralism plus free elections was tried in the 1989–1991 period with catastrophic consequences. The extreme crisis of the state's finances, which gave Paris great leverage over the regime from 1988 to 1998, is a thing of the past. Algeria's buoyant revenue from hydrocarbons and consequent financial independence are enabling the regime to renegotiate its relations with its foreign partners and enlarge its ability to maneuver once more. This fact alone is likely to rule out Western intervention in Algeria's internal politics for the time being.

In the longer term, the necessary condition for democratization is that the Algerian legislature acquires important decision-making powers. Only if this happens will the legislature be able to hold the executive to account (and thereby curb corruption) and, by so doing, guarantee the independence of the judiciary. Only if the national parliament becomes a real locus of decision making, in which the major interests in society need to be effectively represented, can social pressure ensure that elections are wholly free and fair and political parties—the kind necessary to a democratic system of alternating governments—develop. And only if the elected representatives of the people become the source of government mandates can the demilitarization of the Algerian political system be definitive.

For the moment, none of this is in prospect. The high oil price and resulting buoyant revenue have given the distributive state in Algeria a new lease on life. As a result, the regime's capacity to co-opt opposition and buy social peace is high and the effective pressure for fundamental institutional reform is low. The most that can be expected in the short term is that Bouteflika's provisional success in restoring order is preserved and that the Algerian political class and intelligentsia are able to use the continued breathing space this offers them to reflect on and draw the right lessons from the dramatic experience of the period since 1988.

It is in the light of these considerations that the U.S. government in particular should review its own policy toward Algeria. It should recognize that it cannot promote rapid positive reform, but it can and should at least abstain from jeopardizing the qualified progress that has been made in recent years. The danger of a reversal of the recent trend to civilian government and a remilitarization of the Algerian political system is intimately linked to the global war on terrorism. It is important that Washington not encourage Algeria's generals to reassert themselves in the political sphere. To this end, the U.S. government should review its own approach to the issue of countering terrorism in general and the Trans-Saharan Counter-Terrorism Partnership in particular. And it should recognize the need to relativize the purely military aspect of the partnership by enhancing its developmental dimensions and thus the role of civilian leadership in its conception and implementation.

Notes

1. The full name of the party is Le Parti du Front de Libération Nationale (Hizb Jebhat al-Tahrir al-Wataniyya); thus both French and Arabic versions of the official discourse—unlike most media and academic commentary—distinguish the party. It was created only after independence in 1962, from the wartime FLN, which was a front, not a party. I propose to do the same by referring to the party as the PFLN.

2. The Néo-Destour became the Destourian Socialist Party (Parti Socialiste Destourien) in 1964; the PSD became the Democratic Constitutional Rally (Rassemblement Constitutionnel Démocratique) in 1987.

3. That is, the so-called Berber Spring (*Tafsut Imazighen*), the movement of protest against the official repression of the Berber language in March–April 1980.

4. The French term used for the factions in Algerian politics is *clan* (derived ultimately from the Gaelic *clann*, meaning an extended family), and the factional struggle is routinely called *la lutte des clans*. But *clan* is a misnomer; the factions are not constituted on the basis of kinship ties at all. The Arabic word used for faction, *jama'a* (literally group), does not carry this misleading connotation of kinship.

5. Without any constitutional warrant, the army commanders set up the HCE as a five-member directorate in January 1992 to function as a collective leadership to fill the vacant presidency for the rest of Chadli's term in office, that is, to the end of 1993. (Its term was actually extended to end in January 1994 to give the army commanders time to agree on the succession.) Its members were Boudiaf (chairman),

Nezzar, Ali Kafi, Ali Haroun, and Tedjini Haddam. After Boudiaf's death, Kafi succeeded him, and Redha Malek was co-opted to make up the numbers.

6. Notably, such parties included the Berberist Rassemblement pour la Culture et la Démocratie (RCD), the ex-Communist Ettahaddi (Defiance) party, subsequently renamed the Mouvement Démocratique et Social (MDS), and Redha Malek's Alliance Nationale Républicaine (ANR), a secular-modernist splinter from the PFLN.

7. Such newspapers included *Liberté* (close to the RCD) and *Le Matin* (close to Ettahaddi-MDS), in addition to the generally pro-army *El Watan*.

8. The RND was established in early 1997 to function as an alternative pro-regime façade party to the PFLN, at that time regarded as discredited. The RND duly won a plurality of seats in the legislative elections of June 1997 and absolute majorities in the local and regional elections the following October. For a discussion of the amount of rigging this involved, see Hugh Roberts, "Algeria's Contested Elections," *Middle East Report*, no. 209 (Winter 1998), pp. 21–4.

9. Namely, two former heads of government Mouloud Hamrouche and Mokdad Sifi, former foreign minister Dr. Ahmed Taleb Ibrahimi, the FFS leader Hocine Aït Ahmed, the prominent Islamist Abdallah Djaballah, and Colonel Youcef Khatib, the commander of ALN wilaya IV (Algérois) from 1961 to 1962.

10. Mouloud Hamrouche (1989–1991), Sid Ahmed Ghozali (1991–1992), Belaïd Abdesselam (1992–1993), Redha Malek (1993–1994), Mokdad Sifi (1994–1996), Ahmed Ouyahia (1996–1998), Smaïl Hamdani (1998–1999), Ahmed Benbitour (1999–2000), Ali Benflis (2000–2003), Ahmed Ouyahia (2003–2006), and Abdelaziz Belkhadem (2006 to present).

11. Chadli Bendjedid (1979–1990), Khaled Nezzar (1990–1993), Liamine Zeroual (1993–1999), and Abdelaziz Bouteflika (1999 to present).

12. Bouteflika's chief success in the composition of the December 1999 government, apart from getting Zerhouni into the interior ministry, was the appointment of three supporters, Abdellatif Benachenhou, Hamid Temmar, and Chakib Khelil, noted for their espousal of the Washington Consensus in economic policy, to the ministries of finance, participation (that is, privatization), and energy, respectively.

13. Notably books by ex-officers of the ANP: Habib Souaïdia, *La Sale Guerre* (Paris, La Découverte, 2001); Hichem Aboud, *La Mafia des Généraux* (Éditions J.C. Lattès, 2002); Mohammed Samraoui, *Chronique des Années de Sang* (Paris, Denoël, 2003). A website launched by the Mouvement Algérien des Officiers Libres (MAOL), a group of officers who had deserted from the intelligence services, was the source of numerous dramatic allegations concerning the real strategy and tactics of the DAF coterie commanding the ANP during the 1990s. The allegations, which concerned the assassinations of President Boudiaf and others, the use of death squads and torture, the manipulation of the Islamist armed movements, and the implication of senior generals in massive corruption, and others, although never properly documented, were sufficiently detailed and plausible to be taken seriously by the Western media, in France in particular.

14. The leader of the GSPC, Hassan Hattab, was undoubtedly interested in nego-tiating an end to his campaign as the AIS had done earlier. He lost control of the GSPC in the summer of 2003, and his successors began stressing their links to al-Qaeda, which tended to rule out any question of a negotiation.

15. That the riots, in which gendarmes killed over 100 Kabyle youths (an unprece-dented and traumatic event), were deliberately provoked is clear from the evidence documented by the report of the Independent Commission of Enquiry chaired by distinguished lawyer Mohand Issad. For an analysis of the Kabyle protest move-ment and the manipulations that were involved, see International Crisis Group, "Algeria: Unrest and Impasse in Kabylia," *Middle East/North Africa Report*, no. 15 (Cairo/Brussels: ICG, June 10, 2003).

16. Belkhadem emerged as the leader of the Islamic current—the so-called Bar-béfélènes (the Bearded FLN)—within the party at its congress in November 1989.

17. It should be noted that, in the view of many Algerian commentators who have strong democratic credentials, some of the attacks on Bouteflika went far beyond the limits of fair comment and represented an abuse of freedom of speech.

18. See, "Nouvelles peines de prison pour la presse: un autre mardi noir," *El Watan*, June 15, 2005.

19. Article 46 of the decree of February 27, 2006, on the implementation of the Charter of Peace and National Reconciliation states: "Anyone who, by speech, writ-ing, or any other act, uses or exploits the wounds of the National Tragedy to harm the institutions of the Democratic and Popular Republic of Algeria, to weaken the state, or to undermine the good reputation of its agents who honorably served it, or to tarnish the image of Algeria internationally, shall be punished by three to five years in prison and a fine of 250,000 to 500,000 dinars." See the Joint Statement by Amnesty International, Human Rights Watch, the International Center for Transi-tional Justice, and the International Federation for Human Rights, *Algeria: New Amnesty Law Will Ensure Atrocities Go Unpunished, Muzzles Discussion of Civil Con-flict* (Paris: March 1, 2006).

20. Ordinary Algerians regularly complain about *la hogra*, meaning the contempt with which they are treated by office holders at every level, and local-level riots against instances of this still occur with great frequency. This refusal of *la hogra* is rooted in the egalitarian code of honor characteristic of the independent tribes of the Atlas Mountains.

21. That is, the tradition of guerrilla warfare. The Algerian term that translates the French word *maquis is jebel* (mountain).

22. See ICG, "Algeria."

MOROCCO:
TOP-DOWN REFORM WITHOUT
DEMOCRATIC TRANSITION

Marina Ottaway and Meredith Riley

In the three decades after it gained independence in 1956, Morocco was characterized by stability verging on stagnation. But during the 1990s, this North African monarchy embarked on a path of top-down reform. King Hassan II took the first steps down this path during the last years of his long reign, and his son Mohammad VI continued the process after ascending to the throne in 1999.

The reform process has produced some significant changes in Morocco. Human rights conditions have improved. Past abuses have at least been partly acknowledged. A more progressive version of the *Mudawwana*, the code regulating marriage, divorce, child custody, and other aspects of family relations, has been enacted. The taboo on discussing corruption has been lifted, and there has been a degree of economic reform.

Further changes undoubtedly will be introduced in the years to come. Nevertheless, as has been the case thus far, these measures are likely to take the form of discrete steps, intended to introduce limited change in very specific areas rather than stimulate a sustained process of democratic transformation. Indeed, reform appears to be driven by a quest for modernization, not for popular participation and government accountability. To date, there is no indication that Morocco is becoming a democratic country in which power resides in institutions accountable to the electorate. Instead, the king remains the dominant religious and political authority in the country and the main driver of the reform process. All new measures have been introduced from the top, as the result of decisions taken by the king and on the basis of studies carried out by commissions he appointed. Moreover, none of the measures impose limits on his power.

So far, Mohammad VI appears to be acting in the best tradition of the enlightened, reforming, and modernizing monarchs of the past, but he has indicated no readiness to allow his power to be curbed by strong institutions, let alone to accept a full transition to a true constitutional monarchy where the king rules but does not govern. Thus, unless the power of the king is curtailed and counterbalanced by that of institutions over which he has no control, talk of democratization in Morocco is moot. Today the king has the power to appoint a prime minister and government without taking election results into account, to terminate the government and parliament at will, and to exercise legislative power in the absence of parliament. A veritable shadow government of royal advisers keeps an eye on the operations of all ministries and government departments. Not only are important decisions made by the palace, but their execution is also managed—some argue micromanaged—by the royal entourage. The question thus is not whether Morocco will continue its democratic transformation, because, contrary to the views of some, such a transformation has not even started. The real question is whether the reforms enacted so far make further change inevitable and whether the balance of political forces that exists in the country today can force the king to accept limits on his power, leading in the foreseeable future to a democratic transformation.

This chapter explores the extent and limits of the reform process in Morocco thus far, the nature of the political actors, the reforms that could change the political dynamics of the country, and what could be done by outside actors, primarily the United States, individual European countries, and the European Union as a whole, to encourage a process leading to democratization.

Morocco Before Reform

The modern Moroccan political system was set up by King Mohammad V when the French protectorate ended in 1956 and remained virtually unchanged until the early 1990s. It was a system that allowed pluralism in name but limited it in practice. At a time when most Arab (and Third World) countries were banning political parties or adopting single-party systems, Morocco remained an exception, allowing parties to exist, though not to operate freely.

Returning from exile as the champion of Morocco's regained sovereignty, Mohammad V was able to sideline the political parties that could have challenged him. These included the Istiqlal (Independence) party, which had led the independence struggle, and the left-wing Union Nationale des Forces Populaires (UNFP), which had split off from the Istiqlal and won Morocco's first postindependence elections. Mohammad V dismissed the UNFP cabinet and formed his own, acting as his own prime minister, and consolidated power by rallying to himself the rural notables and the security apparatus. He also capitalized on his personal charisma, the popularity of the monarchy, and powerful webs of patronage. The system his son Hassan II inherited in 1961 was thus characterized by direct monarchical control, centralization of power, and a weak and fragmented political party system. Over the next thirty years, Hassan consolidated his position even further, undermining the opposition and stifling all independent political life through a mixture of institutional manipulation, reliance on clientelistic networks, and outright repression.

The 1962 constitution confirmed the pattern of royal domination by giving the monarch the power to nominate and dismiss the prime minister and cabinet at his discretion without regard for election results, to dissolve parliament, and to assume unlimited emergency powers. Revisions of the constitution in 1970, 1980, 1992, and 1996, the latter two taking place after the reform process had started, left that pattern of domination intact, even enhancing it in key ways. After rising to the throne in 1999, the present king, Mohammad VI, tried to give the system an aura of modernity and democratic respectability by defining it as an "executive constitutional monarchy"—a clever label that obfuscates the fact that the constitution in no way limits the power of the "executive" monarchy.

King Hassan II's strong constitutional power was enhanced by other factors. One was religion. The Moroccan king is considered to be a descendant of the prophet and, as *Amir al Mu-minin,* or Commander of the Faithful, the supreme religious authority in the country. Furthermore, Hassan could draw on the traditional network of monarchical institutions, known as the *makhzan,* an imprecise term originally denoting an elite of palace retainers, regional and provincial administrators, and military officers, but eventually embracing all persons in the service of the monarchy and connected to it by entrenched patronage networks. With the monarchy controlling not only power but also economic resources, being part of the *makhzan* was key to social mobility and even security.

Political parties were allowed to exist, but Hassan's strategies of division and co-option rendered them largely ineffective. He co-opted party leaders, pitted parties against each other so that no group could become strong enough to challenge his power, and encouraged the rise of new political organizations to divide and check old ones he saw as threatening. During the

1990s, for instance, he allowed an Islamist government to form in order to check the power of the left.[1] Finally, when all else failed, Hassan II did not hesitate to resort to repression. The 1960s and 1970s, a period in which the king faced considerable challenges, including attempted coups d'état, were particularly brutal. During these *années de plomb* (years of lead), hundreds of palace opponents were abducted and "disappeared," and thousands were imprisoned and sometimes tortured. Victims included anyone perceived as a threat to the regime: The majority was made up of leftists, but Islamists, advocates of Western Saharan independence, and military personnel implicated in several unsuccessful coups all experienced their share of repression.

Introducing Reforms: Hassan II

Morocco remained in political stasis until the early 1990s, when, in response to a changing international situation and the approaching end of his long reign, King Hassan II changed tack and started a slow process of opening up the political system. With the end of the Cold War came a new international climate strongly supportive of democracy. External pressure on the monarchy to conform to the new trend mounted, particularly in 1992, after the European Parliament denied Morocco an aid package because of its poor human rights record. Furthermore, the example of neighboring Algeria, plunged into a bloody war between security forces and Islamists who had turned to violence after being deprived of an election victory, provided a sharp reminder of the new vulnerability of authoritarian political systems. Domestically, a series of severe droughts had forced many rural residents into the cities, resulting in unprecedented levels of both unemployment and social discontent. Discontent led, in turn, to increasing support for Islamist groups, which brought home to the monarchy the danger of ignoring social disaffection. The fact that Morocco faced an imminent succession because of the king's advancing age provided further incentive for Hassan II to introduce changes while he was still fully in control, rather than lose his grip on power or entrust the challenge of transformation to his successor.

Reforms enacted by Hassan II fell into four broad categories: improved respect for human rights, a limited increase in the power of parliament, enhanced opportunities for political participation by parties and civil society, and some attempts to curb corruption. Most of King Hassan's initiatives were aimed at improving Morocco's record on human rights. They included the formation of a human rights council, the Conseil Consultatif des Droits de l'Homme (CCDH), and later of the Ministry for Human Rights; the release of some political prisoners; the reform of laws on preventive detention and public demonstrations; the ratification of major international human rights conventions; and the formation of a special committee to investigate forced disappearances. Although important as signals of a new openness on the part of the government, these steps were limited in scope. Thousands of political prisoners remained in jail and would only be set free years later by Mohammad VI. And while Hassan II admitted shortly before his death that forced disappearances had taken place, he never acknowledged state responsibility.

The same pattern of partial reform could be found in other areas. Constitutional amendments in 1992 and 1996 turned parliament into a bicameral body, with a lower chamber elected entirely by universal suffrage (whereas only two-thirds of the old unicameral body had been directly elected), and broadened the scope of parliament's competence to include approving the budget and questioning ministers. But the move to bicameralism actually solidified the king's control over parliament, because the upper chamber was indirectly elected by professional organizations and local councils close to the monarchy. Furthermore, the 1996 constitution specified that the king could not only veto bills approved by parliament but also amend them at will without resubmitting them to the legislators, and that he could issue laws without consulting parliament.

Of greatest political significance was King Hassan's decision to reach out to political parties and to bring formerly hostile organizations into government. He involved all parties more directly in the discussion of a new electoral law and in other decisions affecting the conduct of elections. He allowed an Islamist organization, Al Islah wal Tajdid (Reform and Renewal) which later formed the Parti de la Justice et Développement (PJD), to participate in the 1997 elections, though only under the banner of a weak, existing party.

Dialogue and improvements in the administration of elections led to better relations between the palace and most political parties, making it possible for King Hassan to bring about the most visible political accomplishment of this reformist period: the *alternance*. Following the 1997 parliamentary elections, the king did not turn to the palace parties to form the new government, as he had always done in the past. Instead, he asked Abdel Rahman Youssoufi, the leader the Union Socialiste des Forces Populaires (USFP), to form the government. (The USFP was the successor to the Leftist Union Nationale des Forces Populaires). Youssoufi was a longtime regime opponent who had spent fifteen years in exile after being imprisoned twice. The decision to bring the former opposition parties into the government was not reached suddenly. Hassan II had been trying to entice the USFP and the Istiqlal for several years, but they had previously refused on the grounds that participation was pointless until the constitution was revised to rein in the king and give more power to the government and parliament. Yet by 1997, faced with the rise of political Islam, the old secular opposition parties swallowed their objections and joined forces with the monarchy.

The Youssoufi cabinet included many ministers drawn from the Kutla, a bloc of parties previously in the opposition, which included the USFP, the Istiqlal, and a number of smaller parties on the left. The king, however, directly appointed the ministers of the so-called sovereignty (as opposed to "technical") ministries: interior, foreign affairs, and justice.

The *alternance* was an ambiguous move. In bringing opposition parties into the government, it clearly signaled that the monarchy was open to a democratic process. The king departed from precedent by linking his choice of prime minister to election results—the Kutla bloc had won a plurality in the elections. But the change did not in any way limit royal power or change the balance between the palace and elected officials. On the contrary, the *alternance* was engineered by the king, who decided that it was a good idea to take such a step; it was not imposed on him by an overwhelming electoral victory of the Kutla parties, which had won only 102 of 325 parliamentary seats. As a result, the Youssoufi government had little power, leaving the king once again the arbiter of Moroccan politics. The government's parliamentary majority in the lower house was small, and the indirectly elected upper house was in the hands of conservatives. The king maintained control over major policy issues, for example, imposing the neoliberal economic policies prescribed by the International Monetary Fund and the World Bank on the left-leaning USFP. In other words, by engineering the *alternance*, King Hassan succeeded in co-opting the two main opposition parties of long-standing without being forced to give up any power or change policies.

The king also allowed more space for civil society organizations to speak out, particularly on the issue of corruption. Spurred in part by a World Bank report on Morocco that singled out corruption as a major impediment to foreign investment and economic development, in the last year of his reign the king permitted the formation of a network of associations committed to the fight against corruption, presented a report to parliament on a major social security embezzlement scheme, and announced a "good management pact" for reform of the civil service. The impact of these initiatives on corruption was negligible, but a previously unquestionable taboo had been lifted.

Moreover, the development of civil society organizations was the beginning of a lasting process extending far beyond anticorruption, most significantly into human and women's rights but also including an array of community associations. Human rights organizations were crucial in making state abuses a matter of public discussion, and women's rights organizations were influential in advocating and negotiating reform of the *Mudawwana*.

Consolidating Reform: Mohammad VI

The rise to the throne of Mohammad VI in 1999 produced considerable initial expectation that Morocco would experience a new, more far-reaching wave of reform. From the beginning, the young king tried to project a public persona quite different from his father's. Hassan II had been distant and aloof and had espoused conservative social values. Mohammad VI cast himself as a modern monarch, interested in meeting his subjects—the "king of the poor" rather than of the elite. Initially, he even hinted that he favored democracy, prompting speculation that he would move Morocco toward constitutional monarchism. In reality, his approach to reform turned out to be strikingly similar to that of his father, simply going further down the same path toward improved human rights, the fight against corruption, and the carefully controlled political inclusion of new groups and political parties. Moreover, the process of reform continued to be driven from the top at the initiative of the king.

The king gave special attention to the human rights agenda, and on this issue he moved considerably further than his father. He released an additional large number of political prisoners. Among them was Abdessalam Yassine, the leader of Al Adl wal Ihsan, Morocco's largest Islamic movement, who was released from house arrest despite his scathing public critiques of both Mohammad VI and his father. The new king strengthened the Conseil Consultatif des Droits de l'Homme somewhat (although its annual reports were still considered too restrained by international human rights organizations). He took further steps to bring Moroccan laws in line with international conventions, for example, amending the penal code to abolish torture.

Most important, Mohammad VI acknowledged the government's responsibility for forced disappearances and other abuses of human rights. Less than a month after succeeding his father, he admitted that the government was responsible for the disappearances and announced the formation of the Independent Arbitration Panel, which would review individual cases and compensate victims. In 2003, the panel was disbanded after paying compensation to only 4,000 victims, but a few months later the king set up the Instance Équité et Réconciliation (IER) to throw light on abuses committed between 1956 and 1999 and help Morocco turn a new page. It is still a matter of dispute whether the two committees went far enough toward truly putting the issue of past human rights abuses to rest. The Independent Arbitration Panel in particular set an extremely short deadline for applications, cutting off thousands of people, and paid monetary damages to victims or their families without any concern for reconciliation. Furthermore, the size of payments varied extraordinarily on the basis of unclear criteria. The IER process was an advance in both organization and mandate, aiming at truth and reconciliation rather than just financial compensation. But it, too, had considerable short-comings. One was that it could not compel testimony from the security forces. Another was that its mandate only extended to 1999, thus excluding investi-gation into allegations that new and serious human rights violations were being committed as part of the "war on terror" at the same time the IER focused attention on the past. Finally, the IER had a contentious relationship with the main independent human rights organizations and missed impor-tant opportunities for collaboration.

Despite such criticisms, and the broader philosophical question of whether truth and reconciliation commissions are the best way of handling the legacy of past abuses, the IER was an unprecedented initiative in the Arab world. It interviewed thousands of victims, conducted field investigations throughout Morocco, organized public hearings (many broadcast on television, radio, or the Internet), and constructed a database of more than 22,000 personal testi-monies. Above all, it dared to air issues of government responsibility for human rights abuses, something that was all the more notable because the government so exposed was not that of a tyrant fallen from power, but that of the king's father.

The reign of Mohammad VI has been marked by other notable reforms. In keeping with his modernizing image, the king pushed through reform of the *Mudawwana*, a project launched by Hassan II a few months before his death. The new family code originally ran into fierce opposition from Islamist groups, which organized a massive demonstration against it in Casablanca, and was only completed in February 2004. The new code raises the marriage age from fifteen to eighteen, allows women to divorce by mutual consent, curbs the right of men to ask for divorce unilaterally, restricts polygamy, and replaces a wife's duty of obedience with the concept of joint responsibility. Despite continuing problems of implementation—such as untrained judges and a lack of information among women about their rights—the scope of the reform is considerable and puts Morocco well ahead of other countries in the region on the issue of women's rights.

Similarly, the king followed in his father's footsteps but pushed further on the issue of corruption, allowing the establishment of a Moroccan chapter of Transparency International, permitting newspapers to report on the issue, and finally, in October 2005, announcing the creation of an independent organization to fight corruption. Unfortunately, the anticorruption organization still does not exist. Nor is there is any evidence that the measures have had a real impact on the level of corruption—a common experience in countries that adopt anticorruption measures—but they have contributed to wider public debate and to the mobilization of civil society organizations.

It would be impossible, given this record, to argue that the reforms Hassan II initiated and his son Mohammad VI advanced were purely cosmetic. The change that has taken place in Morocco is real. The country is more open, once-taboo subjects are being discussed by a newly independent press that has been allowed to develop alongside the official one, women genuinely have more rights than they did previously, and past abuses have been recognized and discussed. To be sure, in many areas the implementation of new policies lags far behind—there is a big difference between recognizing the right of women to ask for a divorce and making it possible for them to do so in practice, or between denouncing corruption and actually curbing it. Nevertheless, Morocco has made real progress in terms of transforming itself into a more open country, with laws that are more in tune with those that regulate life in a democracy. Furthermore, the reform measures taken thus far have the potential to generate new reforms and create momentum for change. Although the IER limited its work to the 1956–1999 period, for example, it is difficult to imagine that similar gross violations of human rights could occur for protracted periods in the future without generating loud and effective protest. Human rights are now on the public agenda, as are the social issues addressed by the revised *Mudawwana*. By the definition used in the introduction to this book, the reforms are significant.

Despite their significance in the social and economic realm and the considerable improvement they made in the Moroccan human rights situation, the reforms enacted by both Hassan II and Mohammad VI are not real political reforms that changed the distribution of power and the nature of the political system. Power still resides in the monarchy, which is untrammeled by constitutional provisions and institutional checks and balances. The king remains free to take into account the outcome of elections when forming a new government or to ignore it. Royal counselors still oversee the operations of government ministries. Almost twenty years into the reform process, democratization has yet to begin in Morocco.

The Missing Link: Political Reform

Notably absent from King Mohammad VI's reform project are measures affecting the political system. Far from continuing and expanding upon his father's reforms, as he has in other areas, the king has brought the process of reforming the political system to a halt.

As noted earlier, the political changes made by King Hassan were extremely modest. The constitutional amendments that created a bicameral parliament, according to some analysts, served to weaken rather than strengthen parliament by actually increasing the number of members indirectly elected by conservative, promonarchy local councils. Under the old arrangement, only one-third of the unicameral parliament was elected indirectly, but now the entire upper house, or 45 percent of the bicameral parliament, is elected in this way. And extending the jurisdiction of parliament did not help either, because in the end the king remains free to veto, amend, or simply stop anything parliament does.

Though unwilling to allow parliament to gain real power, Hassan II acknowledged the need to do something to change the face of a regime that had remained unaltered for thirty years—hence the *alternance*. But the *alternance* did not modify the political dynamics in the country. In bringing the USFP and the Istiqlal closer into the fold, co-opting their leadership, and turning them from opposition parties into servants of the monarchy, it failed to generate a self-sustaining process of change.

Mohammad VI has not followed up even on these modest steps. On the institutional side, he has repeatedly stated that no further constitutional reform is necessary. In terms of political process, in 2002 he reverted to the practice of naming a prime minister without consideration of election results, even though selecting a prime minister from the party receiving the most votes in the parliamentary elections was one of the most significant aspects of the *alternance*. Instead, after the 2002 elections the king picked as prime minister Driss Jettou, a loyal technocrat not aligned with any political party. Furthermore, Mohammad VI did not try to change the informal system of personal, clientelistic networks on which the monarchy has always relied: he simply replaced individuals loyal to his father with individuals loyal to himself. To the extent that he tried to change the way the government worked, he aimed at making it more efficient rather than more democratic. Finally, the king continued to rely on the time-honored practice of co-opting adversaries and responded to pressure for reform by appropriating the reform agenda through the establishment of hand-picked royal commissions to study issues raised by the opposition and then implementing policy changes on his own terms.

In summary, under Mohammad VI royal power has been used to bring about change in the human rights situation, to advance the cause of women's rights, and to air past injustices and the problem of corruption, but not to open the way to genuine political participation and even less to increase the capability of institutions that could check imbalances of power. His is indeed an executive monarchy, but most definitely not a constitutional monarchy, neither in the normal sense of one in which the king rules but does not govern, nor even in the broader sense of a system in which the king has some executive power, but that power is clearly defined—and limited—by a constitution.

Prospects for Political Reform

There are two ways of thinking about political reform in Morocco (or in any other country). The first is to enumerate the measures necessary to transform the political system into one that is more democratic. The second is to envisage the political process that might lead to the enactment of these measures.

In the case of Morocco, the needed reforms are obvious: To become a democratic country, Morocco must restrict the power of the monarchy; institutionalize the separation of the legislative, judicial, and executive powers that now all converge in the hands of the king; and allow elected institutions accountable to the voters to play a real role in governance. In other words, Morocco has to move from being an executive monarchy toward becoming a constitutional one.

In theory, all political parties support constitutional amendments to bring about that transformation. In practice, they are not making a deliberate effort to make this happen, being more concerned at present with defending their position against the Islamists in the 2007 elections than with furthering a democratization agenda. The king has repeatedly stated that he does not see the need for further amendments to the constitution, and the parties are not pressing him. Political reform will not come from the top spontaneously, and so far there is no pressure from the bottom that the king must heed.

For Morocco to move toward democracy, the initiative, or at least the pressure, will have to come not from the palace but from other political forces. But is it possible to envisage a political process that would convince—or force—the king to alter course and accept a diminished role for the monarchy? Can a new balance of political forces emerge in the country that would lead to such a result? Without a change in the balance of power, Morocco might become a somewhat more modern and efficient country, but not a more democratic one.

Furthermore, absent such a change in the balance of power, the royal initiatives to improve human rights and allow more public discussion of important issues in the press and elsewhere remain fragile. While it is highly improbable that the king will reverse the changes in the family code, and that violations of human rights will once again be as blatant as they were during *les années de plomb,* the regime could once again become more repressive. Some Moroccans believe this is already happening. For example, many independent journalists express concern that their freedom to write critically has been curtailed since reaching a high point at the end of Hassan's reign. Also, the fight against corruption has not gone far and is unlikely to do so because real progress would inevitably implicate people who are part of the *makhzan*—anticorruption does not come easily in a clientelistic system. Nor is the king's latest major project, the National Initiative for Human Development, likely to do much to ease poverty and unemployment, since the overall economic structure that creates joblessness, want, and illiteracy remains unchanged.

Reform of the political system, as well as more far-reaching policy reform, depends on the emergence of independent political forces that the king can neither suppress nor co-opt. By definition, such forces would have to be political movements with large political bases and thus not dependent on the king's largesse for their survival or for their standing relative to other groups.

There are three real or potential major political actors in Morocco today. The first is the palace, what Moroccans call the *makhzan* or, in French, simply and tellingly, *le pouvoir.* The second is the old opposition made up of the long-established secular parties. Although they appear to be a spent force without much dynamism or initiative, these parties cannot be dismissed completely. They still get electoral support, have party structures that could be used effectively, and, with more dynamic leadership, could become much more significant players. The third noteworthy political force is the Islamist parties and movements, undoubtedly a rising power but still difficult to fathom. Above all, it is far from clear whether the PJD has the political skills to be effective were it to join the government, and whether the broader Islamic religious movements would have the capacity to keep Islamists in government from being manipulated by the palace, as the representatives of other parties have been before them.

The assets of the palace are enormous, given the formal power bestowed on the monarchy by the constitution, the informal power accrued through tradition, and the religious legitimacy enjoyed solely by the Commander of the Faithful. Just as important, the palace has a level of political experience and savvy that all other players lack. For decades it has been able to outmaneuver every domestic adversary, aided when necessary by the less subtle support of the security apparatus.

Secular Parties

The secular political parties that used to be in the opposition are important players formally, because they are part of the government and parliament. But they are also old, tired, and lacking in initiative. They are as much in need of reform as the political system itself. And the term *secular parties* needs to be understood correctly in the context of Morocco. There are no militantly secularist parties in the country. All parties stress that the values of Islam underpin everything they do, just as they underpin the deeply religious society they represent. Secular parties do not advocate the complete separation of state and religion. On the contrary, they recognize that in Morocco the two perforce converge in the person of the monarch, who is both the supreme political and religious authority. Paradoxically, the one major organization that dares to challenge the king as both a political and a religious leader is the Islamist movement Al Adl wal Ihsan. Liberal and left-leaning parties, in contrast, apparently have no problem recognizing the legitimacy of Mohammad VI as the Commander of the Faithful as well as the king of Morocco. In other words, Morocco's non-Islamist parties are secular only in the sense that they neither advocate the establishment of an Islamic state nor argue that Sharia should be the source of all legislation. It can be said that they are secular but not secularist.

The secular parties are highly fragmented. In the 2002 parliamentary elections, twenty-five secular parties competed, with all but four winning seats. (By contrast, only one Islamist party fielded candidates.) All together, there are now more than thirty registered parties (almost all of them secular). The most important among them are still the organizations that emerged before or at the time of independence: the Istiqlal and the USFP. The Istiqlal still has historical legitimacy as the most prominent party in Morocco's struggle to regain complete sovereignty. Incidentally, the party, now considered secular, was founded by a religious scholar who rooted the idea of independence in the country's Muslim identity. The USFP also has historical legitimacy as Morocco's militant socialist opposition at a time when ideologies of the Left dominated much of the Arab political world. Although these parties lost the power struggle with Mohammad V and were further marginalized by Hassan II, they remained the core of the opposition until the rise of Islamist movements. Recently, the two parties have become the nucleus of the Kutla bloc, an unusual alliance of liberal and leftist organizations that also includes smaller parties. With *alternance,* the Kutla parties left the ranks of the perennial opposition. Today the USFP and the Istiqlal consider themselves "government" parties, as if this were a permanent characteristic. Having come in from the cold, they have trouble conceiving of a new *alternance* that might once again put them, even temporarily, in the opposition—in other words, they have not fully accepted a democratic process.

The Kutla parties do not provide much momentum for change at present. They joined the government and do not have much to show for it, but they do not want to compromise their position by demanding further reform. Like all officially registered political parties, they recognize the legitimacy of the monarchy—this is a condition for registration—but they also favor political reforms that would give more power to other institutions. The 2002 election platform of the Istiqlal called for the transition from "façade democracy" to "authentic democracy." The current platform of the USFP is even more explicit, proposing specific constitutional amendments that would increase the power of parliament vis-à-vis that of the king. Yet, like most secular political groups in the Middle East, these well-established parties find it difficult to communicate a new and more vibrant message that would allow them to build stronger constituencies. Their platforms are generic and almost indistinguishable. They promise to address the issue of unemployment, to stimulate the development of key economic sectors, to improve education, and to build affordable housing—all measures Morocco badly needs, but that, in the absence of a clear strategy, have a "chicken in every pot" ring to them.

Despite their obvious problems, it would be a mistake to dismiss the Istiqlal and the USFP completely as potential participants in a process of political reform. When they accepted King Hassan's invitation to enter the government in 1998, many analysts predicted that they would be destroyed by the decision. Instead of bringing about real change and demonstrating their effectiveness to Moroccan citizens, they would be tainted by their association with the king, prevented from implementing a real reform project, and thus would be discredited. But only half of the prediction has proven correct. The Kutla parties failed to establish themselves as effective implementers of a vigorous reform agenda, in part because of the limited power of the government, but also because of their own lack of competence and their timidity about taking advantage of that power to the maximum extent. Moreover, King Hassan made sure that he, not the government of Prime Minister Youssoufi, got the credit for any positive changes. But the second half of the prediction, that the Istiqlal and the USFP would become discredited and consequently lose votes, has not come about. Support for the two parties has been remarkably stable. The USFP secured fifty-seven seats in the 1997 elections, dropping only slightly to fifty in 2002; the Istiqlal improved its position considerably from 1997 to 2002, from thirty-two seats to forty-eight. The two parties have apparently secured a stable niche in Morocco's fragmented political system, possibly aided by the absence of other credible non-Islamist parties.

The historical opposition parties thus have a solid base of support. They also have well-established party structures: some 600 offices around the country for the USFP and more than a thousand for the Istiqlal. The two parties' effectiveness as instruments of political change, however, is decreased by their fear of the Islamist organizations and therefore their reluctance to challenge the king—on whom they count for protection against the new rivals. As a result, while they proclaim the need for constitutional reforms that would enhance the power of parliament and the independence of the judiciary, they also make it clear that reforms can only go as far as the king will allow and that he must continue to play a central role. This is more than an admission of powerlessness by the parties; it is also a recognition of the fact that they prefer their own control of a weak government under his continued tutelage to the possibility of stronger institutions controlled by the Islamists.

The secular parties also include many that were historically allied with the monarchy. These are tame organizations that never challenge the king, but only vie for participation in the circles of power close to him. Many have been kept small and weak by rivalries, often encouraged by the palace, that lead to frequent splits and reorganizations. But some parties do have support, particularly the Mouvement Populaire and the Rassemblement National des Indépendants, especially in rural, and, in the case of the Mouvement Populaire, Berber areas. With more than sixty seats in parliament, the Mouvement Populaire is a force to be reckoned with, although more as a monarchy-allied counterweight to the Islamists than as an independent force for change.

Islamist Parties and Movements

In comparison with the secular parties, the Islamist parties and organizations are young and vigorous but also untried. They are less fragmented and more tightly organized than the secular parties. They are also more ideological—by contrast, the socialism of the USFP has become watered down over the years to nothing more than a vague concern for the poor and downtrodden. There was only one Islamist party, the PJD, until the recent formation of two new small parties, which may not survive the 2007 elections. In addition, the panoply of nonviolent Islamist organizations includes a religious movement affiliated with the PJD (Al Tawhid wal Islah), and the larger, more militant (though nonviolent), and vocally antimonarchist Al Adl wal Ihsan. The jihadist groups are not included in the present discussion, as they are not actors in any conceivable political reform process. They do not seek participation and do not appear to be strong enough to bring down the regime through violence. While it is all too likely that the jihadists will engage in more acts of violence, as they did with the Casablanca attacks in May 2003, they will most likely remain a background, low-level threat that may help the government justify a degree of continuing repression.

Islamist parties and organizations likely pose the most serious challenge to the king's monopoly on power. They could inject a new dynamic into Moroccan politics, possibly leading to political reform, although it is far from a foregone conclusion that they will succeed in doing so. This will depend largely on the PJD's capacity to resist co-option by the palace and its success in maintaining the support of the religious organizations if it joins the government. The outcome will also depend on how the secular parties respond—whether by joining the Islamists in pressing for reform or by joining the king to stop the Islamists' rise, simultaneously undermining the reform process.

The PJD, so far the only Islamist party to compete in elections, has established itself as a major force in Moroccan politics. In the 2002 elections, it gained the third-highest number of seats in parliament, despite presenting candidates in only fifty-five of the ninety-one constituencies. This restraint resulted from the fear that too large an electoral victory might provoke the government into nullifying the election results and banning the party, as the Algerian government had done ten years earlier when faced with the prospect of a victory by the Islamic Salvation Front.[2] The party could well win the largest number of votes in the 2007 parliamentary elections, though not the majority: the large number of political parties makes it virtually impossible for any one party to do so. A new election law will further limit the margin of victory of any one party—some analysts even argue that no party is likely to win more than 20 percent of the seats.

Given the obstacles to a strong electoral victory and the proven capacity of the palace to outmaneuver and co-opt political parties, it is hardly certain that the PJD will have the power to force real change in Moroccan politics.

Indeed, if the Islamist movement in Morocco only included the PJD, there would be good reasons to doubt that the party would be any more successful at avoiding co-option and strengthening the power of the government vis-à-vis the palace than the Kutla parties have been. But the Islamist movement also includes the two large religious organizations, which may increase the PJD's resolve and ability to resist co-option. Furthermore, the PJD is a stronger party, in terms of organization and leadership, than the Istiqlal and the USFP. It has more open and democratic governance and thus extensive internal debate. This means that the leaders know their actions are observed, and thus that they need to satisfy their constituents rather than simply pursue personal ambitions.

To understand how the religious movements might influence the political scene, it is necessary to go back to the history and different intellectual legacies of the two major nonviolent groups. The origins of all contemporary mainstream Islamist political movements in Morocco can be traced back to the 1970s. This was a crucial period in many Middle Eastern and North African countries, during which the character of opposition movements shifted away from the nationalism and socialism that had dominated the political scene and toward Islamism. This change, encouraged in many cases by governments seeking to combat leftist influence by encouraging an Islamic revival, did not receive much attention at the time. There was good reason for this in Morocco, because the full impact of the shift toward Islamism did not manifest itself until the 1990s.

The PJD and the religious movement al-Tawhid wal Islah, from which the PJD stems and with which it is associated, have their roots in a radical group that developed in the 1970s called Islamic Youth. The Rabat branch of the movement broke off in the early 1980s, because of disagreement over the autocratic tendencies of the group's leader and, most importantly, because the movement was taking an antagonistic stance toward the government. From the beginning, the hallmark of the breakaway group, originally called al-Jama'a al-Islamiyya, was the decision to become a recognized association and a legitimate participant in Moroccan politics. It took some ten years, and a new name that omitted references to Islam (al-Islah wal Tajdid), before the government recognized the group as a legitimate association. But when the newly relabeled Islah immediately tried to form a political party to participate in local elections, the government denied it registration, frustrating the organization's attempt to enter electoral politics.

During the next five years, al-Islah wal Tajdid explored various strategies for political participation. It considered joining the Istiqlal, but the party rejected collaboration with Islah as an organization, although it declared itself ready to accept Islah's members into its ranks as individuals. In 1996, however, Islah managed to attach itself to a moribund party, the Mouvement Populaire Démocratique et Constitutionnel (MPDC), itself a splinter group from an older Berber movement. Because the MPDC was an empty shell at that time, Islah was able to take it over, presenting its own candidates in the 1997 parliamentary elections and gaining nine seats in parliament. The quest by the movement to become an official political player, initiated in the early 1980s, had finally succeeded.

There is some dispute about why Islah was successful in taking over the MPDC and what role the king and the *makhzan* played in the maneuver. Certainly, Hassan II decided to accept the entry of the Islamists into politics as legitimate players. Whether the palace actually organized the takeover, as the more conspiracy-minded observers argue, is less clear. But the takeover was complete. In 1998 the MPDC changed its name, becoming the PJD. Islah, which had in the meantime joined with another small Islamist movement, had also changed its name to al-Tawhid wal Islah (Unity and Reform). The two names and the formal separation of the organizations persist to this day, with the PJD as the political party and al-Tawhid as the broader religious movement.[3]

The dominant theme running through this long and convoluted story is the movement's determination to gain official recognition, not only as an association, but also as a legitimate political party. This determination has had a major impact on how the PJD has acted as an official party. After 1998, it carefully positioned itself as a constructive critic of the new *alternance* government, always going out of its way to stress its complete acceptance of the legitimacy of the monarchy. In the 2002 parliamentary elections, in which it enjoyed great success and emerged as the third-largest party, it was careful to limit the number of districts in which it competed, to avoid alarming the king, the other political parties, and Moroccan society as a whole. In the 2003 local council elections, it agreed to compete in only 25 percent of localities. As an important player in parliament, with a caucus composed of forty-two members, it decided it would support laws adopted democratically by majority vote after ample discussion, including the reform of the *Mudawwana*. Although the PJD initially opposed the new family code and helped organize massive demonstrations in Casablanca against it, in the end it explained to its followers that adoption of the new code was the result of a democratic process and thus had to be accepted. Participation and legitimacy remain paramount in the policies of the PJD. This is its strength but could also be its downfall, causing it to become co-opted, with its leaders—like those of other parties—settling into the comfortable role of mildly critical, loyal, and ultimately ineffectual supporters of the monarchy.

The other major Islamist movement, the larger and more militant al-Adl wal Ihsan (Justice and Charity), has refused to participate in the Moroccan political system, which it considers corrupt, with as much determination as the PJD has shown in striving to join it. Organized around the figure of its founder, Abdessalam Yassine, a combination of spiritual guide of the movement and charismatic leader, al-Adl wal Ihsan is a complex and at times bewildering organization. In part, it is an organization in the mold of Morocco's numerous traditional Sufi brotherhoods, nonviolent and suffused with a strong current of mysticism, including a belief in the importance of dreams. In part, it is a very political movement, with some of its leaders prone to using the radical language of dependency theory and Third World revolution. The two at times combine in ways that worry the Moroccan government. For instance, in early 2006 many of the movement's followers started reporting that they had dreamt about a major but unspecified upheaval that would occur sometime before the year was out; this triggered a wave of arrests by security forces concerned that the dreams might be related somehow to an actual plot.

Yassine launched al-Adl wal Ihsan in 1974, with an open letter to Hassan II attacking the legitimacy of the king as a political and religious leader. The organization has maintained this antagonistic position toward the monarchy ever since. The king, in the movement's view, has used Islam to serve his own interests and maintain monarchical control rather than devote his efforts to serving the interests of the Islamic community. Abdessalam Yassine's message of nonviolence and forthright opposition to the monarchy, reiterated constantly by his daughter Nadia Yassine (also an important figure within al-Adl), has won the father prolonged periods of imprisonment and house arrest and his daughter constant trouble with the authorities.

While al-Adl continues to reject political participation, it has undergone changes recently that have led to speculation that it might be preparing to alter its position. First, while the aging Abdessalam Yassine has retreated increasingly into mysticism, other people in leadership positions are unquestionably moving in the opposite direction; they are political operatives, not mystics. Al-Adl has also evolved organizationally, putting in place two separate leadership bodies for the movement's two tendencies: the political Majlis al Shura, which provides the political and organizational direction of the movement, and the Majlis al Irchad (or Majlis al Rabbani), which provides spiritual (or ideological) guidance. This is not the same kind of separation between political party and religious organization that occurred with the PJD and al-Tawhid, but it is perhaps the beginning of a change in that direction. The fact that the organization launched a new membership drive as the country started preparing for the 2007 elections certainly suggests at the very least a sensitivity to the political cycle.

The existence of al-Adl, a membership-based organization with an estimated 25,000 to 30,000 members and tens of thousands of additional followers, and of the smaller but still large al-Tawhid wal Islah, makes it more difficult for the palace to co-opt the PJD. Al-Tawhid is a source of strong support but also a challenge for the PJD. It is an organization whose members adhere to strong religious principles and are less inclined than the politicians in the PJD to accept the need for compromise and pragmatism required by participation in politics and government. The PJD must use constant care in managing relations with its religious base, a task that has not always been easy. For example, the PJD received enthusiastic support when it organized a demonstration against the new, supposedly un-Islamic family code, but found it more challenging later to explain to its supporters in al-Tawhid why it ultimately decided to accept the reform. The PJD probably does not have infinite room for maneuver if it wants to maintain the allegiance of its religious base, but nobody, including the PJD, knows just how much room it has. The perception that the PJD had been co-opted would also cause it to lose the support of many Moroccans who are attracted to it not because it is an Islamist party but because they believe that it is the only honest party in Morocco today, untainted by compromises with the palace.

If the PJD managed to avoid co-option, driven by the danger of losing the support of members of the religious movements or, worse, by the emergence of a rival movement, Morocco could embark on a process leading to political reform. Yet even then, other pieces would have to fall into place. If the PJD enters the government after the 2007 parliamentary elections, it can only avoid accusations of co-option and a consequent loss of support if it manages to accomplish something. This means taking the utmost advantage of whatever power the system allows ministries to exercise, which lies not so much in their formal mandates but in exploiting the interstices of a system controlled by the palace. Although ministries are ultimately controlled by the king's counselors, ministers can take some initiatives and initiate policies, as long as they can do this without challenging the palace. PJD leaders, and even some of the more dynamic members of other political parties, argue that this is possible, but there is no proof that this is the case; in any event, it has not happened yet.

The willingness of the PJD to stand up to the palace has not been tested. As an opposition party in parliament, it has been careful not to antagonize the monarchy. As a result, some dissidents, even in the leadership of the PJD, already complain of co-option. A critical moment will occur after the 2007 elections if the party is given the opportunity to join the government, and accepts it. The capacity of the PJD to work from within the legal political process while maintaining an independent voice and challenging the palace to give up some power in the short run is the key to starting a democratic process in Morocco. But it is not enough: In the long run, a paradigm change in the Moroccan political system requires that more than one party stand up to the king. In turn, this requires internal reform in the secular parties, particularly the convening of regularly scheduled congresses, leading to the election of new officers and the renewal of the party leadership. It is difficult to imagine parties such as the Mouvement Populaire and the Rassemblement National des Indépendants, the so-called feudal parties based on networks of rural notables, transforming themselves. But the Istiqlal and the USFP in particular, both of which already have real party structures (however fossilized), have at least a potential for their own, and thus Morocco's, transformation.

The final element in a process leading to political reform would be the willingness of the monarchy to surrender some power if faced by a party that maintained its independence. The monarchy will not give up power if it is not pressed; nor will it do so if it feels threatened. The palace has the capacity to resist pressure for political change, thanks to its networks of clients and, above all, to the strength of the security apparatus. Less accommodating Islamists have already been subjected to the scrutiny of the security system, and no one is certain how willing the monarchy would be to use repression against more mainstream Islamist opposition.

So far, the parties have not succeeded in exerting sufficient pressure on the monarchy to force a democratic opening, in part because they have been co-opted and in part because secular parties have chosen the king's protection against the Islamist parties over a drive for reform. The parties would have much a better chance of achieving the reforms they ostensibly want if they joined forces, but this would require an alliance between secular parties and the PJD, which would not be easily forged. Pressure on the monarchy to relinquish power will not come from civil society either; nor will it come from a poor, politically disaffected population.

In other words, while real political reform in Morocco is not impossible, it certainly will not be easy. It will require that the PJD avoid co-option and take advantage of every possibility for action the system offers, that other parties meet the challenge by renewing themselves, and that all parties exert combined pressure on the monarchy to give up some power. Finally, it will require that the monarchy respond positively. Realistically, though, such a scenario is less likely than the continuation of economic, social, and human rights reforms without any change in the political system.

Promoting Political Reform in Morocco: A Limited Role for Outsiders

The context in which the United States and Europe work to promote democracy is much more benign in Morocco than in most other Arab countries. But it is also one in which outsiders will find it difficult to have an impact, in part because Morocco has already taken the easier steps concerning human and women's rights, and now confronts the core issue of the distribution of political power.

The context in Morocco is relatively favorable to change, though not to democracy. Since the 1990s, when Hassan II decided to deal with the opposition by inclusion rather than repression, and, at the same time, took steps to improve the country's human rights record, Morocco has become a relatively open society. The fact that secular opposition parties have become government parties and that the PJD is by far the most moderate Islamist party in the Arab world has helped in maintaining this benign environment. To be sure, there is a darker side to the Moroccan situation. A violent Islamist element exists, manifested most dramatically in the attacks that took place on May 16, 2003, in Casablanca, an event etched as deeply in the minds of Moroccans as the terrorist attacks of September 11, 2001, are in the minds of Americans. And the government is still ready to use some repression against even nonviolent movements it cannot co-opt, as shown by the wave of constant arrests (though followed by quick releases) with which the authorities responded to "open houses" held in mid-2006 by al-Adl wal Ihsan to recruit new members. And the lack of countervailing political forces means that all reforms are fragile and dependent on the will of the palace. Nevertheless, Morocco competes with Lebanon as the most open Arab country, but is more stable.

Nevertheless, the prospects for outside influence on a process of democratization are not good. First, there is the question of whether, given the country's excellent comparative standing, the United States and Europe should make it a priority to encourage real democracy in Morocco. Valid arguments can be made both in favor of neglect (efforts should be concentrated on countries where the situation is worse) and of greater engagement (it would be easier to help bring about democracy in Morocco than in a more repressive state). The result has been a rather uncertain policy, particularly on the part of the United States. Morocco has received praise from Washington for the changes that have taken place so far and has been rewarded with a free trade agreement.[4] At the same time, the level of U.S. assistance to Morocco has fluctuated, having recently being reduced drastically and then restored. Europe has a more linear policy, but it has focused on economic relations and cultural exchanges.

The United States enjoys good relations with the Moroccan monarchy, which has never challenged U.S. interests. This was true during the Cold War and is true today. Morocco has cooperated on issues regarding international terrorism. Except for the occupation of the Western Sahara, it has not pursued an adventurist foreign policy (and the United States has no particular interest in how the issue of the Western Sahara is resolved, as long as it does not lead to conflict and instability in the region). There is, in other words, no good reason for the United States to antagonize Mohammad VI's regime by pressing hard for democratic reforms. Furthermore, the administration of George W. Bush, anxious to be able to point to cases of successful democratization in the Arab world, is much more interested in stressing Morocco's successes than its shortcomings. Morocco has also been an easy partner for both the European Union and the individual European states.

The United States has established fairly good relations with the PJD. The party is legal, is as moderate as can be expected of an Islamist party, competes democratically, is a significant political player, and can be expected to be even more important after the 2007 elections. Whether or not U.S. officials believe that the PJD is truly committed to democracy and would not try to turn Morocco into an Islamist state, they know that the power of the palace will keep the PJD under control. Good relations with the PJD thus suit the U.S. government's need to show, at very little risk, that it is not against Islamic organizations, only against Islamic extremists. As a result, PJD leaders have contacts with U.S. embassy officials, are invited along with leaders of all other parties to embassy receptions, and have no trouble obtaining visas to the United States. This has created a minor backlash against the United States on the part of some secular parties and nongovernmental organizations in Morocco, which have become convinced that the United States wants the Islamists to come to power in Rabat. (Indeed, some secular Moroccans are also convinced that the United States is behind the success of other Islamist movements in the Arab world, including the illegal Muslim Brotherhood in Egypt.) Despite this highly conspiratorial perception of relations between the United States and the PJD, the superficial cordiality does not denote closeness, much less U.S. influence over the PJD. Indeed, the concept of the United States encouraging the PJD to remain steadfast in its independence of the king to push for true democratic reform taxes the imagination of even the most suspiciously minded.

The most important contribution to true democratic reform in Morocco that the United States and European countries could make would be to facilitate the transformation of the major secular parties through pressure on their leaderships. The United States is already trying to strengthen political parties in Morocco through the work being done by the National Democratic Institute for International Affairs and the International Republican Institute, nongovernmental agencies tied to the two major U.S. political parties. Both organizations provide training for political parties, at either the national or the local level. In the name of nonpartisanship, the training is provided to all legal political parties. Such training does not hurt, but it is unlikely to help very much either in this case. No amount of training will convince parties whose strength resides in networks of local notables with ties to the peasantry of their districts to abandon a structure that may be outmoded and anachronistic but gives them their comparative advantage. And training for lower-level cadres will not break the stranglehold of the incumbent leaders on political renewal in the Istiqlal and the USFP, because the relevant issue is not knowledge but power. The real challenge is to convince the leadership of the secular parties that their best chance for both competing successfully against the Islamist parties and for achieving some of the constitutional reforms they want is to take seriously the task of reforming their organizations. Helping the process of internal reform of the political parties is an important contribution that outsiders could make to political reform in Morocco. And they could do so without undermining their relations with the monarchy, which shares the goal of party renewal—though not to give the parties more power.

U.S. democracy promotion programs in Morocco have targeted not only political parties, but organizations of civil society as well. During the last fifteen years, Morocco has developed a significant network of secular civil society organizations. The reforms implemented from the top have encouraged—and allowed—the formation of such organizations, which have thrived thanks not only to the opening of the political space created by the reforms but also to the support they have received from U.S. and European organizations.

The most significant civil society organizations are those focusing on human rights and women's rights. They have done impressive work in their respective areas, thanks to their own efforts but also to the fact that they have worked toward goals supported by the palace and the international community. Women's organizations in particular played a key role not only in generating support for the reformed *Mudawwana*, but also in lobbying for changes in the nationality law (so that women could transmit citizenship to their children) and a gender quota for women in parliament. Anticorruption organizations, bound to challenge vested interests if successful, have had a more limited impact, lifting the taboo on the discussion of corruption but achieving no concrete results.

In Morocco, as in all other countries, civil society organizations have shown a capacity to arouse and foster debate on major issues, as long as they work in a reasonably permissive environment. But, again, as is the case for such organizations everywhere, they have been successful in bringing about concrete change only when they have worked with the regime, rather than against it. While support for civil society organizations in Morocco should continue, because their existence will make it more difficult for the monarchy to slip back into more authoritarian ways, such support is unlikely to lead to true political reform. Civil society groups cannot stand in for political parties in forcing the palace to surrender some of its power and open the way to a democratic process. They lack the clout to compel the regime to implement reforms it does not want, and they would certainly fail if they tried to challenge the monarchy to give up some of its power.

Morocco's success in moving from top-down reform to a democratic transition is not a foregone conclusion. It will require a successful balancing act by the PJD, renewal within the major secular political parties, and ultimately the willingness of the monarchy to surrender power rather than revert to autocracy. The influence of outsiders in facilitating a democratic transition will be limited and will depend on how successfully their efforts relate to the very complicated political game that will unfold after the 2007 elections.

Notes

1. Ellen Lust-Okar, "Divided They Rule: The Management and Manipulation of Political Opposition," *Comparative Politics*, vol. 36, no. 2 (January 2004): pp. 159–79, and Michael J. Willis, "Political Parties in the Maghrib: Ideology and Identification. A Suggested Typology," *e-Journal of North African Studies*, vol. 7, no. 3 (Autumn 2002): pp. 1–28.

2. Michael J. Willis, "Morocco's Islamists and the Legislative Elections of 2002: The Strange Case of the Party That Did Not Want to Win," *Mediterranean Politics*, vol. 9, no. 1 (Spring 2004): pp. 53–81.

3. For more detail, see Michael J. Willis, "Between Alternance and the Makhzen: Al-Tawhid wa Al-Islah's Entry into Moroccan Politics," *Journal of North African Studies*, vol. 4, no. 3 (Autumn 1999): pp. 45–80.

4. Members of the U.S. government frequently commend Morocco for its reforms. See, for example, the statement by Under Secretary for Public Diplomacy and Public Affairs Karen Hughes at the Moroccan Foreign Ministry, Rabat, June 5, 2006, and statements by Reps. Ileana Ros-Lehtinen (R-Fla.), John B. Larson (D-Conn.), and Robert I. Wexler (D-Fla.), quoted in an article by the state-owned Moroccan wire service Maghreb Arab Press, "US Congresspersons Hail Morocco's 'Courageous and Strong' Measures to Consolidate Democratic Process," June 10, 2006. Morocco is also the only country in the Middle East approved for funding through the U.S. government's Millennium Challenge Account development assistance program.

THE SAUDI LABYRINTH:
IS THERE A POLITICAL OPENING?

Amr Hamzawy

Recent years have witnessed unprecedented political dynamism in Saudi Arabia. Since 2002 the government has pursued various reform policies. Its most relevant measures have included reforming the Shura Council, holding municipal elections, legalizing civil society actors, implementing educational reform plans, and institutionalizing national dialogue conferences. Although these measures appear less significant when compared with political developments in other Arab countries, such as Lebanon and Egypt, they constitute elements of a meaningful opening in authoritarian Saudi politics.

In the 1970s and 1980s, Saudi Arabia represented a clear case of authoritarian consolidation. The al-Saud royal family used high oil revenues to boost its control and to expand existing networks of patrimonial allegiance across the country. The state apparatus swelled, and with it the role of the security forces and the Wahhabi religious establishment grew dominant. The government's authoritarian grip over society tightened. A degree of pluralism rooted in the tribal structures of the Saudi society and in the benevolent rule of the first kings was replaced by an emerging repressive state and an aggressive, fundamentalist Wahhabi ideology.

There were a number of changes that signified this transformation. The government abolished the municipal elections that had been held regularly up to the 1960s. Dissenting views on political, social, and moral issues were no longer tolerated. Minorities, in particular the Shi'i community in the eastern provinces, suffered from systematic discrimination and hate campaigns. Saudi politics became the monopoly of royal princes, Wahhabi clerics, and their allies in the state bureaucracy.

Although modernization and urbanization processes changed the social map and created a stable middle class, popular demands for reform remained weak. Saudis seemed to either consent to the patrimonial logic of "no taxation, no representation" or approve of the conservative turn taken since the 1970s. The few examples of opposition groups challenging the authoritarianism of the royal family—such as the 1979 seizure of the Great Mosque in Mecca by a fundamentalist group and the initial rise of the Islamic Awakening Movement (al-Sahwa al-Islamiyya) in the 1980s—were efficiently contained.

In the 1990s, however, this political scene began to change slightly. The 1991 Gulf War hurt the Saudi economy, and the presence of U.S. troops in the cradle of Islam undermined the legitimacy of the royal family. Rising unemployment and poverty rates led intellectuals and religious scholars to demand substantial political and economic reforms. Most significant, a Memorandum of Advice was addressed to late King Fahad in 1991 in which nearly fifty signatories—religious scholars and others—called on him to create a legislative council, enact anticorruption measures, and promote equal distribution of the country's resources among its citizens. After harsh reactions by the security forces against the signatories, the king announced in 1992 the establishment of an appointed national consultative council, the Shura Council, and detailed a plan to appoint municipal councils in all provinces of the kingdom. However, neither the Shura Council nor the municipal councils were endowed with legislative or oversight powers. In the second half of the 1990s, other minor reform measures, primarily administrative, were implemented to quiet growing popular dissatisfaction.

However, the authoritarian grip of the royal family has not loosened. Indeed, by the end of the 1990s, the government, faced with the rise of violent jihadist groups, resorted to outright repressive instruments to deal with dissenting views in general and leaned heavily on the religious establishment to generate legitimacy among the population. In return, official Wahhabism stiffened its control over three focal points in society: mosques, courts, and schools.

The terrorist attacks of September 11, 2001, exposed Saudi society to the catastrophic outcomes of its authoritarian lethargy. The most immediate impact of the 9/11 attacks was to subject the royal family to increasing international pressure to introduce significant reforms to combat terrorism and extremism. The attacks also served as a catalyst for wide-ranging debates among the political and intellectual elites about "what went wrong" and "what should be done." Domestic calls for reform were suddenly given a better hearing. In recent years these two factors—international and domestic reform demands—have injected new elements of dynamism and openness into Saudi

Arabia's political reality. They have also generated sufficient incentives for the government to embark on the road of reform.

Mapping Political Actors

Recent reform measures in Saudi Arabia have stemmed from power relations among the major political actors. To a great extent, the interplay between the royal family and the Wahhabi religious establishment has determined the pace as well as the scope of implemented reforms. Other actors, however, have also entered the political arena and now play an important role in shaping the reform process. Though far from organized and viable opposition movements, these dissenting groups—most notably liberal reformist groups, moderate Islamists, and conservative religious scholars critical of official Wahhabism—have increasingly placed reform issues in the public space and as such have induced the royal family and the religious establishment to address their demands. Apart from a few confrontational moments, the newcomers have avoided direct clashes with the two giants of Saudi politics. Instead, they have pushed for gradual government concessions in key spheres and tried to sustain the momentum of political opening.

Royal Family

Article 5 of Saudi Arabia's Basic Law of Government issued in 1993 states that

> [T]he system of government in the Kingdom of Saudi Arabia is that of a monarchy. Rule passes to the sons of the founding King, Abdel Aziz bin Abdel Rahman al-Faysal al-Saud, and their children's children. The most upright among them is to receive allegiance in accordance with the principles of the Holy Koran and the Tradition of the Venerable Prophet.

Since its ascent to power in the first quarter of the twentieth century, the al-Saud family's rule has rarely been challenged. The royal family controls state institutions to such an extent that it becomes difficult to distinguish between them. The executive, the cabinet, and the provincial authorities across the country are directly run by the al-Saud princes and their close allies in the state bureaucracy. Powerful princes head the security apparatus—the Ministry of interior and various intelligence agencies—as well as the armed forces. State resources, in particular oil revenues, flow into the royal budget, which is not differentiated from that of the state.

In the absence of any institutionalized mechanisms for accountability, the royal family has always allocated state resources in the manner of absolute monarchs. Increasingly since the oil boom of the 1970s, much has been invested not only to modernize the country but also to sustain, along tribal structures, networks of patrimonial allegiance instrumental for preserving the al-Saud family's power and legitimacy among the population.

A second constant means of preserving power has been official Wahhabism. Since the establishment of the modern Saudi state in 1932, the royal family has ruled this vast heterogeneous country in the name of Wahhabi Islam, a fundamentalist interpretation of Islamic teachings that dates back to the second half of the eighteenth century. Wahhabi clerics—organized in a powerful and popular religious establishment that will be discussed in the following pages—have in return given legitimacy to the royal family.

The royal family also has effectively constructed international and regional alliances aimed at preserving its power. Most significant, its strategic alliance with the United States since the discovery of oil in 1938 has protected its rule in moments of regional turmoil, in particular during the confrontation with pan-Arab Nasserism in the 1960s and in the aftermath of Saddam Hussein's invasion of Kuwait in 1991.

With regard to reform preferences, the royal family has been clearly divided into two factions in recent years. King Abdullah bin Abdul-Aziz heads the moderate faction that in recent years has advocated gradual opening and more citizen participation in politics, but only in ways that do not threaten the dominance of the royal family over the country. This faction has also endeavored to inject elements of moderation into official Wahhabism and lessen the discrimination against communities and groups that have suffered most from Wahhabi exclusion, primarily women, Shi'i citizens, and dissenting groups.

In the second half of the 1990s, most of the executive authority of ailing King Fahad was moved to then Crown Prince and Prime Minister Abdullah. Long before his ascent to power in the summer of 2005, Abdullah had been the de facto ruler of Saudi Arabia. He promoted most of the reform measures the government has introduced since 2002.

A second prominent representative of the moderate faction is Prince Saud al-Faisal, Saudi Arabia's foreign minister for thirty years. Recently, Saud al-Faisal has openly challenged the Wahhabi religious establishment regarding its conservative positions on women's civil and political rights. In a recent statement he maintained that "nowhere in the Koran is it mentioned that women are not allowed to drive cars, have the right to vote, or choose their career." The most outspoken representative of the moderate royals has always been Prince

Talal bin Abdul-Aziz, half-brother of King Abdullah. Prince Talal has repeatedly called for reforming the religious establishment and limiting the power of the executive by turning the Shura Council into a partially elected body and vesting it with budgetary oversight.

The second faction in the royal family is less inclined to promote reforms, fearing that the house of al-Saud might lose control over society as a result. The most powerful representatives of the conservative royals are Crown Prince Sultan bin Abdul-Aziz, Prince Nayef bin Abdul-Aziz, who serves as minister of the interior, and Prince Salman bin Abdul-Aziz, who governs the Riyadh region. All of them are renowned for their adherence to official Wahhabism, which they view as the essential instrument for keeping the country together. They have also been reluctant to grant minorities and dissenting groups more freedoms, accusing them of destabilizing the social order. In recent years, the conservative faction has worked to slow the pace of reforms and used the backing of the religious establishment to generate popular support for its position.

It is not clear how the power balance between the two royal factions is unfolding. Some observers argue that Abdullah's faction has gained momentum in recent years, while others assert that Nayef and Salman have marginalized Abdullah and other moderates. Regardless of the validity of these competing claims, tensions generated out of the differences between the two royal factions are real. These tensions are documented in public statements and reflected in divergent policy preferences. The differences go beyond an alleged division of labor between moderates, who act to quiet internal and external calls for political opening with friendly statements and minor reform measures, and conservatives, who side with the religious establishment and manage the murky reality of repression. Instead, there is a real conflict between members of the royal family who want to handle discontent with reform and those who advocate doing so with security measures. This conflict explains to some extent the limits of the current political opening in Saudi Arabia.

Religious Establishment

Article 23 of the Saudi Basic Law of Government affirms that the "state protects Islam; it implements its Sharia; it orders people to do right and shun evil; it fulfills the duty regarding God's call." These stipulations embody the legal foundation of the immense authority the Wahhabi religious establishment enjoys. Public and private morality, education, and the justice system are the spheres of Wahhabi hegemony over society. Fortified by the alliance with the royal family, the religious establishment has evolved into a vast network of institutions, universities, schools, and specialized centers.

The most significant religious institution is the Council of Senior Ulama, which was established by royal decree in 1971 and is Saudi Arabia's highest religious authority. It is composed of twenty clerics appointed by the king and headed by the Grand Mufti. As stipulated in the Basic Law, Article 45, the council's duty is to issue religious informed opinions, or *fatwa*, based on Sharia on all matters submitted to it by the king. A second important institution is the notorious Committee for the Promotion of Virtue and the Suppression of Vice, which has developed into a powerful law enforcement organ. Its members, who include state employees and volunteers, have the task of safeguarding true Islamic teachings, as defined by official Wahhabism, and penalizing those who violate them. Regular targets for the committee's zeal in the public space are either "inappropriately" veiled women or "ill-mannered" men. The religious establishment also includes other institutions that are directly or indirectly controlled by the Council of Senior Ulama. Among them are the Ministry of Islamic Affairs, Endowments, and Guidance; the Ministry of Pilgrimage; the Religious Supervision of the Holy Mosque; and various specialized directorates that supervise the educational system.

Since the 1970s, the religious establishment has grown more assertive and developed an aggressive fundamentalist dogma. It has exercised and perpetuated its power within the framework of a mutually beneficial relationship with the royal family, whereby legitimacy has been traded for the Wahhabi's authority to regulate society. This reciprocal arrangement has given both sides the ability to contain the influence of other political actors, ranging from liberal reformists to conservative religious scholars, and has curbed the reform drive.

In recent years, reform measures advocated by the moderate faction in the royal family have generated much discontent within the religious establishment. Wahhabi clerics, apart from a few marginal moderate voices, have always been critical of political openings. Indeed, the massive increase in their power came after the end of the last liberal period in Saudi Arabia during the 1960s. Since 2002, the clerics have been organizing support among the conservatives in the royal family. In particular they have issued many public statements denouncing the limited measures promoting educational reform and women's rights implemented by the government and have thus far managed to impede the reform process.

Saudi intellectuals and observers differ in their assessment of the balance of power between the royal family and the clerics. On the one hand, some liberal reformists contend it is the royal family that retains the upper hand. For them, several episodes, ranging from the late King Faisal's decree in the 1960s to permit female education despite fierce Wahhabi opposition, to the recent decree to end the ban on mobile telephones with cameras, show that the Wahhabi clerics will ultimately bow to the will of the ruler. They would not venture to openly oppose current reforms should the royal family demonstrate a resolve to pursue such a course. This view holds that the tension between moderates and conservatives within the royal family has enabled Wahhabi clerics to restrain the reform drive and influence the power balance between the two factions in favor of the conservatives. On the other hand, an opposing view held most notably by moderate Islamists stresses the autonomy of Wahhabi clerics. Although the religious establishment is sustained by generous royal allocations, the religious establishment itself has not been co-opted but instead continues to defy the royal will.

Regardless of which view is most accurate, in today's Saudi politics the religious establishment remains antireform and the only major political force that is the least influenced by moderating trends.

Liberal Reformists

In recent years, nonviolent dissenting groups in Saudi Arabia have continued to suffer from various restrictions on political freedoms. Government regulations ban political parties and, to a great extent, limit the right to assemble freely in nongovernmental organizations (NGOs). Given these conditions, liberal reformists—mostly secular-minded lawyers, university professors, intellectuals, political activists, and journalists—have worked in the aftermath of the 9/11 terrorist attacks to mobilize popular support for their demands and to obtain the ear of the moderate faction in the royal family. Both strategies succeeded in further pushing the envelope for reform and in granting liberal reformists more room for maneuver in the public space.

Since 2002, the liberal reformist platform has focused on granting basic political freedoms and civil rights for men and women. It has also stressed promoting equality between the Sunni majority and the Shi'i minorities and enhancing political participation in public matters through empowering existing consultative institutions and transforming them into elected bodies. Legalizing NGOs and combating terrorism and extremism by limiting the control of the religious establishment over the educational system have been integral components of the liberal reformist platform as well.

Obviously these bold demands have brought liberal reformists into confrontation with the conservative faction in the royal family and with the Wahhabi religious establishment. The lack of institutionalization in parties or opposition movements as well as the absence of organized constituencies outside the urban educated elite makes liberal reformists highly vulnerable to repressive measures and easy to target individually: For example, university professors have been banned from teaching; travel documents of critical intellectuals have been confiscated; and individuals have been jailed for extended periods of time.

The imprisonment of three of the signatories of the petition calling for the establishment of a constitutional monarchy in 2004 is the best-known example of punishment inflicted on liberal reformists in recent years. In December 2003, 116 liberal reformists and moderate Islamists signed a daring petition calling on the government to establish a constitutional monarchy in Saudi Arabia. The signatories advocated comprehensive constitutional reform and enhanced political participation in public matters within the framework of Islamic teachings. Their major demands included (1) granting full-fledged political freedoms and civil rights to all citizens, anchored in a permanent constitution; (2) granting gender equality; (3) introducing the principles of separation of powers and rulers' accountability; (4) electing a house of representatives to serve as the legislative branch of the government; (5) establishing an independent judiciary and introducing procedural mechanisms to ensure its impartiality; (6) creating a supreme constitutional court; (7) lifting restrictions on the formation of civil society organizations and guaranteeing the right to free assembly and peaceful protest; and (8) combating corruption and granting an equitable distribution of state resources.

The signatories called on the government to form an independent national committee composed of constitutional law and other legal experts, religious scholars, and public figures to draft a permanent constitution based on true Islamic teachings and universal principles of democratic governing. They also demanded that the draft constitution be confirmed in a national referendum within one year of its announcement and that the government embark on implementing its provisions in a transitional period that would not exceed three years.

Although the petition calling for the establishment of a constitutional monarchy was not the first liberally inspired public document in recent years—it was preceded by other less significant petitions—its bold character outraged both factions within the royal family. The involvement of Shi'i religious figures also infuriated some Wahhabi clerics, who denounced the petition as blasphemous and the signatories as renegades. In March 2004, police authorities arrested twelve of the signatories but subsequently released nine of them on the condition that they refrain from reiterating similar demands in public and that they end their political activities. The remaining three activists—Ali al-Dumaini, Matruk al-Falih, and Abdullah al-Hamid—refused to agree to these restrictions.[1] Their detention continued, and in May 2005 a court sentenced them to prison terms of six to nine years. King Abdullah, however, pardoned them a few days after his ascent to power in August 2005.

The experience of the petition calling for the establishment of a constitutional monarchy demonstrates the vulnerability of the liberal reformists. Many of them have learned the lesson and have largely kept a low profile, stressing the need to cooperate with the government in promoting the reform process. This less confrontational strategy recently led to the appointment of a few liberal reformists to the Shura Council.

Moderate Islamists

Moderate Islamists agree with liberal reformists on the need to press for reform, but they have a different destination. Moderate Sunni Islamists, mostly religious scholars critical of the fundamentalist Wahhabi interpretation of Islam, place more emphasis on reforming the religious establishment. They assert that without garnering religious approval and without ensuring the full compatibility of reform demands and Sharia provisions, broad segments of the Saudi population will ultimately view any reform measures as endangering their values and way of life.

Scholars such as Abdel Aziz al-Qasim, a lawyer based in Riyadh, and Hassan al-Malki, a former instructor at the religious Imam Muhammad bin Saud University, advocate an innovative interpretation of religion that can help ground the modern ideas of accountable government, political participation, human rights, and formation of civil society organizations into a legitimate Islamic framework. They contend that without opening the mosque and the school—the two strongholds of official Wahhabism—to moderate thinking, the battle for reform and the struggle against extremism cannot be won.

Moderate Shi'i Islamists, however, take a position similar to that of liberal reformists. Having had to endure Wahhabi discrimination in the last decades, they place no hope in the possibility of reforming the religious establishment. Instead, they have called on the royal family to limit the powers of the Wahhabi clerics and promote the plurality of Islamic schools of thought. Their ultimate objective has been to persuade the royal family that its legitimacy would be established by stressing the commonalities between the Sunni and Shi'i communities, instead of depending on official Wahhabism as its only frame of reference.

A second significant difference between liberal reformist and moderate Islamist platforms relates to their views on social and cultural reform issues. Moderate Islamists in Saudi Arabia have remained trapped in illiberal stances that draw on religion to legitimize various restrictions regarding gender equality and freedom of opinion and expression.

Because they challenge official Wahhabism, both Sunni and Shi'i moderate Islamists have been frequently targeted by the religious establishment. Some of them—like Hassan al-Malki—lost their teaching jobs at higher education institutions; others found themselves faced with public denunciation campaigns. Nevertheless, the partial convergence of the moderate Islamist platform and liberal reformist demands in recent years has secured the participation of moderate Islamist voices in public debates on reform. However, in today's Saudi politics these voices remain weak. Their new interpretations of Islamic teachings have yet to appeal to the moderate faction in the royal family as an alternative source to legitimize reforms among the population and forgo the restraining influence of Wahhabi clerics.

Remnants of the Islamic Awakening

Throughout the 1980s and 1990s, Saudi Arabia witnessed the emergence of a conservative Islamist movement that aimed at freeing Wahhabism from the bonds of the alliance between the royal family and the religious establishment. Activists of the Islamic Awakening Movement, primarily graduates of religious universities, accused Wahhabi clerics of being co-opted by the Saudi rulers. For them, the clerics had degenerated from defenders of Sharia to subservient mouthpieces always willing to legitimize the ruler's policies.

Especially in the 1990s, the Islamic Awakening Movement grew more politicized and attracted an increasingly popular following. In fact the movement even found some adherents within the religious establishment itself, mostly among young clerics. Its platform addressed two major concerns common to Islamist movements in the Arab world at that time: doctrinal purity and social justice. First, it attempted to purify Wahhabism from traces of political co-option. Second, it raised demands for equitable distribution of state resources and for anticorruption measures, reflecting the widespread popular discontent created by the severe economic and financial crisis that followed the 1991 Gulf War.

The government reacted by imprisoning the leaders of the Islamic Awakening Movement and empowering the religious establishment to tame its critics. New Wahhabi universities and institutions were established to curb dissenting views—often through co-option. In a move to address popular concerns, the government also introduced a series of administrative reforms to combat corruption in the state bureaucracy. The strategies were successful, and by the end of the 1990s the Islamic Awakening Movement had lost momentum.

In recent years, however, two conflicting trends have emerged from the remnants of the Islamic Awakening. First, violent jihadist groups operating within and outside Saudi Arabia have attracted many former followers of the movement, preaching a radical ideology and becoming a real security threat to the state. While the terrorist attacks committed by these groups have enabled the conservative faction in the royal family to push for more stringent security measures and to slow down reform, they have simultaneously strengthened the liberal reformists' and moderate Islamists' belief that reform is the only viable strategy to cure the root causes of terrorism and challenge radical ideologies.

Second, some leading figures of the Islamic Awakening Movement have partially altered their views and moved closer to the liberal reformist and moderate Islamist platforms. Inspired by general trends toward moderation in the Islamist spectrum in the Arab world, scholars like Salman bin Fahad al-Auda, head of the nongovernmental institution Islam Today, and Sifr bin Abdel Rahman al-Hawali, former professor at the religious Um al-Qura University in Mecca, have gradually come to endorse calls for basic political freedoms and popular participation. Al-Auda now even goes so far as to state that nothing in Islam is in conflict with democracy (understood as a system of participation and accountability), provided that it does not contradict Sharia provisions. Although both al-Auda and al-Hawali remain critical of the religious establishment, they have softened their stance with regard to the royal family. They have called on the government to enact meaningful reform and offered cooperation in combating the jihadist threat.

Reform Measures Between 2002 and 2007

The partial convergence of the platforms of liberal reformists, moderate Islamists, and conservative religious scholars and the support of the moderate faction of the royal family have given new momentum recently to the reform process, leading to significant, incremental measures including the strengthening of the Shura Council, the holding of municipal elections, the legalization of a number of civil society organizations, educational reform, and the launching of national dialogues. U.S. pressure has also been an important factor, particularly in the case of the municipal elections and the legalization of civil society organizations. Indeed, many Saudi intellectuals and observers rate this last factor as the most crucial for sustaining the reform process in recent years.

Reform of the Shura Council

Appointed consultative councils, which have neither legislative nor oversight powers, have a long history in Saudi Arabia. Founding King Abdel Aziz al-Saud authorized the first consultative councils in the 1920s. In 1992 King Fahad changed the Shura Council's regulatory provisions and expanded its role and responsibilities in response to demands by religious scholars presented in the 1991 Memorandum of Advice. In addition to the council's original duty of offering nonbinding opinions on matters referred to it by the king, the enacted amendments granted it the right to voice concerns about public matters, send suggestions to the cabinet, and question ministers, but stopped short of endowing it with legislative powers. In its first cycle in 1992, the council consisted of sixty members and a president. By the inauguration of the fourth cycle in 2005, its membership had increased to 150. At present, almost half the council's members are drawn from the Wahhabi religious establishment, and the remainder is made up of university professors, technocrats, and representatives of the business community.

In the 1990s the council's deliberations focused primarily on legal issues pertaining to Sharia, socioeconomic development plans, and annual reports of ministries and other government agencies. On all these matters, the council's practice was to issue short, nonbinding recommendations to the cabinet based on simple majority rules.

In recent years, however, the Shura Council has undergone two meaningful transformations. The first transformation was that its regulatory provisions have changed—albeit slowly—to give members a higher degree of autonomy. In December 2003 King Fahad announced that the council would be empowered to play a more active role. In 2005 several amendments were finally enacted. Most significant, Article 17 of the council's regulatory provisions was changed to allow the council to present its recommendations directly to the king, instead of the cabinet, ensuring an improved degree of responsiveness on the side of the executive. Also, Article 23 was amended to give council members more freedom in proposing, discussing, and enacting new internal regulations. However, the reformists' expectation that the amendments might provide for partial elections of the council's members and endow it with some oversight powers over the cabinet did not materialize.

The second transformation is that the council has grown more political due to the diversification of its membership and agenda as liberal reformists and moderate Islamists have been increasingly appointed to the council. The new members have voiced concerns about political reform and challenged the dominance of Wahhabi clerics over the inner workings of the council. In addition, since 2003 the president of the council—while making it clear that full membership for women is not on the council's agenda—has frequently extended invitations to female scholars and activists to attend open sessions and to consult members on social issues relevant to women. The content of debate in the Shura Council has clearly moved beyond the unpoliticized legacy of the 1990s.

Debates in the Shura Council have also become public due to media coverage that includes uncensored televised broadcasts. Council members have discussed prominent issues such as strategies to combat terrorism and extremism, fiscal policies, public expenditures, corruption allegations against government officials, and educational reform plans. They have also acquired enough autonomy to tackle matters that were previously declared taboo for public discussion. A telling case was the council's debate on the new traffic law in the summer of 2005. Muhammad al-Zulfa, a liberal reformist member of the council, proposed to include the legalization of driver licenses for women on the agenda. Although it was not allowed to reach the floor, al-Zulfa's proposal forced the council to address this highly explosive matter in public for the first time.

These changes have not led to concrete policy outcomes so far. The Shura Council still has no real legislative power and is not a representative institution because it is not elected. Nonetheless, the position of the council in Saudi politics has shifted from that of a marginal body dominated by Wahhabi clerics to a venue for vibrant public debates reflecting the plurality of views on reform concerns.

Municipal Elections

In 1993 a royal decree introduced a revised system of provincial government. Appointed municipal councils were to be established across the country to monitor local developments and advise executive authorities. The decree detailed the municipal councils' duties and responsibilities, which were mostly of an administrative nature, including preparing budgetary programs, supervising regulations regarding public services, monitoring public revenues and spending, and voicing opinion on issues referred to them by the executive.

In 2005, in direct response to domestic and international reform demands, the government decided to hold partial elections for the country's 178 municipal councils. The elections took place in three stages over a period of three months from February to April 2005 and were highly contested. In Riyadh, for example, 646 candidates competed for seven municipal seats. The voter turnout ranged from 25 to 35 percent of eligible voters. Moderate Islamists, in both Sunni- and Shi'i-dominated provinces, emerged as winners in most races. Women were excluded as voters and candidates.

Most Arab and Western observers were quick to dismiss the municipal elections as irrelevant, merely a cosmetic step taken to ease domestic and international reform pressure. Their analyses highlighted the various shortcomings of these partial elections, particularly the exclusion of women, the triviality of the councils' duties, and the great influence of tribal loyalties and confessional affiliations in determining voter preferences.

But such a hasty dismissal reveals a lack of understanding of Saudi politics. The tribal loyalties and confessional affiliations clearly manifested in the municipal elections did not represent incurable elements of backwardness. Rather, they entailed an important moment of pluralism. Throughout most of the twentieth century, the Saudi government suppressed diversity in society. The surfacing of tribal and confessional affiliations in today's politics represents a reassertion of pluralism and ultimately serves to push the reform process forward. After all, only a consensus-oriented participatory political system is capable of accommodating diversity peacefully.

The municipal elections have served three important purposes with regard to the reform process. First, as Saudi Arabia's first elections since the 1960s, they reinvigorated the forgotten memory of popular participation. Second, they set a precedent for opening existing consultative bodies for pluralist contestation. And, third, the elections garnered great attention among the Saudi population and helped strengthen the debates on reform.

Legalization of Human Rights Organizations and Professional Syndicates

Over the past four years, the Saudi government has approved the establishment of two human rights organizations, institutionalized professional syndicates, and permitted the participation of women as voters and candidates in some of their board elections. These changes indicate a greater readiness on the part of the government to expand civil society and create modern mechanisms for better representation.

In April 2004 the government approved the establishment of the country's first nongovernmental human rights organization, the Saudi National Organization for Human Rights (NOHR), whose mandate is monitoring human rights violations and reporting them to relevant government organs, especially the ministry of the interior.[2] Since its establishment, the NOHR has organized visits to prisons in all regions and devoted special attention to longtime detainees being held without charges. The organization has also investigated cases of prisoner mistreatment. It has, however, kept a low profile on issues pertaining to freedom of expression and politically motivated detentions. For example, the NOHR never took a public position on the detention of the three signatories of the petition calling for the establishment of a constitutional monarchy. It has also failed to address discriminatory practices against women and Shiite citizens. Indeed, since the creation of the NOHR, there has been no substantial improvement in the Saudi human rights record. These weaknesses have negatively impacted the organization's image. Dissenting groups have come to view the NOHR as a co-opted arm of the government created to quiet international criticism.

The establishment of the first governmental human rights agency in December 2005 has only increased these doubts. The Saudi Human Rights Agency (SHRA) is concerned with spreading awareness about human rights and contributing to implementing those rights in accordance with Islamic teachings. The SHRA, whose members are appointed by the king, has the mandate of consulting and supervising the government on human rights issues. Regardless of the real motives behind the creation of the SHRA, it is difficult to imagine that it will be able to transcend the legacy of governmental human rights organizations elsewhere in authoritarian countries, where activities are geared to disguise and justify human rights violations.

On the level of less politicized NGOs, Saudi Arabia's first-ever syndicate for journalists was authorized in June 2004. Two female journalists were appointed to the syndicate's nine-member board. This opening for women in professional syndicates has gained more momentum over the few last years. In December 2005 the Saudi National Agency for Engineers held its board elections and, in a bold move, admitted women as both voters and candidates. Seventy male candidates and one female engineer contested seven seats. The female engineer won a seat. Lastly, the government has authorized in 2006 partial elections in provincial chambers of commerce. Female members could either vote—as in elections for the Riyadh Chamber of Commerce—or participate as both voters and candidates—as in the Jeddah Chamber of Commerce and the elections of the Eastern Region Chamber of Commerce.

Undoubtedly the legalization of various NGOs has opened up Saudi civil society and created new opportunities for citizen participation. The government's measures in this regard—modest in absolute terms but bold when compared with steps taken in other areas—have also highlighted the fact that the reform process in Saudi Arabia is bound to be uneven. Women acquired the right to vote and run for syndicates' board elections only after being completely excluded from the municipal elections. And even though the role of women in civil society has improved greatly, the Wahhabi religious establishment has retained the ability to coerce the government into upholding conservative stances on female personal freedoms.

Educational Reform Measures

Although there were some signs of governmental interest in modernizing education in the 1990s, the real push in this field followed the attacks of 9/11. Since then, educational reform has been framed in the context of combating terrorism. External actors, primarily the United States, have systematically accused the Wahhabi-controlled educational system of being a hotbed of extremism and pressured the Saudi government to introduce meaningful reforms to promote the values of tolerance and pluralism. Domestically, liberal reformists have also included educational reform in their platform, calling on the government to limit the influence of the religious establishment and inject elements of moderation into the curricula. The shockwaves of 9/11 and the rising jihadist threat have enabled liberal reformists to focus public attention on the importance of educational reform in promoting a culture of pluralism and sustaining the current political opening.

In recent years, the moderate faction in the royal family has clashed several times with the religious establishment over educational reform plans. Specifically, Western pressure concerning educational reform has hardened the position of Wahhabi clerics fearful of losing one of their strongholds in society. Therefore, considerable opposition to government measures has emerged, greatly diminishing the moderate royals' room for maneuver. The result has been a series of hesitant reform measures that have stopped short of introducing a significant shift in Saudi education.

Between 2002 and 2007, the ministry of education undertook several steps to remove extremist ideas from the curricula and create a balance between religious and nonreligious topics. In 2002, discriminatory references to Shi'i Muslims and non-Muslims were partially removed from textbooks and replaced by passages calling for the respect of other religions and cultures. In 2003 and 2004, liberal-minded Minister of Education Muhammad al-Rashid merged the administrative structure of the male and female branches of education and unified the curricula in nonreligious topics for both branches. He also announced a plan to introduce English language instruction in primary schools.

All these steps were vehemently opposed by Wahhabi clerics, particularly the unification of male and female curricula as well as the minimal increase in credit hours devoted to nonreligious sciences. Although the Wahhabi opposition has not persuaded the government to reverse its measures, as 156 clerics demanded in an early 2004 petition, it has clearly diminished the government's ability to push for more. Al-Rashid was ousted from the cabinet in February 2005 after an orchestrated denunciation campaign against him. Abdullah Salih al-Ubaid, a graduate of the ultraconservative Imam Muhammad bin Saud University, replaced him.

In fact, during the last two years the moderate faction in the royal family has come under more pressure with regard to implemented reforms. Recently, King Abdullah had to state publicly that there is no compromise on the Islamic nature of the educational system, affirming that "this country is either Islamic or nothing at all."

Institutionalization of the National Dialogue Conferences

In June 2003 the government announced an initiative to host national dialogue conferences to discuss needed reforms and promote freedom of expression. The government-sponsored Abdul-Aziz Center for National Dialogue subsequently launched a series of meetings, extending invitations to male and female university professors, intellectuals, and activists. Representatives of the Shi'i minority and liberal reformists participated in the meetings alongside Wahhabi clerics and government officials. To date, seven rounds of the national dialogue conferences held between June 2003 and May 2007 have addressed the future of political reform, radicalism and moderation, women's status, youth problems, intercultural dialogue, education, and employment.

Participants put forward some bold proposals, ranging from electing the members of the Shura Council, recognizing equal political rights for women, promoting equitable distribution of state resources, enacting antidiscrimination measures in favor of the Shi'i community, and empowering civil society organizations. Controversial discussions culminated in a number of recommendations that, while not binding, have been selectively implemented by the government; the reform of the Shura Council and the municipal elections are two important examples.

The national dialogue conferences have had other significant consequences. They have offered dissenting groups a platform to articulate their reform demands and exposed the Saudi public to a plurality of schools of thought, which official Wahhabism has long suppressed. The national dialogue conferences have gradually evolved into open marketplaces for reform ideas and visions. They have also inspired the emergence of nongovernmental intellectual forums across a country that has long lacked uncensored venues to voice public concerns and promote citizens' participation. In the absence of democratic deliberations in politics, the growing margin of freedom of expression in the public space has become the focal point for pluralist contestations in Saudi Arabia.

Potential for Further Significant Reform

Reforms implemented by the Saudi government in recent years have revitalized existing consultative councils and introduced the mechanism of elections at the municipal level. New opportunities for citizen participation in civil society have emerged, and the margin of freedom in the public space has expanded significantly. In addition, the political spectrum has grown more diverse with the entry of new players, who have garnered popular support for their reform platforms.

. Although these changes represent a significant opening in Saudi politics, they have not fundamentally altered the authoritarian nature of the political system. The royal family and the Wahhabi religious establishment have sustained their dominant positions in society. Their ability to block, stall, and even reverse reforms has not diminished substantially. In the absence of competing power centers, the reform process has remained inherently vulnerable and limited. In spite of the expansion of its functions, the Shura Council has not acquired real legislative or oversight power to hold the government, let alone the royal family, accountable. Government promises to ensure the independence of the judiciary and limit Wahhabi control over it have not materialized beyond a series of minimal administrative reform measures with no significant impact. As the experience of the petition calling for the establishment of a constitutional monarchy has demonstrated, the empowerment of liberal reformists and other dissenting groups has not protected them from government repression or Wahhabi denunciations. And although two human rights organizations were legalized, human rights violations and discriminatory treatment of specific groups of the population have not decreased significantly.

Within these limits and given the unchanged concentration of power in the hands of the royal family and the religious establishment, there are four realistic avenues to sustain the reform process and expand political freedoms in today's Saudi Arabia: consolidating Shura and municipal councils, expanding civil society, promoting educational reform, and promoting gender equality.

Consolidating Shura and Municipal Councils

Increasing the number of Shura Council members to 150 and gradually empowering them in recent years have made the council a relevant institution in Saudi politics. One possibility to enhance this positive development is to introduce elections of at least a portion of the council's members. Indeed, liberal reformists and moderate Islamists alike have called on the government to do just that—with the proposed share of elected members ranging from 25 to 50 percent. A few members of the council have voiced similar demands in public and, in an attempt to garner support in the royal family, have proposed that elected members be approved by the king in the final instance.

There have been growing signs since 2002 that the moderate faction in the royal family has transcended the fear of elections. Holding elections in municipal councils and professional syndicates has not threatened the stability or the legitimacy of the house of al-Saud. In a recent televised meeting with members of the council, King Abdullah indirectly embraced the demand for introducing a partial election stating that "the nation looks to you—members of the Shura Council—as its representatives and we will ensure that you truly be so."

Vesting limited oversight powers in the council represents a second realistic priority for further empowerment. In contrast to maximalist demands of some liberal reformists who ask for immediate accountability of the executive before the council and full budgetary oversight, a minimalist, incremental approach might prove to be more effective. Extending the council's purview to allow questioning ministers and civil servants on public expenditures and resource allocation would allow members to acquire a more supervisory role over government workings and ensure more continuity than the current practice of only discussing ministerial annual reports.

With regard to municipal councils, two reform measures are within reach. One measure—the gradual extension of the election mechanism to cover all seats in the councils instead of the current 50 percent—seems acceptable to the royal family. A second measure also within reach—democratizing the internal functioning of the councils —would transform them into more vibrant places of political deliberations. At present, local councils' presidents, who are chosen from among appointed members, determine the final agenda, proposals, and recommendations. Limiting their powers and delegating more responsibilities to members appear essential. Indeed, in 2005 and 2006 the Shura Council announced proposals to this effect, calling on the government to vest more authority to its members than to presidents of municipal councils.

Expanding Civil Society

In spite of the significant opening in Saudi civil society, the legalization of NGOs has remained—even by regional standards—restrictive. Legalization depends on authorization by various officials, and government agencies continue to hold sway over the inner workings of approved organizations such as the NOHR. An important step to change this situation is to gradually ease restrictions on the legalization of new organizations, particularly those that address issues such as political freedoms and human rights. In recent years, the great majority of liberal reformists, moderate Islamists, and reform-minded religious scholars have been forced to rely on informal networks to coordinate their activities. The move to legality would allow these groups to enhance popular participation in public matters and enable them to inject more elements of moderation into society. Due to the continued absence of political parties, NGOs are bound to acquire the significant role of defending citizens' civil rights, representing their demands to the government, and safeguarding a degree of pluralism in the public space.

As mentioned earlier, the government has recently authorized the establishment of a few professional syndicates and permitted partial or full elections of their boards. The possibility of expanding this precedent in the near future to cover more professions is real. Obviously the government fears that the emergence of syndicates as modern patterns for organized interest representation might challenge existing networks of patrimonial allegiance and lead to increased politicization in the public space. Indeed, in other Arab countries—Morocco, Tunisia, Egypt, Jordan, Kuwait—opposition groups have used professional syndicates to articulate their platforms in public and build popular constituencies, especially in urban centers. Islamist movements, in particular, started establishing themselves as key actors in Arab politics by participating in, and often winning, the syndicates' internal elections, evoking in some cases government repression to contain them. Saudi authorities are aware of this history, and they can be expected to subject the leadership of the syndicates to restrictions and co-option. Yet, the mere increase in the total number of syndicates would constitute a significant step forward in the institutionalization of civil society.

Finally, since the terrorist attacks of 9/11, the government has taken measures to regulate the explosive terrain of nongovernmental Islamic charity. The Saudi government has banned many nongovernmental charitable organizations or prohibited them from operating outside the country because of their widespread radical leanings and the suspicion that these organizations finance terrorist groups. Although understandable and indeed necessary in many cases, such government restrictions have unfortunately inflicted harm on some organizations that never indulged in illegal practices. As in other countries of the Arab world, Islamic charity organizations in Saudi Arabia have always been a pillar of civil society. Most of them have served to protect underprivileged citizens and therefore attract a broad following. In fact, some—in particular those directed by moderate Islamists—have been partially dedicated to civic education and human rights projects. Easing restrictions on charity organizations, while holding their boards accountable for abiding by government regulations and encouraging them to direct part of their activities toward disseminating a culture of tolerance and pluralism, would add immensely to the current momentum in the Saudi civil society.

Promoting Educational Reform

Education is perhaps one of the most sensitive areas for future reform. Efforts since 2002 have failed to generate a significant change in the educational system because the religious establishment has blocked many changes and because liberal reformists and moderate Islamists differ a great deal regarding educational reform and have thus been unable to present a united front. Liberal reformists favor a substantial change in the educational curricula to ensure a balance between religious and nonreligious subjects. Many of them rightly contend that the current curricula are generally superficial and detached from present-day issues. Moderate Islamists would like to keep the overall religious orientation of the curricula unchanged and focus primarily on omitting extremist ideas regarding the Shi'i community, Christians, and Jews from textbooks.

Despite these obstacles, small-scale reform steps remain plausible. Textbooks have by no means been completely purged of the extremist baggage of the last decades. Discriminatory references to the Shi'i community and other minorities in Saudi Arabia have not disappeared fully. Infusing tolerance and respect for the plurality of Islamic schools of thought has lagged in recent years. On all these issues, incremental improvement remains possible even without a complete overhaul of the educational system.

Another area where incremental improvement is possible is teacher training. Since 2002 the ministry of education has regular started international training and exchange programs for teachers. These programs, designed to expose Saudi instructors to moderate regional and international teaching environments, can be intensified in the future.

Admittedly, these steps, should the government undertake them, would not substantially alter the fundamental reality of the Saudi educational system, which is the hegemony of the religious establishment. That problem cannot be overcome in the short run. But by focusing on existing free spaces to get around the main obstacle, reforms can at least change to some extent what is being transmitted in classrooms.

Working Toward Gender Equality

Gender equality is the most emotional of all reform issues being discussed in Saudi Arabia at present. The domestic debate on women's status in society has moved beyond the set of demands that have become popular in the West—for example, permitting female driver's licenses and eliminating Sharia-imposed restrictions on women's mobility. At the core of the current debate are women's civil rights and political participation.

Saudis are extremely divided on this issue and, as a result, contradictory trends are emerging. Women were excluded as voters and candidates from municipal elections but shortly thereafter were allowed to participate in both capacities in professional syndicate elections. The religious establishment still upholds its position insisting that women be banned almost entirely from the public sphere, but liberal reformists and a few moderate Islamists have become more outspoken in demanding equal rights for women, often with the endorsement of moderate royals. As a result, female intellectuals and scholars have participated in the national dialogue conferences, voicing their concerns with an unprecedentedly daring resolve. At the same time, however, the number of female appointments to high-ranking government positions has remained almost stagnant.

Given the contradictory nature of recent developments, only additional minor steps are attainable in the short run. Women's involvement in the public space can and will continue to increase because the precedent-setting participation of women in syndicate elections cannot be reversed. It is also possible that the government will adopt and implement legal measures aimed at improving the status of women in the private sphere; the problem of domestic violence has been debated in recent years in a rather taboo-breaking way. It is imaginable that women will be granted the right to cast their ballot in next municipal elections. But the recognition of equal rights for women in Saudi Arabia remains, at best, a long way off.

Role of the United States

Promoting the current political opening in Saudi Arabia presents the United States with a set of difficult challenges. In the Saudi case, the United States lacks the leverage of economic or military aid that can be conditioned to the implementation of further reform measures. And in fact in Saudi Arabia the economic leverage runs quite the reverse with the U.S. economy depending a great deal on Saudi oil. The domestic dynamics in Saudi Arabia also generate very few possibilities for a significant U.S. role.

As a result of these challenges, U.S. pressure for reform since 9/11 has been inconsistent and has met with only limited effect. Shocked by the fact that most of the 9/11 hijackers were Saudi citizens, the Bush administration pressed the royal family to combat terrorism and extremism. In 2002 and 2003, prior to the invasion of Iraq, the administration also unleashed an unprecedented barrage of rhetoric about the necessity for Saudi reform, targeting in particular the absence of political participation and the educational system. Fearful of losing its strategic alliance with the United States and amid growing domestic demands for change, the royal family did respond and implemented some reforms, as discussed earlier.

However, the emergence of the Iraqi turmoil has pushed the pendulum of U.S.–Saudi relations back in the opposite direction. Over the past three years, the Bush administration has softened its stance vis-à-vis Saudi Arabia and kept a low profile on Saudi domestic issues. The royal family, for its part, has resorted to scare tactics, arguing that rapid, uncontrolled reforms would undermine its authority, leading to a jihadist takeover. The United States, worried about the possibility of total destabilization in the Gulf region, has abated its pressure for reform. U.S. security needs in Iraq and dramatic increases in oil prices have also contributed to this change. Today's bilateral relations demonstrate growing areas of convergence. The rift that 9/11 created between the U.S. and Saudi Arabia has largely been repaired.

In its search for entry points to promote reform in Saudi Arabia, the United States is also constrained by Saudi domestic realities. Although the current political opening is undoubtedly significant, it is by no means the beginning of a Saudi democratization process. This is not a country that can be expected to legalize political parties or organize truly competitive elections in the near future. By the same token, the emergence of a powerful legislative authority or an independent judiciary is unlikely. Reforming the authoritarian polity in Saudi Arabia is bound to follow a slow path—an uneven process that would entail the gradual expansion of political representation and the creation of new spaces where citizens enjoy limited freedoms. Disagreements about certain issues such as the mélange of religion and politics as well as the role of women in public life are integral parts of introducing reforms in a country like Saudi Arabia.

Given these conditions, the United States has two realistic entry points to encourage political reform in Saudi Arabia. First, at the government-to-government level, the administration should support the demands of Saudi groups advocating reform. The demands for broadening the power of the Shura Council, electing at least some of its members, and legalizing more NGOs and syndicates deserve particular support. Pressing the Saudi government on these issues would also allay popular suspicion of U.S. intentions because domestic actors have articulated similar demands.

Second, at the nongovernmental level, the United States should offer to intensify its contacts with civil society actors. Such an endeavor will necessitate joint efforts by the administration and U.S. NGOs operating in the fields of democracy promotion and human rights. The Saudi government must be pressured to allow freer cooperation between international and domestic NGOs, something that remains extremely difficult at present. Gradually including Saudi NGOs and professional syndicates in ongoing regional programs as well as devising country-specific measures can help develop their capacities and embolden their reform platforms by exposing them to the international democracy promotion agenda.

However, on other issues such as educational reform and gender equality, the United States would be better advised to keep a low profile. These two issues, often seen as soft entry points by democracy promoters, are highly sensitive in the Saudi case. Previous U.S. interventions in favor of liberal curricula and women's empowerment between 2002 and 2004 were discredited in public by all domestic actors, including female activists. Furthermore, domestic actors remain highly divided on these issues.

The steps advocated here are modest. But in a country like Saudi Arabia, which is only now beginning to take the first steps toward liberalization, it is better for the United States to set modest goals and promote them consistently than to indulge in grand rhetoric about democracy that cannot be backed by a clear policy.

Notes

1. Compared with Ali al-Dumaini and Matruk al-Falih, who have been active in liberal reformist circles in recent years, al-Hamid's background is more rooted in the moderate Islamist spectrum.

2. The NOHR is composed of forty-one members, mostly of the liberal reformist group. Nine of its members are female scholars and activists.

KUWAIT:
POLITICS IN A
PARTICIPATORY EMIRATE

Paul Salem

Kuwait has a long history of consultative government, constitutional-ism, and participatory politics unique among the monarchies of the Gulf region. The ruling al-Sabah family's place in the political system was established by agreement—not force—among the leading families of the trading city of Kuwait in the mid-eighteenth century; administration by consultation continued until the late nineteenth century. In the twentieth century, while the country was a British protectorate, authoritarian tenden-cies within the ruling family were countered by a strong constitutional movement that started in the 1920s, bore fruit in parliamentary elections in 1938, and resulted in a fairly democratic constitution when the country became independent in 1961. Since then, Kuwait has had eleven parliamen-tary elections, and the National Assembly has continued to play a very powerful role in the state.

Nevertheless, there has been a long power struggle between the ruling al-Sabah family and the parliament, leading to the suspension of both the constitution and parliament in 1976 and again in 1986. The system became more stable after the liberation of Kuwait from the Iraqi invasion of 1990 for two reasons: first, the al-Sabah family had performed poorly during the war and needed to rebuild its legitimacy with the Kuwaiti public; second, the United States insisted on a return to parliamentary constitutionalism after the war. Since then, parliament has played a central role again, and the country has seen various reforms.

The year 2006 was particularly eventful. In January, the National Assembly resolved a succession crisis within the al-Sabah family by intervening consti-tutionally in favor of Sheikh Sabah al-Ahmad over the ailing Sheikh Saad

211

al-Abdullah. In the spring, after a number of lawyers successfully challenged a ban on public gatherings in the constitutional court, youth and other social groups led public protests for a change in the electoral system. The movement, joined by members of parliament, led to a standoff with the government. The emir dissolved parliament and called for new elections, which an opposition coalition decisively won. The new government accepted the opposition's redistricting proposals, which amounted to a major reform of the electoral system. Since then, the government has also responded to pressure from the National Assembly on a number of issues, including anticorruption, press and television freedoms, and reform in the educational, sports, and business sectors.

The process of reform in Kuwait is neither systematic nor linear. There are many players with competing agendas, and the political pulling and pushing that characterizes the relationship between the government and the National Assembly is often more about showboating and capturing newspaper headlines than about comprehensive, well-thought-out reform. The government often sees the contentious parliament as an obstacle to top-down reforms that it or the emir might be interested in implementing. Yet there is no doubt that the Kuwaiti political system is fluid and responsive, that the emir and the executive branch do not have a free rein on power, and that the National Assembly, civil society, the business community, and public opinion have important roles in the Kuwaiti decision-making process.

Roots of Reform

Origins of Kuwaiti Politics: Shura, Authority, and Opposition

The origins of the Kuwaiti political system go back to the late eighteenth century, when the merchant families of the small fishing and pearl-diving town of Kuwait appointed a respected member of one of the families, Abdullah al-Sabah, as emir—in effect, governor. The appointment was essentially a practical division of tasks between governance (*imara*) and commerce (*tijara*) among different families, rather than the ascension of one family to a position of dominance over others. Indeed, until the twentieth century, it was usually the al-Sabah family that was the weaker party, dependent as it was on precious revenues from the merchant families, rather than the other way around.

This period contains the germs of many elements that are essential in understanding the basic political ideas and attitudes in Kuwait. First, the ruler was not seen as superior, but simply as performing a particular function as part of the necessary division of labor within a growing economy and society.

Second, the ruler was tasked with looking after the interests of the city as a whole, not with promoting the interests of his family, and there was no question that other groups or families were in any way his—or his family's—subjects. Third, the political sphere was not seen as superior to the economic or civilian spheres, but rather parallel to and supportive of them. Fourth, rule was not imposed by force, but by consent and agreement. Fifth, rule was established within the firm context of consultation (*shura*), and the emir did not have absolute power—this was no Hobbesian contract to quell dissension by establishing an all-powerful monarch, but a more businesslike arrangement to appoint a chairman to help look after the interests of a growing concern. Sixth, the arrangement was bolstered by representation with taxation, because it was the tax revenues generated by the merchant families' activities that sustained the emir and his fledgling administration.

This spirit of cooperative *shura* was broken at the turn of the twentieth century by Sheikh Mubarak al-Sabah, who leaned on newfound British support to impose a more authoritarian style of politics on Kuwait. His attempts led to several waves of protest and dissent, culminating in the demand for a written constitution. A first constitutional document, agreed upon by leading opposition notables and the al-Sabah family, asserted the right of the community to resolve succession crises within the al-Sabah family and called for the election of a Shura Council charged with the "administration of the affairs of the country on the basis of justice and fairness" under the guidance and leadership of the emir. A twelve-member Shura Council was appointed, not elected; it was not given any real authority and soon dissolved, quickly ending this first attempt at a constitution.

In 1938 the British urged the al-Sabah family to shore up its rule by accepting a number of political reforms. Elections for a National Assembly were held that June, with voting restricted to the leading notables of the main families. The assembly, headed by the reformist Sheikh Abdullah al-Salem of the al-Sabah family, drafted another constitutional document, one promptly accepted by the ruling emir. The document asserted that the people were the source of all authority, that they were represented by their elected deputies, that the National Assembly alone had the right to produce legislation, and that all treaties and concessions must go through the National Assembly. But the assembly soon began to flex its muscles and question the petroleum concessions granted by the Sabah family to the British, prompting the emir to quickly dissolve it with enthusiastic British backing. New elections held in early 1939 produced another assembly, but attempts by the new legislature and the emir to agree on a constitution failed, and the assembly was soon dissolved again.

The third and decisive attempt at a constitution came in the late 1950s, again with a nudge from the British. Reacting to the growing appeal of Nasserism after the Suez War of 1956 and the union of Egypt and Syria in 1958, the British tried to preempt trouble by promising independence to Kuwait. They also again urged the emir to allow wider participation in government to shore up the state's weak Arab nationalist credentials with at least some democratic credentials. The British were also eager to create a Jordanian–Iraqi–Kuwaiti Arab Union led by the pro-British Hashemites to counter Nasser's Egyptian–Syrian United Arab Republic (UAR). Although the Iraqi monarchy soon fell to an Arab nationalist coup and Nasser's UAR itself collapsed in 1961, the momentum for independence and change in Kuwait had already taken root.

Struggle over Constitutionalism: 1961–1990

Kuwait received its independence in June 1961. This was followed in December by elections for a constituent assembly (*majlis ta'sisi*) tasked with drafting a constitution for the country. The constitution was drafted in cooperation with the emir and promulgated in November 1962. The emir at that time was Sheikh Abdullah, who had headed the constitutionally minded assembly of 1938. His presence was crucial in legitimizing and institutionalizing the new power-sharing arrangements between the ruling family and the public.

The 1962 constitution is a detailed and strong document that effectively curbs the power of the emir and the ruling family in a way that falls short of a true constitutional democracy but is unparalleled among other monarchies in the region. It declares Kuwait an independent sovereign state in which the head of state is a hereditary member of the Sabah line. Sovereignty resides in the Kuwaiti people, and they choose their representatives to a National Assembly in regular and free elections. The heir to the throne, who is nominated by the emir, must be approved by the parliament, and the emir must swear an oath before parliament. The emir appoints a government that helps him exercise executive authority; this government does not require the approval or confidence of parliament, but any and all ministers, including the prime minister, can be questioned by parliament and removed from office by a parliamentary vote. The emir and parliament shared legislative authority in two ways: first, ministers (no more than fifteen) in the emir-appointed cabinet become ex officio voting members of parliament alongside the fifty elected deputies, and second, all legislation requires the approval of both parliament and the emir.

But the successors of Abdullah, Sabah al-Salem al-Sabah (1967–1977) and Jaber al-Ahmed al-Sabah (1977–January 2006), were not as favorably inclined to constitutionalism and parliamentary democracy as was Abdullah. The increasing oil revenue of the state enabled the al-Sabah family to rid itself of its original dependence on the big trading families for financial support and thus change one of the main dynamics of the system. They suspended the constitution and dissolved parliament twice, in 1976 and 1986, each time for four years. In the first case, domestic pressure led to fresh elections and a resumption of parliamentary life; in the second, the Iraqi invasion intervened.

Reaffirmation of Constitutionalism: 1991 and Beyond

The Iraqi occupation and its aftermath represented an important watershed in Kuwaiti political development. The return of Sabah rule to Kuwait after its poor performance during the war and after the attempts to roll back constitutionalism in the 1970s and 1980s required a renewed commitment to that principle from both the Sabah family and the Kuwaiti public. In addition the U.S. government had no choice but to press the Sabah family to commit itself to a restoration of the constitution and parliament so Washington could justify its military investment in Kuwait to Congress and its own public.

When Iraqi forces took over Kuwait, most of the Sabah family fled the country, a severe blow to their credibility. At the same time, the population who suffered under the occupation developed a sense of unity, nationalism, and entitlement. The outlines of the new political contract that would emerge after the war were hammered out in a meeting organized in Saudi Arabia in which members of the Sabah family and other leading Kuwaitis met under Saudi and American auspices. The conferees in Saudi Arabia agreed to renew their support for the rule of the Sabah family in return for a permanent and unequivocal return to regular constitutional and political life. Although authoritarian and anticonstitutional tendencies persist within the Sabah family, they have remained in check. Postwar elections were held in 1992 and again in 1996, 1999, 2003, and 2006, often with a very strong showing for the opposition, without leading to a suspension of constitutional or parliamentary life.

The long-reigning Sheikh Jaber died in mid-January 2006, inaugurating a year of extraordinary political dynamism in Kuwait. The assumption of power by the heir-designate, Sheikh Saad al-Abdullah, who was virtually incapacitated by illness, was contested both within the family and by parliament. It soon became clear that the new emir was not even well enough to take the required oath of investiture before parliament. As the deadline for taking the oath passed, parliament moved to depose the emir-designate and invest instead Prime Minister Sheikh Sabah al-Ahmad of the al-Sabah family's Jaber line. As the parliamentary motion was taking place, a letter of abdication from Sheikh Saad arrived, thus avoiding a direct parliamentary deposition. Sabah took the oath of office as emir and appointed his brother, Nawwaf al-Ahmad, as the new crown prince and his nephew, Nasser al-Muhammad al-Ahmad, as prime minister.

The extraordinary events of January were followed in the spring by equally significant developments. A group of lawyers, contesting a political case, challenged the constitutionality of the law banning public gatherings that had been on the books for over two decades. The challenge went to the constitutional court, and in a bold move, the court struck down the law. This emboldened a number of opposition and youth groups, mobilized around the demand to amend the election law, to organize an escalating series of public gatherings and demonstrations. Their main demand was that the number of electoral constituencies be reduced from twenty-five to five.

The twenty-five constituencies had been put in place by the government in the run-up to the first postliberation elections in 1992. Opposition leaders alleged that the constituencies were gerrymandered in such a way as to favor allies of the government and were small enough so as to enable the easy buying of votes to decide the outcome. They argued that five large districts would reduce the influence of gerrymandering and money and bring about fairer representation. The youth-driven public protests quickly garnered the support of a majority within the National Assembly. The government, hoping to stem the tide, proposed a ten-district compromise, which the National Assembly rejected. Facing growing opposition within parliament and among the protestors, the emir acted on his constitutional prerogative to dissolve parliament and call new elections, albeit on the basis of the old twenty-five-district law—hoping to reshuffle the parliamentary deck in his favor.

Government supporters did poorly in the elections, with a loose opposition alliance—supporting the five-district reform—taking more than two-thirds of the fifty seats in parliament. After the elections, the government promptly dropped its old ten-district proposal and agreed to five districts. With victory in the electoral districting battle, public and parliamentary attention shifted to other issues, particularly those of corruption and waste, oil and land resources, and the sports and youth sectors. The succession crisis of January, the protests of the spring, and the elections of the summer all demonstrated the extent to which the public and parliament wield significant influence in the Kuwaiti political system.

The Context of Competition

Despite the realities of constitutionalism, regular elections, and an important degree of popular participation and parliamentary influence, the Kuwaiti system remains restrictive in a number of ways: the ruling family, though weaker than others in the region, remains the dominant player in the system; the political system up until only two years ago excluded women and still excludes a large number of other Kuwaiti inhabitants; the economy is state dominated, which creates a dependent labor force and prevents the emergence of a truly independent business class; and civil society is active but still stunted.

Social Structures: Between Heterogeneity and Exclusion

In a resident population of over 2.5 million, not quite 1 million are Kuwaitis. The remainder is largely Arab and South Asian workers, along with a number of Westerners. It is only the Kuwaitis, of course, who are officially included in political life, and even among Kuwaitis, the extension of suffrage has been very slow. The first "elections" in 1920 involved a few dozen notables gathered at a home of one of their own. Suffrage was gradually extended in successive stages to include, by the 1990s, the majority of male Kuwaitis twenty-one years of age or older. Still excluded were a large number of male citizens who had only recently been naturalized and another 100,000 stateless inhabitants of Kuwait, known as the *bidoon* (in Arabic, "without"). The question of suffrage and citizenship remains highly contested in Kuwait.

The exclusion of women from political life was the most glaring until the last elections. Women's suffrage had been a demand of reformers since the 1960s, but conservative forces in the Sabah family and in Islamist organizations represented in parliament opposed it. The law granting women the right to vote was finally passed in 2005, and women were enabled to vote and run for parliament for the first time in the 2006 elections. While several women ran, none won seats, due to a lack of political experience and continuing resistance by voters. Female candidates, however, might fare better next time Kuwaitis go the polls because of changes in the electoral law and because political organizations, above all Islamist groups, have now realized the weight of the women's vote and seek to include them in the political process as supporters and candidates.

Although almost the entire Kuwaiti population is urbanized, there is lingering identity segmentation between self-described urban (*hadari*) Kuwaitis, who consider themselves the original or early settlers in Kuwait City, and tribal (*qabali*) Kuwaitis, who made the transition to urban life and, in some cases citizenship, more recently. In the current Kuwaiti population, about 65 percent are considered *qabali* and 35 percent *hadari*. The tribal populations, although living in urban conditions indistinguishable from those of others, still have a social structure and identity that flows from their tribal group. Their social and cultural values tend to be more conservative, and their politics were originally more sympathetic to the Sabah family.

The main leftist, liberal, and Arab nationalist movements in Kuwait originated largely in the *hadari* communities and continue to find most traction there. Islamist groups have been able to make inroads into the tribal communities since the 1980s. Before several elections, the tribal groups have organized their own "primaries" to choose candidates for office, and the old 25-district electoral system districts were gerrymandered to ensure the ample representation of tribal groups allied with the government. In recent times, inroads by the Islamists into tribal communities together with the broad opposition alliance of Islamists and non-Islamist forces since the 1991 liberation have somewhat reduced the rift between these two elements of society.

Although official figures are kept under wraps, estimates of the sectarian distribution put the Shi'i community in Kuwait at between 15 and 25 percent. Some are from among the *hadaris* and trace their roots to Arab and Iranian merchant families; others are of Arab tribal origins. Initially led by various Shi'i merchant notables, the Shi'i leadership has been increasingly supplanted by Islamists inspired by movements in Iraq and Iran. In the wake of the Islamic revolution in Iran, Shi'i Islamists organized protests demanding wider participation and more recognition of their presence and role. The government reacted forcefully to the challenge and quelled the movement, but Shi'i Islamists were allowed to enter mainstream politics and won seats in all subsequent parliaments. After an initial policy of repression, the state shifted to a policy of co-option and containment by legalizing some of the associations and allowing them to participate in elections, while gerrymandering districts to ensure that Shi'i representation remained quite limited. For their part, by allying with the broad constitutional opposition since the mid-1980s, Shi'i Islamists have been able to limit the Sunni–Shi'i divide and avoid confrontation.

Young people are also a potent and rising force in Kuwait. Making up over half of the population, empowered by education, and raised on satellite television and the Internet, Kuwaiti youth are an informed and dynamic force. Demonstrations organized by young people in May 2006 broke the long-standing taboo relating to public demonstration and opened the gates to wider protests that eventually brought down the government, led to early elections, an opposition victory, and the change in the electoral law. Young

Kuwaitis organized into a number of formal and informal groupings, working together in 2006 to launch the popular campaign to amend the election law. The agenda adopted by youth in the spring of 2006 was eventually adopted by a large cross-section of the business and political elite and became the heart of the successful opposition campaigns leading up to the June 2006 elections.

Youth in Kuwait have traditionally mobilized around university student bodies. The main student body, the National Students Union, has been dominated by conservative Islamist students since the mid-1980s. However, secular, liberal, and nationalist currents among the student body have also found voice in other organizations, some of which have been set up by students after graduation. In any case, student organizations from most sectors of the political spectrum joined together in the reform movement of spring 2006, and much of this cooperation has continued in the postelection period. Nevertheless, youth leadership is divided over some social and cultural issues. Islamists wish to introduce more conservative rules and habits into Kuwaiti society and culture, amend Article 2 of the constitution to render Sharia the only source of legislation, and introduce more segregation and separation of women in society. Non-Islamist youth, while grateful for the support of their Islamist cohorts in the electoral reform and anticorruption struggles, are wary of them on other issues.

At the higher reaches of the social pyramid there is also heterogeneity. The ruling family is just that—a ruling family, that is, tasked with the troublesome job of governing—not a royal family. While respected, members of the al-Sabah family—including the emir, the prime minister, and ministers—are not treated as exalted royalty, as they are in some of the other Arab monarchies in the Gulf Cooperation Council (GCC), but rather with professional respect. In social settings, other elites interact with them on an equal footing. In parliament and the press, while the emir himself is generally shielded from direct criticism, other members of the ruling family—in and out of office—come in for much direct and freewheeling challenge and even attacks. The presence of a fair number of prominent, wealthy, and powerful merchant families with historic roles in Kuwait (such as the Sager, Kharafi, Ghanem, and Budai families) also adds to the sense of openness and power-sharing at the higher reaches of the Kuwaiti social pyramid.

Monolithic Economy

In contrast to this sociopolitical heterogeneity, the economy of Kuwait tends very strongly toward the monolithic and top heavy. Over 90 percent of the labor force is employed by the state, and the bulk of the economy is dependent on the single, state-controlled resource of oil. This heavily state-centric structure has been a longstanding point of agreement between the ruling family and the traditional nationalist opposition, which shared the statist economic thinking of most Arab nationalists in the region in the 1950s and 1960s. The merchant families might have put forward an alternative point of view, but undertaking divestment and privatization and risking unemployment were never politically popular viewpoints; privatization, in particular, was too closely linked with a fear of Western, especially American, influence. In addition, the Kuwaiti merchant and private sector became a successful but dependent partner of the state and thus was co-opted into the politico-economic structure. Oil remains the sole, significant driving force of the Kuwaiti economy, and foreign direct investment does not exceed a few million dollars.

The monolithic and statist aspect of the Kuwaiti economy is the main factor that gives the state a large measure of ultimate control and influence over society. Although Kuwaitis agitate, oppose, and complain, their economic interests tie them firmly to the state and dissuade them from more openly shaking or challenging the system. Students and youth agitate for change, but when they graduate they invariably turn to the public sector for jobs. Even the so-called liberal reformers, who complain about the limited role the private sector plays in the economic development of Kuwait, suggest—without a hint of irony—increased government subsidies for private companies as a way to bring about such change.

It is important to note that the oil income accrues to the Kuwaiti state, not—as is the case in many other GCC states—to the ruling family. The ruling family has a set allowance, currently fixed by parliament at KD50 million ($173 million). This goes to the emir to cover the expenses of his office as well as the income of other members of the Sabah family. Otherwise, the vast oil revenues of Kuwait accrue to the Kuwaiti treasury. Thus, dependence on the oil sector and state employment in Kuwait does not mean dependence on the Sabah family but on the state in general. Nevertheless, the monolithic aspect of the economy and employment in Kuwait is one of the strongest forces that promotes apathy in the society and protects the status quo. There is little in Kuwait that cannot be resolved by co-option or throwing money at the problem or the person.

Civil Society: Standing but Stunted

The absence of a strong ruling regime has prevented the state from crushing or absorbing civil society—a rare situation in Arab countries. The original establishment of Sabah rule and the constant dialectic between state and society in the development of the state's institutions in the past century consolidated a state-society relationship that is fairly open and balanced. Much of this balance was established not on the strength of modern associational patterns, but on that of tribal and family groupings and traditional patterns of consultation and decision making. Between 1920 and 1960, modern forms of association, such as professional syndicates, nongovernmental organizations (NGOs), and youth and cultural groups also joined this balance.

The 1962 constitution enshrined the right to form associations and unions in Article 43, and many such organizations bloomed in the 1960s and early 1970s. Despite these constitutional guarantees, successive emirs and governments tried to maintain restrictions on associational life. Until recently, the establishment of any association required the express permission of the emir himself; even today the government's permission is necessary. Political associations—that is, political parties—are not mentioned in the constitution and are still not allowed in Kuwait, although political groupings are strong and active. They are discussed below. There are approximately 300 registered NGOs functioning in Kuwait at present, according to the ministry of social affairs, with interests ranging from education to welfare, health, environment, and social awareness.

Much of the NGO sector has strong links with the state, as many are dependent on government cooperation or funds or are dominated by elites who for other reasons have strong links to the state-centric elite, or both. Only a small portion of the NGO sector has been a source of sociopolitical dynamism, hosting debates and participating in public movements. The majority of other NGOs have remained focused on narrower sectoral or service functions, preserving a nonantagonistic relationship with the state and other elites. The student unions are very active. Labor organizing among public sector workers, who constitute 90 percent of the labor force, is not allowed.

Somewhat specific to Kuwait is the influence of *diwaniyat*, informal salon gatherings that are part of traditional practices. *Diwaniyat* mushroomed in the 1990s and early post-2000 period as main centers of gathering, debate, and opinion formation. Shielded by the privacy and integrity of the home, they provided additional civil space and became organized into various types and topics; for example, there were *diwaniyat* that brought together businessmen and focused on economic matters, others that brought together youth and focused on education and sports, and so on. They remain an important pattern of associational life.

In the realm of the news media, Kuwait has a significant print media tradition outside of government control. The country's five main newspapers are privately owned and fairly opinionated and influential. To be sure, their editorial policy often reflects the orientation or interests of their well-connected owners, or both, but they still provide a wide arena for airing of issues and criticism of government policy. Parliament recently gained concessions from the government that loosen restrictions on the establishment of new newspapers, but there are fears that members of the ruling family will rush to move into the newspaper business more widely to crowd out their traditional rivals.

Television and radio has long been a government monopoly, although Kuwaitis have easy access to numerous other channels from neighboring countries and satellite TV. But even in this sector there has been movement. The government licensed the first private television station, al-Rai, in 2006, and parliament and the government have had heated debate in recent months about the rules and regulations for licensing other new private television stations. It is yet to be seen whether the private audiovisual media will emerge as a sociopolitical force in Kuwait like the private press was previously and in the way that private and satellite television has emerged as a force elsewhere in the region.

Political Groupings: Protoparty Patterns

The establishment of political parties is a central question for Kuwait, since it is hard to contemplate the further development of the Kuwaiti political system unless modern political parties are allowed, even encouraged, to form. However, the Sabah family and conservative elites remain predictably reluctant to allow the organization of parties. Even among the opposition, there is hesitation to broach the issue, because legalizing political parties would require amending the constitution, and many fear that tampering with the constitution might lead down a slippery slope and roll back the gains made after 1962 and 1991.

Nevertheless, associational life in politics goes back many decades in Kuwait and has considerable vigor and dynamism. Many ostensibly nonpolitical associations that were established in the pre-independence period were actually closely associated with the constitutional opposition and with Arab nationalist movements. Arab nationalists played a prominent role in the 1960s. They did well in the elections of 1963, but the next elections of 1967 were rigged expressly to weaken their power in parliament, and the Arab defeat in the 1967 war led to the splintering of the movement into various nationalist, leftist, and liberal subgroups.

Islamists entered political life in earnest in the early 1980s, winning numerous seats in parliament and taking control of the National Union of Kuwaiti Students, thanks in part to the government's efforts to encourage Islamist organizations to counter the traditional nationalist opposition. Shi'i Islamists became active and influential only after the 1979 revolution in Iran but succeeded in getting deputies into parliament in 1981 and 1985 and have been a presence in parliament ever since.

Elected in June 2006, the present parliament demonstrates the lively political life of Kuwait but also the endless splintering and divisions that make decisions difficult. Of the 50 elected members, seventeen are Islamists—six Muslim Brothers organized as the Islamic Constitutional Movement, three Salafis, and eight independents. Eight other deputies belong to the National Action group (al-Amal al-Watani), which brings together liberals, former socialists, and nationalists. Another eight are grouped in the Popular Action bloc (al-Amal al-Sha'bi), a loose alliance of more hard-line nationalist deputies who oppose economic liberalism—the Popular Action bloc also includes the Shi'i Islamists. The remaining seventeen deputies are government allies who ran as independents. The Islamists, the National Action bloc, and the Popular Action bloc contested the elections together in a loose opposition alliance of thirty-three deputies referred to in parliament as the Bloc of Blocs (kutlat al kutal). They have not always voted together on all issues, but they remain the dominant parliamentary force.

The political landscape in Kuwait thus remains pluralistic and competitive. The Islamists are a strong but not overwhelming force, and they have not been able to get their way on a number of issues, such as changing Article 2 of the constitution or blocking the women's vote. They have had some success, such as the recent imposition of a 1 percent *zakat* (Islamic tithe) on corporate profits and older regulations restricting the mixing of the sexes in universities.

The non-Islamist forces have a harder time mobilizing public enthusiasm and support in the wake of the decline of socialist and nationalist ideologies and their inability to give democratic and liberal discourse wide popular appeal. Significantly, Islamist and non-Islamist forces have been able to find common ground on some fundamental reform issues—such as electoral law reform and fighting corruption—work out common plans of action and move together during and after elections to effect change.

Process and Priorities of Reform

Horizons and Limits of Reform

Gradual and negotiated reform has been part of the practice and legacy of Kuwaiti politics for the past century. Politics has often been a fairly fluid process based on power balances, negotiation, and accommodation. Reform—in the sense of issue-specific, domestic change—has been a focus of political activism and pressure in postliberation Kuwaiti politics in ways quite different from other Arab countries, where the discourse is much more radical and general. This is so for a number of reasons.

First, there is a fairly wide consensus within Kuwait in support of the basic outlines of the political system: respecting the rule of the Sabah family, the constitution, basic freedoms, and the political process. Second, there has been a fair margin of public space throughout the past decades to develop and refine reform ideas. Third, the state has not radicalized the opposition through repression and persecution but rather moderated it through accommodation and participation. Fourth, authoritarian regimes in Iraq, Iran, and Saudi Arabia have continually served as a sobering example for Kuwait. Fifth, the Iraqi invasion and the support of the Palestine Liberation Organization (PLO) for the invasion shattered the credibility of pan-Arabist ideology and reinforced Kuwaiti nationalism. In a sense, Kuwait's focus on domestic reform is the result of not only its political traditions and history but also its inoculation against the temptations or illusions of the ideologies that have seized other political communities in the region.

Because the constitution is the backbone of the system, there is a sense among many reformers that one can push for reform within the system, but one must not tamper with the constitution itself. For example, there is considerable debate as to whether members of the ruling family should refrain from occupying ministerial posts and the prime ministership—a change that does not require a constitutional amendment—but very little debate about whether cabinets should require a vote of confidence by parliament, because such change would require a constitutional amendment.

The recent record of reform in Kuwait has been significant. In the past two years alone, women were given the right to vote and run for office; the ban on public gatherings was effectively lifted; the election law was changed, decreasing the number of districts from twenty-five to five; the press law was changed to allow the licensing of new newspapers and magazines; and the government's monopoly on audiovisual media was loosened.

In addition, the heated elections of 2006 and the resulting parliament have raised the level of parliamentary influence. Shortly after the election, all opposition deputies agreed to a six-month, written reform plan. It specified a month-by-month schedule of activities, including engagement with the government, and proposed new legislation on taxation, public concessions, business competition, oil wealth management, health and health insurance, Islamic banking, social security, handicapped rights and services, electoral law, sports, and other matters, including changes in parliamentary bylaws.

Indeed, the elections of 2006 have introduced a new dynamism into Kuwaiti political life. Parliament feels more empowered, and opposition deputies have been able to achieve a workable level of collective action. It is not clear, however, whether this threshold will last. The Sabah family was particularly weak during 2006 and is likely to reassert its power; it has many financial and political tools at its disposal to co-opt and defuse opponents. The opposition alliance itself is shaky, and a number of deputies have already voted with the government on a number of key appointments and decisions, and this lack of unity and discipline could grow. The public itself was very involved during 2006, but this level of engagement has already died down considerably, thus weakening parliament in relation to the government and the Sabah family. The true test of the course of Kuwaiti politics lies in the next parliamentary elections in 2010.

The Reform Debate

Kuwaitis agree on the need for further reform in their country but not on what changes the country needs. There are considerable divisions between the government and the opposition as well as among opposition groups. The main sources of tension between the government and the opposition are corruption and economic management and, to a lesser extent, the participation in the cabinet of members of the al-Sabah family. The opposition is deeply divided on cultural issues and to some extent on political strategy.

Fighting corruption has been the rallying cry of the opposition, and parliament has been quite aggressive in questioning key ministers—of energy, health, sports, and education, among others—on public spending and contracting. Although Kuwait has a major advantage over other GCC countries in that oil revenues accrue to the state treasury rather than to the ruling family, the opposition contends that the ruling family and their allies use their political influence for private gain and unfairly channel resources and assets to themselves. In the controversy over corruption, both sides use the information provided by the government audit bureau, which keeps fairly accurate and transparent accounts of public revenues and expenditures.

Controversy over the government's economic plans is great, to the point where the government charges that it threatens economic progress. Project Kuwait, a government plan to encourage foreign companies to invest in the country's northern oil fields bordering Iraq, has been blocked for years by dissension. The government argues that rapid development of the fields requires a level of investment and technological know-how beyond the capacity of Kuwait's publicly owned oil company; it also points out that Western investment on the precarious border with Iraq will guarantee Western interest in protecting Kuwait. A majority of parliamentarians insist that Kuwait can and must develop the fields alone. As a result, the oil remains unexploited.

More controversy has surrounded the government's granting of build-operate-transfer (BOT) contracts for lucrative projects, such as hotels and malls, and its granting of permits for the use of public lands in valuable areas. This has been a main source of enrichment for members and allies of the ruling family and government officials in the past. The post-2006 parliament forced the government to abrogate or renegotiate many of these contracts. Still, there is no agreed plan for the use of public land.

There are also many tensions among the various opposition groups. To begin with, the opposition remains quite divided about the participation of the Sabah family in the cabinet. The decision of the emir not to appoint the crown prince as prime minister after the 2006 elections was seen by most as a step forward, because it left parliament free to criticize the prime minister and even question him without directly implicating the emir and his heir. However, the idea of moving to a true parliamentary system, where no ruling family members would be part of the cabinet and thus the cabinet would be fully responsible to the parliament, remains controversial among opposition groups. Some see it as a step toward greater democracy, but others believe that the presence of al-Sabah members in the cabinet increases the system's dynamism and checks and balances, and gives the executive some independence from the legislature. Some of the smaller opposition groups fear a true parliamentary system, calculating that their rivals would end up getting the lion's share of power.

The opposition is still not satisfied with the electoral law and wants further changes to reduce the influence of money and patronage and create a more transparent and fair process. However, they are divided about the legalization of political parties. While nobody disagrees that it would be desirable in theory, many prefer to keep the issue on the back burner, because it would require a constitutional amendment and possibly open a Pandora's box of constitutional revisions.

The major differences that pit different opposition groups and even different factions in the government against each other are those concerning the role of Islam in the political system and society. Islamists, led by the Islamic Constitutional Movement, would like to amend Article 2 of the constitution to make Sharia the sole source of legislation. Pragmatically, they have shelved the issue, realizing that they were alienating other opposition members and in any case could not get the change approved as long as the emir opposed it. Indeed, they are playing down the Islamist agenda, focusing on electoral and governance reform in general. As far as the Islamization of laws, they have restricted themselves to highlighting and supporting the work of the emir-appointed committee officially tasked with bringing legislation in line with Sharia, although the committee's progress is deliberate and slow.

Nevertheless, tensions remain between Islamist and non-Islamist opposition groups. The latter fear that the Islamists would insist on amending Article 2 if they gained more seats in parliament, leading to a revision of all legislation. Kuwait is a conservative and Islamic society; however, it is more liberal than many of its GCC neighbors or its other large neighbors, such as Iran or the emerging Iraq. The non-Islamists fear that even the narrow margin of secular freedoms that Kuwait enjoys might be under threat in the near future and that Kuwait could move toward a more rigidly Islamist future even as it might become more democratic.

Although there is much discussion about reform in parliament, in practice there is also a lot of horse trading and pork-barrel politics. Parliamentary seats are a source of patronage for politicians and a platform from which they can position themselves for ministerial posts, lucrative deals, or prestigious assignments. This leaves parliament open to accusations that it is impeding reform rather than promoting it.

The argument is most often set forth by members of the ruling family and their associates. In their view, the power of the Kuwaiti parliament is the main reason why the country has not been able to modernize its economy and match the phenomenal growth of Dubai or even Abu Dhabi and Qatar. Kuwait, once the leader in the region, has now fallen behind countries it used to regard as backward. The ruling family sees parliament as a drag on quick decision making and growth-friendly policies, a body that blocks government initiatives and craves patronage. While the opposition argues that more democratization is necessary for more rapid and sustainable growth, many within the emir's circle argue quite the opposite.

Looking Ahead: Prospects for Fundamental Reform

To some extent, the political life of Kuwait resembles that of many countries with a reasonably democratic and open political system. There are plenty of tensions in the system—between government and opposition, among groups within the opposition, and even within the government. There is disagreement on policy issues, horse trading, and grandstanding—in other words, there is a lot of normal politics.

Below the surface, however, there runs in Kuwait a much deeper tension about the unresolved nature of the political system. On the one hand, there is a drive, or at least an expectation among some, that Kuwait eventually must become a constitutional monarchy, with the Sabah family slowly reducing its direct role in day-to-day government. The separation of the offices of crown prince and prime minister can be seen as a step in that direction, as can the dropping of key Sabah ministers from the cabinet through a reshuffle when they were challenged by parliament. It would be highly premature to say Kuwait is moving toward a constitutional monarchy, but the potential exists.

In contrast, many Kuwaitis do not rule out the possibility that the ruling family could suspend the constitution and parliament, as it has done twice before in recent times—and as it was rumored to be considering after the last elections. Many within the ruling family feel that the concessions of 1962 went too far and that the present weakness of the Sabah family and strength of the opposition are worrisome developments that must be remedied at the earliest opportunity. This view is shared by the ruling families of other Gulf monarchies, who fear that the example of the more open political system of Kuwait will encourage similar demands in their own countries. So far, it seems likely that the balance of power between the ruling family and the opposition will continue more or less as is. However, unforeseen shocks, such as a sudden escalation of conflict in the Gulf region—if the Iraq sectarian war spreads to other countries or if hostilities erupt between the United States and Iran—could upset this delicate balance.

The next real test of the system will be the legislative elections in 2010. They will be held under the new law of five ten-seat districts, in which voters can cast only four votes each. This will be a challenge for large groups like the Islamic Constitutional Movement, which would face the difficult choice of either running slates of only four candidates in each district thus limiting their maximum number of seats to twenty, or running more than four candidates per district and running the risk of splitting their votes and losing seats. The law was designed to try to limit vote buying and client-centered politics; it is likely to bring about a fairly heterogeneous parliament with a slightly better chance for a few women to make it and with no clear majority for any one group. As for whether the elections of 2010 will elicit as much participation and polarization as the 2006 elections, much will depend on the politics of the time. No doubt the emir will have drawn many lessons from the chaotic experience of 2006, and the government will try to be much better prepared for the next elections.

Meanwhile, Kuwait appears to be moving forward—even if fitfully at times—along the path of reform. The opposition has taken a clear initiative in identifying key areas of governance that need reform and is keeping its level of engagement and action high. The emir and the government have accepted the legitimacy of many of these reform ideas and proposals and also have realized that accepting policy reform is politic, both strategically and tactically, as a way to develop the state and its institutions and to keep the emir and the family ahead of demands for reform. In that sense, Kuwait is in a fairly healthy dynamic in which the fundamentals of the political system are not threatened—hence major players do not feel forced to fight back—while the system is responsive enough to allow the airing of public needs and demands, their articulation into proposals and programs, and their occasional adoption by government or parliament. Kuwait may witness significant policy reform in various areas, including electoral law, political association, media, civil society, social services, education, and sports as well as the management of public funds, public property, and public resources.

Role of External Actors

The elements and dynamics of participatory and constitutional politics are deeply rooted in Kuwaiti history and the Kuwaiti experience. Reform has not been imported from abroad, nor is it an ill-fitting vestige of colonial influence. To be sure, Kuwait does not exist in a vacuum, and constitutional ideas that swept the Middle East in the 1930s and 1940s found their way into the constitution of 1962; similarly, the U.S. liberation of Kuwait in 1991 influenced postliberation politics. All these influences, however, have played into a preexisting reality of a country where there have always been several centers of power.

The main challenge for external actors who want to see reform continue in Kuwait is not to find ways to influence Kuwaiti leaders and institutions toward instituting specific changes, but to protect Kuwait from being overwhelmed by new regional wars. Kuwait was saved from the Iraqi invasion by U.S. forces in 1991 and has so far survived the collapse of the Iraqi state and the serious deterioration of the security and sectarian situation there. But the dangers emanating from Iraq are still of grave concern to Kuwait, as is the possibility of a confrontation between the United States and Iran. Kuwait is a small country among large neighbors in an explosive corner of the world; it has weathered the regional storm so far but cannot afford further tensions and escalations. It has a strong interest in helping external players—both regional and international—find negotiated and peaceful resolutions to their differences.

From Arab countries, Kuwait only needs stability, but the Arab countries have much to learn from Kuwait, a country that has been able to match traditional power structures with a growing margin of democracy. For most of the past decades, Arab republics looked down on Kuwait as a conservative country dominated by a ruling family, and Arab monarchies feared that the Kuwaiti example would encourage demands for similar empowerment at home. While the Arab republics have regressed into military or one-party dictatorships or collapsed into failed states, and even recently promising Arab monarchies like Jordan have pulled back from real democratic accommodation and empowerment, Kuwait increasingly stands out as an important, even if imperfect, example.

From the West and other international players, Kuwait, as noted, needs the safeguard of regional security and stability. Kuwait is on a fairly positive trajectory, and regional instability, not domestic reversal, will threaten it most. Otherwise, it is important that the community of democratic nations understand and appreciate the realities of Kuwaiti politics. There is an important opportunity in the coming years to proceed with further reforms in governance and policy in Kuwait. This should be encouraged, for it will have a great impact on the economy and society. Otherwise, in terms of political reform, it seems important to help Kuwait figure out how to build on its public engagement and political dynamism to develop more efficient and productive political associations or parties that can do a better job of aggregating interests and developing policy and legislation.

Finally, it might also be important for the world's constitutional monarchies to share the history of their evolution and internal debates that led them to where they are today. Constitutional monarchy might be the long-term destination of Kuwait as well as of many of the Arab world's current monarchies, but the most active Western player in the Middle East, the United States, has no such sensibility and offers a radically different perspective.

YEMEN:
THE CENTRALITY OF PROCESS

Sarah Phillips

Since the Republic of Yemen was created in 1990 through the unification of the northern and southern states, the Yemeni regime has very consciously framed its policies in the language of democracy, while simultaneously muzzling initiatives that might help facilitate democratic consolidation. There has been a marked increase in the level of popular political activity, but the country's power structures have proven resilient to political reform.

Although the same president has been in power since before unification, Yemen is regularly portrayed as having made genuine moves toward democracy. The country was recently pushed into the spotlight by the 2006 presidential election in which a credible opponent officially captured nearly 22 percent of the vote. The director of the National Democratic Institute's Middle East Program stated: "Having watched democratic developments for ten years in the Middle East, this may have been the most significant election so far."[1] Yemen also has lively parliamentary and public political debates, in which citizens and opposition figures routinely criticize the government. The number of parliamentary votes for the main opposition party increased roughly fourfold between 1993 and 2003, and there is generally enthusiastic participation in the electoral process. President Ali Abdullah Saleh regularly makes declarations about the importance of democratic values. Indeed, the idea of an unfolding transition to democracy has become an important legitimizing platform for the Yemeni government, domestically and internationally.

In practice, however, the situation is more complex. Alongside some progressive changes, there is a president approaching his thirtieth year in power, a government that is perceived to be increasingly corrupt, and a deeply fragmented political opposition that has been unable to force real concessions from the regime. There has been a worrisome increase in the harassment of journalists in recent years, but even government-run newspapers still sometimes publish articles criticizing the narrowing of press freedoms. In other words, there are some aspects of democracy in Yemen's political system, but not enough to constrain the regime or hold it accountable.

The changes that Yemen has witnessed since 1990 thus do not represent a clear democratic transition but contain elements of several broad patterns of political change in the Arab world, where limited openings, controlled pluralism, and regime endurance are related processes and where all too often repression tends to follow periods of relaxed control.

Yemeni Political System: Pluralized Authoritarianism

The Republic of Yemen was created when the historically and politically divergent northern Yemen Arab Republic (YAR) and the southern People's Democratic Republic of Yemen (PDRY) unified in 1990. The current political system is superimposed on a society with strong tribal structures that are often quite autonomous from the state, considerable regional differences, and extreme poverty. Yemen's experiment with democratic procedures and institutions must be viewed against the backdrop of this tribal structure and of unification, a task that has been the overriding concern of the regime since 1990, even though the rhetoric has given more prominence to democratization.

The YAR was a traditionalist, free market state heavily dependent on foreign aid from the West, whereas the PDRY identified itself as Marxist and was propped up by the Soviet Union. Considerable debate exists over the reasons behind the sudden unification, but it is clear that both sides were attracted by the short-term political and economic benefits and probably thought they could outfox their counterparts to expand their own power. The atmosphere of intense distrust between the leaders under which unification was conducted meant that despite initial appearances of democratic willingness, intense interparty and regional rivalry undermined cooperation.

Unification was achieved by essentially merging the two former regimes in what was theoretically a reasonably equitable power-sharing arrangement. Even though South Yemen's population was only around a quarter of that of North Yemen, the Yemeni Socialist Party (YSP), which ruled the south, and the General People's Congress (GPC), which controlled the north, agreed to share power on a roughly fifty-fifty basis until the first elections could be held. Neither state had an established history of electoral or democratic politics. Political parties had been banned and, except for the small-scale parliamentary elections held in each state in 1988, institutionalized political participation had been virtually nonexistent. Nonetheless, the public was very optimistic about the democratic foundations of the new unified state and enthusiastically embraced the rights it was granted.

Like many states in the Arab world that have embarked on a process of limited reform, Yemen developed a political system best described as pluralized authoritarianism.[2] The regime is authoritarian, and although some space is granted for alternative voices, there are severe restrictions on the establishment of alternative institutionalized power centers that might threaten the elite. Elections are usually regular and at times even somewhat competitive, but the officials are much less focused on policy formulation than on building and reinforcing patronage links between themselves and society. In pluralized authoritarian states, opposition groups can unintentionally strengthen the regime they seek to weaken. The managed and curtailed political space that regimes grant opposition groups can mean that the opposition's actions serve to either legitimize the regime, providing them with access to funding from donors advocating democracy, or act as a pressure valve for popular discontent. Formal, and therefore identifiable, opposition groups provide avenues for dissent that are more manageable for the regime than if discontent were simply left to bubble below the surface unchecked. Regimes in pluralized authoritarian states thus maintain their positions in part through the type of openings that might normally be expected to dislodge them.

The granting of some political space, however limited, and the holding of somewhat competitive elections also provide certain benefits to members of the opposition. As a result, the opposition has been wary of provoking a harsh response from the regime by manifesting its dissent too boldly. As a leader of the al-Tajammu al-Yamani lil-Islah (Yemeni Gathering for Reform, or Islah Party) told the author in late 2004, "[President] Saleh could call a state of emergency and dissolve Islah, other political parties and the parliament, and arrest thousands of Islahis ... Right now we are pushing for progress but we avoid [the] more sensitive issues." Although opposition members complain vocally about the limits and controls placed on them, they have been disinclined to champion systemic changes too aggressively for fear of losing ground gained since 1990. Opposition members may see the current system as flawed, but many also believe that the likely alternative is chaos or further repression. Thus they see political demands that threaten the regime too dramatically as counterproductive. In Yemen, the perception that the regime's removal would lead to a power vacuum and to strife reinforces the view that negotiating with the regime is more prudent than aggressively working to topple it. It is likely, however, that if economic and political stability continue to deteriorate, opposition groups will become more willing in this regard.

The opposition's fear of creating a power vacuum and provoking the regime into unleashing its security apparatus has further reinforced the preference for coexistence over unrestrained confrontation. Equally important is the opposition's perception of its own weakness and what it sees as the lack of realistic alternatives to the present regime. President Saleh played on the opposition's weakness when he announced in the lead-up to the 2006 presidential elections, "Yes, some opposition figures say it is very necessary [for me] to accept [the presidential] nomination for there's no alternative ... Why are there not alternatives?"[3]

Early Reforms and the Challenge of Unification

When the two former Yemeni states unified in 1990, the new Republic of Yemen declared itself a participatory parliamentary democracy—the first in the Arabian Peninsula. Voting rights were granted to all citizens over the age of eighteen, and far greater freedoms in expression and political association than existed previously were written into law. The new constitution, which was adopted after a nationwide referendum in 1991, gave voting and candidacy rights to all adult citizens; it recognized the legal equality of all citizens, judicial independence, and a directly elected parliament; and it guaranteed a democratic political system. Islamic Sharia was to be the "main source" of legislation, a view that was challenged in 1994 by the Islamist Islah Party, which believed the wording could lead to a secular state. Islah succeeded in having Sharia declared the "sole source" of all legislation. In reality, Yemen's legal code has remained an often incoherent and poorly enforced blend of Sharia, tribal, and Western-style laws that is frequently administered on the basis of political or personal affiliation.

The political reforms introduced in the early 1990s were dictated by the necessity to cobble together the two parts of the country rather than by a genuine desire to transform Yemen into a democracy. As a result, reforms were only partial, with new laws granting rights that were quickly watered down. The Press Law of 1990, for example, made considerable promises regarding the right to the freedom of knowledge, expression, the press, and access to information. It led to an almost overnight explosion in the number of publications in the country, and it increased the public's ability to scrutinize the government. However, the new law also stipulated strict qualifications that journalists had to meet and other restrictive conditions under which an organization could publish material. The Yemeni penal code allows journalists to be imprisoned for humiliating the state or for distributing "false information," and the regime has not hesitated to avail itself of these rights. Material deemed to be harmful to national unity, security, the economy, Islam, or the president is also technically prohibited from publication.

Likewise, the Parties and Elections Law of 1991 removed many of the previous restrictions on political association and facilitated the establishment of an unprecedented number of grassroots organizations and political parties. However, the law again aimed to prevent people from using their new rights to the detriment of such loosely defined entities as "Islamic precepts and values," "the sovereignty, integrity, and unity of the country and the people," "the republican system," or "the national cohesion of the Yemeni society." These ambiguous articles have been used by the regime to protect itself from the spirit of the constitution.

Yemen's first postunification elections were held in April 1993 and marked by a great deal of popular enthusiasm. Roughly 3,000 candidates participated in the elections, and voter turnout was quite high. International observers deemed the process relatively free and fair although electoral violations were still blatant. Significant flaws notwithstanding, the process was a huge departure from the practice of politics just three years earlier.

Three major political parties participated in the elections: the GPC, the YSP, and the Islah Party. The GPC, President Saleh's party and the ruling party of North Yemen, was and remains the largest of the three. It retains the ideological incoherence that justified its inception in 1982, when political parties were banned and a broad political umbrella was the preferred method of accommodating competing political factions. It comprised a vast number of diverse elites that supported the regime and helped formalize the system of patronage available to politically relevant supporters of President Saleh's rule. The YSP, the ruling party of the former South Yemen, was the most ideologically radical ruling party in the Arab world. Identifying itself as Marxist, it called for revolutionary socialist struggle. The party was wracked by factional violence, which culminated in a two-week civil war in January 1986 that killed thousands of party members and civilians. After the bloodletting, the YSP began to look to pluralism in an attempt to recover from the massive societal and political rifts that the conflict exacerbated. The YSP entered into Yemen's unification in 1990 as the weaker of the two partners but pushed to ensure that a commitment to pluralist politics was part of the unification arrangement.

The Islamist Islah Party was created a few months after unification, largely from members of the GPC in an effort to marginalize the YSP and give a distinct political voice to the GPC's more religiously inclined members. In the early years, Islah's organizational structure and policies were almost identical to those of the GPC, although this changed incrementally when the party officially became a member of the opposition in 1997. Islah is a moderate Islamist party and is not averse to formal, multiparty political participation. Like the GPC, Islah rests on a diverse coalition of tribal elites, moderate and hard-line Islamists, and conservative (tribal or Islamist) businessmen. As a result of the diversity that exists particularly at the elite level, the party is difficult to pin down ideologically. Islah also maintains strong connections with the international Muslim Brotherhood.

In Yemen's first parliamentary elections in 1993, the YSP polled better in the former south than the GPC did in the former north, where the Islah Party also found considerable support, but the socialists were still dismayed by the overall results. They came in considerably behind the GPC and a close third behind the upstart northern-based Islah Party. As a result, the YSP lost the privileged position that it had held in the 1990–1993 interim government. The GPC and Islah established a coalition government, an alliance the disempowered southerners viewed as creating a serious imbalance of power between North and South Yemen. The two sides descended into a series of worsening accusations and violence.

In the hurry to solve the pressing short-term concerns of unifying the two states, the enormity of the project had been seriously underestimated. Democracy was seen as a convenient mechanism with which to blend two dramatically different political systems, and many of the difficult questions of state building were put on the backburner indefinitely. The result of pinning such high hopes on a poorly defined democracy was a great range of amorphous debates and little concrete progress toward fixing the problems of the fledgling state. Yemenis were soon to discover the difficulty of hastily combining unification and democratization, and authoritarianism was reconsolidated, albeit never officially.

Civil War and the Reversal of Reform

Relations between the two former ruling parties became increasingly antagonistic after the 1993 elections, with each denouncing the other's supposed lack of commitment to unity and power sharing. In an attempt to cool the mounting crisis, a group of respected northern elites established the National

Dialogue of Political Forces to publicly thrash out potential solutions to the situation. The solutions they recommended were outlined in the Document of Pledge and Accord, which called for further limits to executive power, a bicameral legislature, and greater decentralization of power. Support for the document was widespread throughout both the north and the south, with all three major parties clambering to be seen as supporting the democratic vision it articulated. By March 1994, the National Dialogue of Political Forces broke down amid the continued struggle between the northern and southern elites, and the stage was set for civil war.

Fighting broke out in April 1994, and the bloody two-month conflict that ensued destroyed much of the buoyancy surrounding the idea of unity and, by extension, the democratization that had been grafted onto it. The GPC was victorious and cracked down on the elements of the YSP that it deemed secessionist. It also quickly adopted constitutional amendments that retracted many of the progressive reforms introduced after unification. In the GPC's view, its efforts at power sharing and democratization had led to the YSP reneging on its commitment to unity. The bloodied YSP felt that it had been maneuvered out of its rightful share of power by the GPC's desire to gain control of the south's valuable natural resources.

In September 1994, barely two months after the fighting ceased, constitutional amendments were passed by a special committee, without a popular referendum. The YSP's defeat in the war cost the party its parliamentary veto, allowing amendments to be drawn up by the ruling GPC–Islah coalition. Close to half of the original articles in the constitution were amended, and 29 new articles were added. The amendments abolished the Presidential Council and broadened the powers of the president. The Presidential Council, which in the 1991 constitution was a five-member body elected by the parliament, was replaced by the Consultative Council (Majlis al-Shura), whose 59 (now 111) members are appointed by the president. Unlike the Presidential Council before it, the Majlis al-Shura was initially an advisory body that could not issue binding resolutions, although it has since been granted some minor legislative functions. The legal code of the former South, much of which was quite progressive, particularly regarding women, was also formally nullified. Further consolidating power in the executive, the amended constitution allowed the president to appoint the prime minister, head the Supreme Judicial Council—overriding the constitutional separation of powers—and decree laws when parliament was not in session. The president led the Supreme Judicial Council until 2006.

Finally, the northern-dominated military flooded into the south, appropriating land and extending the hegemony of northern elites in the region. The once-robust southern court system that was removed by the constitutional amendments has been gradually replaced by a system more prone to patronage-based affiliation, much to the infuriation of many southerners. The consolidation of the patronage system is one of the most important legacies of the postwar period and probably the most antithetical to the development of democracy. The selective distribution of benefits and application of punishments grant a huge amount of power to the regime. Unlike the situation in some other Arab states, Yemeni oppositionists are less curtailed by legal restrictions—which would require a stronger system of formal institutions—than they are by the regime's discretionary application of the law and distribution of favors.

Additional constitutional changes were approved in 2001 by referendum, although the substance of the amendments was not made widely available prior to the vote. The changes further relaxed the restrictions on the president and his ability to dissolve the parliament. Whereas the 1994 constitution had required that a nationwide referendum be held before such action could be taken, the 2001 amendments required only that voters "elect a new House of Representatives within sixty days from the date of issuance of the decree of dissolution." Nevertheless, the president has never dissolved the parliament, although the threat remains. The amendments also extended the presidential term from five to seven years. The local press has since been rife with speculation that this was to allow time for Saleh's son, Ahmed Ali Abdullah Saleh, to reach 40 years of age, the constitutional minimum age for the president. When President Saleh was subjected to a barrage of negative articles in the press about the issue of political inheritance in 2004, he told the army that the press and the opposition were "hostile forces" and "mentally ill." This confrontation marked the beginning of a further narrowing of political space, and shortly thereafter the harassment of journalists and political activists increased significantly.

The Nongovernmental Organization (NGO) Law of 2001 and its 2004 bylaw reiterated the government's formal commitment to political pluralism but allowed room for considerable government monitoring and control of NGO activities. Yemeni NGOs are also controlled through the informal government patronage available to groups that do not overstep the government's redlines. The regime places a high level of pressure on NGOs to accept a semi-official role, by granting state funding in exchange for a degree of political acquiescence. Thus, while there is legal space for NGOs, the regime's redlines are perpetuated by a civil society aware of the consequences and probable futility of aggressive dissent, and aware of the rewards of at least partial compliance. Yemen's economic turmoil compounds this situation because while there remains the background threat of political violence, economic scarcity makes government "offers" of financial assistance hard to turn down. Many organizations are faced with the difficult choice of either having a very minimal political impact or having no impact at all because they are forced to close down.

Despite the regime's political dominance, President Saleh still emphasizes his need to at least appear to be sharing power, stating publicly that: "We want all political powers under the parliament's dome. We want all the parties to have a chance, and we don't want a 99.9 percent majority."[4] The heavily lopsided distribution of power aside, the idea of electoral competition and political pluralism still carries significant weight within the Yemeni system. The regime's greater interest in unity than reform has meant that Yemen has charted an uncertain political path, but a number of reforms still warrant assessment.

How Significant Are the Changes?

Despite the reversal of reform that followed the civil war, there is still a degree of openness in the Yemeni political system. The country has not reverted completely to the authoritarianism that marked both North and South Yemen before unification. A multiparty system, regular elections, and a sometimes vocal opposition still exist, but their significance in putting Yemen on a path to democracy remains questionable.

To assess the significance of Yemen's limited reforms and the changes they have spurred, one must ask whether they have merely reinforced an authoritarian regime, or whether they may still precipitate a more significant shift away from centralized control. From the regime's side, there is little to suggest that electoral politics and managed pluralism have been intended to greatly expand the circle of decision makers. On balance, the postwar period has witnessed far more major retreats from reform than progress. The YSP boycotted the 1997 parliamentary elections, and the GPC, lacking a unified opposition, won a landslide victory. Following these elections, Islah left the ruling coalition and joined what its leaders termed the "loyal opposition," that is, a party with a growing grassroots support base but with enduring patronage ties between its leadership and the regime. The GPC's increase in dominance can be traced from the 1993 parliamentary elections where it won 145 of 301 seats, to 187 seats in the 1997 elections, to its near total victory in the 2003 elections, with 229 seats occupied by GPC members and several more occupied by officially independent candidates with strong ties to the GPC.

Political reform does not depend on the government alone but also on other actors. It is, therefore, helpful to look at whether there have been any changes on the demand side to the successes and failures of actors outside the regime in expanding their room to maneuver under the conditions of pluralized authoritarianism. Although Yemen's political opening has not fundamentally altered the distribution of power, it appears that some oppositionists have recognized the potential to open up further space for themselves. This recognition may seem a small step considering the obstacles that any group faces in wresting actual power, but it bears the potential to become more significant in the foreseeable future, particularly if the regime's support base continues to narrow. The fight for further political space in an essentially closed system can be seen in the functioning of the parliament, the establishment of an opposition coalition, and, most important, in the 2006 elections.

Significance of the Parliament

On paper, the Yemeni parliament has considerable power, but in practice it is severely constrained. The constitution gives parliament the responsibility to propose and approve legislation; question the prime minister, ministers, and their deputies; approve the government's program or withdraw confidence in the government; review and approve the budget; and, with a two-thirds majority, impeach the president if he is found to have violated the constitution or committed grand treason. Unlike in other Arab states, Yemen's executive does not have the constitutional right of veto.

The regime has undermined the parliament's constitutional right of oversight, and the parliament has not, as an institution, vigorously demanded these rights to be upheld. There is a feeling of powerlessness among the members and a sense that their primary purpose is to rubber-stamp decisions made by the executive to provide a veneer of democracy to citizens and foreign donors. The provision of democratic semblance is the most obvious function of the parliament, but its significance goes deeper.

Parliament extends patronage to a large section of local elites and gives them a stake in the political system without offering them sufficient power to alter it. It also serves as a gauge of public opinion—an early warning system for mounting tension in society. It is a relatively safe way for the executive to judge popular political sentiment and address grievances before they grow to

YEMEN: THE CENTRALITY OF PROCESS | 241

the stage where a more forceful response is required. Parliament functions as a sounding board that can alert the executive to broader discontent and provide it with advice to buffer some of the excesses of its policies. The parliament is a tool to widen the net of political opinion and allow a limited, controlled amount of upward communication from society. In this sense, parliament appears mainly to reinforce the power of the existing regime by softening its relations with the society.

There are, however, some members of parliament who have started to see their institution as a potential vehicle for change and also as a place to voice dissent and raise public awareness of Yemen's problems. In the last few years, parliamentarians have rallied against corrupt deals that were being passed by the regime without oversight. This was most notable in parliament's outrage in 2004 at the regime's attempted sale of a sizeable concession for oil exploration in "Block 53" at well below its market value. In 2005, around 100 members of the GPC broke ranks and signed a petition against the reduction of fuel subsidies. Even though the protest was ultimately ineffective, it remained noteworthy as a coordinated effort against a policy that was important to the regime. The parliamentarians were ultimately strong-armed into complying with a decision that was made behind closed doors, but this time they did not lend credibility to the process, instead making their own inability to act against a highly unpopular bill a matter of public record and debate.

There have also been a number of high-profile resignations and defections from the GPC, each of which was a calculated protest against the status quo. In late 2005, a group of sixteen progressive parliamentarians established YemenPAC (Yemeni Parliamentarians Against Corruption) in an effort to combat rising corruption. In the wake of the 2006 elections, YemenPAC successfully drafted and lobbied for amendments to the Anticorruption Law to form a stronger and more independent anticorruption commission. They also managed to remove the president from the commission selection process, despite the government's initial objections. These may each seem like small steps, but they represent an attempt by those outside the regime to create further space for themselves in an unpromising situation.

Yemen's parliament is neither genuinely independent nor effective, but it forms part of the softer end of the regime's drive to retain control and is an attempt to monitor and in some cases respond to citizens' concerns. Though sometimes only barely tolerated by the regime, the parliament has also been used to provide feedback from the society, and some changes in the regime's stance have occurred as a result. On balance, parliament's function has been more cosmetic than anything, but it is conceivable that this could change in times of popular discontent or if enough members of parliament begin to see their interests as opposed to the regime that constrains them.

Significance of Civil Society

The notion that civil society is a key base from which to propel a transition to democracy is a dominant theme in the literature on reform in the Arab world and in the democracy advocacy programs found throughout the region. After Yemeni unification, many civil society organizations emerged to fill the political space that was deliberately vacated by the regime, but they have not been sufficiently equipped to protect that space or fight for more once the regime began to retract it. Yemeni civil society's inability to successfully counteract the regime has meant that it has not emerged as a key actor in promoting a democratic transition.

There are three key barriers to civil society forming an effective counterbalance to the regime in Yemen. The first is that civil society tends to rearticulate the same system of patrimonialism that drives the ruling elite— the effectiveness of actors in the civil sphere is derived largely from their proximity to the leadership. Without personal connections to regime figures, political activists, advocacy groups, newspapers, and professional syndicates are unlikely to stay solvent or have their interests heard.

Second, the way in which the concept of civil society has been applied to the Middle East by Western scholars and democracy promoters often presupposes an American lobby-group style of politics, where organized groups are empowered to bargain with the state to achieve specific goals. This assumes the rule of law and respect for the sovereignty of the state by those bargaining with it, neither of which are consistently apparent in Yemen. The law, or more often the lack of its enforcement, does not consistently protect civil groups, which makes it extremely difficult for activists to press beyond the regime's redlines without risk of punishment. If civil society is to counteract the state, it must be clear where and what the state is, but Yemen's tangled web of patron–client links makes this identification difficult.

Finally, and most important, gains by civil society in Yemen, such as the growing number of organizations and the slightly more liberal regulatory laws, have not corresponded to losses in the regime's power. In a pluralized authoritarian state, the presence of an active though stifled civil society can actually help to protect the state's key political elites. The dilemma is that waiting for the state to grant genuine reforms is not an attractive option either.

Opposition Coalition

The opposition Joint Meeting Parties (JMP) coalition was formed in 2002 in an effort to protect its members from the GPC. It is a rather unlikely partnership among the Islamist Islah Party, which dominates the group, the YSP, and three other minor parties. The unusual nature of a coalition between Islamist and secular parties should not be overlooked, particularly considering that Islah was in coalition with the GPC against the YSP just five years before they joined forces and that the two parties fought a bloody civil war just eight years prior to that. It is one of Yemen's many ironies that Islah and the YSP have found common cause—an indication of the importance that interest-based alliances hold over ideology in Yemeni politics. The parties' willingness to cooperate is also a sign of increasing electoral pragmatism within the Yemeni opposition.

The JMP coalition is based on an agreement among its members not to compete against one another if the outcome would favor an outsider but it is also an endeavor to create an alternative political home for elites who are not under the GPC umbrella. In its first attempt at cooperation in the 2003 parliamentary elections, the JMP was largely ineffective and characterized by distrust, particularly between Islah and the YSP. By early 2006, however, the regime was plagued by so many problems that the opposition smelled blood in the water and began to frame its desires more sharply than it had previously dared. In the months immediately prior to the 2006 presidential and local elections (which were held simultaneously), the willingness of JMP members to cooperate increased enormously, much to the surprise of most Yemenis. There was considerable optimism domestically and internationally that a formidable opposition was rising to capitalize on the regime's failures.

Ultimately, the JMP did not do as well as it might have in either the presidential or the local elections. Instead, the party achieved what had been the opposition's unspoken mandate for the past several years: to provoke debate and apply pressure on the president to reform himself, without actually targeting his job. The many electoral violations notwithstanding, Yemeni voters also preferred the idea of a strong and familiar leader who had been pressured to improve, over the prospect of unpredictable change with a new untested leader. President Saleh was officially awarded 77 percent of the vote, and the JMP's presidential candidate, Faisal bin Shamlan, received 22 percent. In the local elections, the JMP did even worse, winning just 9 and 14.5 percent of seats at the governorate and district level, respectively.

The JMP did not launch an official challenge to the results despite its initial—and clearly exaggerated—claims that bin Shamlan received 2 million more votes than he was officially awarded. Instead, the party released a statement that it wanted "to avoid a clash or confrontation with the authorities which (might) derail the process of change that has begun." The JMP accepted that it did not yet have the capacity to challenge for the presidency and so accepted that its role was mainly educational. Bin Shamlan even stated several weeks after the elections that he would continue his political life as an independent, not a member of the JMP, whom he said he had campaigned for only to "extend the desire [for] change among Yemeni people." The elections thus provided the opportunity for a flurry of coordination among the opposition against a common opponent, but once the elections were over the opposition broke into more disparate parts and remained lackluster until a surge of popular discontent returned them to prominence in mid-2007.

For all of its failings, the JMP (particularly Islah) has become the only organized, nonviolent, potential threat to the regime. That such a threat even exists represents a significant shift in the last fifteen years. This time, the JMP alliance proved to be weaker than the sum of its parts, but it is likely that its members will learn from this experience and regroup for the parliamentary elections in April 2009. For the JMP's performance to become more significant in the next elections, it will have to see its function as being less a political lobby group and more of an alternative power center.

2006 Elections

The September 2006 elections were a victory, at least on one level, for popular participation and electoral administration. The vocabulary of democracy that characterized the rhetoric during the campaign period underlined that, if nothing else, recourse to the concept of democracy has become the most legitimate way to frame a political debate. The elections also showed that people are increasingly expecting politics to be conducted through the electoral process, which is conceivably an unintended form of institution building, and a consequence of the regime's use of democracy to legitimize itself.

The campaign period was the most vigorous the country had seen, and the regime appeared genuinely worried by the level of competition mustered by its opponents. As a result, there was intense pressure placed on both Islah and the YSP to abandon the JMP: Islah was offered cabinet positions, and the YSP was offered the return of confiscated property and offices, in return for leaving the coalition. The sheer number of pictures of the president adorning nearly every building in the country pointed to the regime's nervousness at the seeming strength of its opponents. Several senior government figures noted privately in the days leading up to the elections that they even expected the

JMP to win "half or more than half" the seats in the local councils. The GPC's sweep of 75 to 80 percent of local council seats belies the extent to which the regime's cage was rattled during this time.

The number of people who worked in the polling booths on election day demonstrated a level of enthusiasm for participation in the political process, and the relatively even spread between GPC and JMP representatives showed considerable pluralism. Around the country there were some 27,000 sub-committees, which watched over the rooms where the votes were cast. Each subcommittee consisted of three people, the members of which were officially divided to favor the GPC to JMP by a relatively small margin—54 to 46 percent, respectively. In every committee, there was at least one representative from the two main competing parties. In addition, each candidate (presidential and local) was permitted to have one representative to oversee the process in each polling station where he or she was competing. This meant that at least 200,000 people, including independent local monitors (which some estimates put as high as 45,000 people), observed the process across the country on election day. Despite the regime's heavy-handed attempt to manipulate the elections earlier on, Yemeni political activists and voters believed that there was still something to be gained at the polls.

Ultimately, the election results showed that the regime was more resilient than many people had expected: It was challenged by the process, but its power was not diminished by the outcome. Despite the fears of the regime and the hopes of the opposition, in the end one phrase summed up the popular mood at the polls, "better the devil you know." And President Saleh proved adept at playing on popular fears of the instability that might occur if he was removed from power. Just days before the elections, attacks by militants on two oil installations reinforced the tenuous nature of stability and security in the country and further exacerbated the climate of fear that had echoed through the campaign. At about the same time, the government paid a "president's bonus" of an additional month's salary to the one million or so people on its payroll, thus reinforcing the image of President Saleh as the provider of the nation. In a country beset with poverty, the impact of such payment should not be underestimated.

Despite the description of the elections by some international observers as a "positive development in Yemen's democratization process," Yemen emerged from the process as more a consolidated pluralized authoritarian state than one necessarily on the path to democracy. The distribution of power and resources remains centralized, and the formal and informal state institutions remain geared toward facilitating this distribution. Nevertheless, the elections were significant, mainly because of the willingness of the diverse members of the JMP to work together.

Priorities for Reform

The deeply entrenched patronage system, including the exclusive distribution of government appointments and resources, is the biggest obstacle to reform that Yemen faces. Democracy is built on the rule of law and the ability of the citizenry to influence the government in a regular, protected, and nonviolent manner. The procedures associated with liberal democracy, such as elections and parliaments, are not ends in themselves. They are considered democratic because they attempt to formalize a feedback mechanism that increases the subjection of decision makers to the political will of those affected by their decisions. Yemen's state-sponsored system of patronage undermines the subjection of the government to the popular will by overriding both the creation of strong institutions and the establishment of law and order. It is clear that without addressing some very basic issues of state building to at least reduce the potency of the patronage system, there is a glass ceiling on the other types of reform that can be realistically achieved.

In the absence of a robust political opposition, the will of the president is central to this pursuit, and the likelihood that he will willingly distribute power away from himself is just the first in a series of hurdles. Of course, not all problems stem from the executive, but the president has the best chance to implement the most changes quickly and thus pave the way for more broad-based reform.

The opposition, however, is still in a position to strengthen its coordination and consistency of message to place additional pressure on the president to commit to more reforms in the short term, with a view to challenging for greater power in the longer term. At this stage, the opposition's capacity to actually seize power in an election is probably less important than its ability to focus popular debates and the attention of the leadership on the necessity of significant reform, which is what the JMP attempted in the 2006 elections. Having achieved this shift in focus, however, the JMP would need to move on to increase its level of internal critique, build its grassroots support base, and create substantive alternative policies.

The 2006 elections placed resistance to the Saleh regime in the most prominent position since the 1994 civil war, and the opposition has never been better situated to focus calls for reform around the window of opportunity that this grants them. This window is wedged slightly wider by two factors:

first, by the regime's public enthusiasm for reform after the challenge it encountered during the elections campaign, and second, by the regime's subsequent bid for increased international aid, which was largely based on the promise of greater reform. The nearly $5 billion in aid commitments that Yemen pledged at the donors' conference in November 2006 means that donors are likely to apply some pressure on the regime to handle this money responsibly.

Devaluing State-Sponsored Patronage

There is widespread consensus among reform advocates in Yemen that to progress toward democracy, the country should ideally reduce corruption, enhance the rule of law, decentralize power away from the regime, and increase the level of cooperation between opposition parties and activists. The feasibility of these goals hinges predominantly on one central though still malleable factor: the regime-sponsored patronage system. As a whole, Yemen's patronage system is a very blurry target, but it can be separated into smaller, more manageable pieces. Starting a reform process by aggressively targeting those at the top without also addressing other entrenched structural impediments is likely not only to be ineffective but also to alienate key actors who might ease the passage of some necessary reforms.

A fundamental element of the patronage system is the regime's encouragement of citizens' financial dependence on the state, whether through government employment or the reliance on personal connections to the regime to succeed in business. Efforts could conceivably be made by international lending agencies, donors, the JMP, and reform-minded members of the government to promote initiatives that increase citizens' opportunities for financial independence from the state and weaken the importance of personal networks for securing basic needs. Yemen's grim economic situation is already leading these actors to consider where potential openings for such reforms exist.

The more readily achievable priorities for promoting lower-level reform include implementing merit-based hiring policies in the civil service and increasing wages to a realistic level. The government is understandably nervous about the political repercussions of rationalizing the bureaucracy as major international lending groups consistently suggest. Although it would be difficult for the government to terminate a large number of existing employees, it would be relatively simple to implement new hiring practices based on merit—in fact it would only require that the government enforce the law already in place. The political cost of enforcing the existing law would be much lower for the regime, and the money saved could be funneled into living wages for employees, thus reducing the lure of the lower-level corruption that undermines the government's capacity. This effort would be logically complemented by a drive to clearly articulate the tasks that government employees are expected to perform, as roles are currently poorly defined and redundancy is high. Better definition of tasks would help support a system of oversight with employee rewards and punishments that are also based on merit instead of patronage ties. The regime might be likely to recognize the benefits of these initiatives, having seen the success of the Social Fund for Development (SFD). The SFD is a Yemeni governmental agency into which donors have been putting considerable—and increasing—amounts of money because of its transparency and effectiveness, both of which are products of the SFD's merit-based hiring policies and the living wages paid to its employees.

The relevance of the patronage system would also diminish should conditions be made more favorable to local businesses and investors. According to World Bank statistics, Yemen's economic climate is one of the least competitive in the Arab world, and in terms of the minimum amount of capital required to set up a business it is the second most expensive country in the world. Businesses are expected to negotiate their tax rates with government officials, as there is no standard rate evenly applied. Personal relationships with powerful officials guide the amount of tax a business has to pay and thus can determine which businesses succeed and which fail. Simplification of the procedures to establish a business is therefore another short-term measure that could be improved to expand people's avenues for financial independence. A World Bank program is already making some progress in this area.

Promoting the Rule of Law

If political reform is to progress significantly, state institutions with not only the capacity but also the political will to enforce the law need to be established. Although many of Yemen's laws meet international standards on paper, the corruption and weakness in the judiciary and the lack of institutional power granted to the police force severely undermine legal enforcement. Yemeni citizens are theoretically equal before the law, but in practice punishments are unevenly applied with little possibility of recourse, particularly where the regime itself is involved. The executive regularly intervenes in judicial procedures, and judges tend to be politically appointed, which further skews the legal balance in favor of those already in power. It is virtually impossible to seek legal redress under this system without the protection of personal relationships. Yemenis' attachment to their formal legal institutions is not nearly as high as in some other Arab states, such as Egypt, and remolding them is not inconceivable, particularly if the benefits of doing so are clear. The majority of Yemenis are sick of the inefficiencies and inequalities endemic in their formal systems, and genuine reform would probably be well received at the lower level. Again the difficulty lies in the unwillingness of those at the top to reform a system from which they draw personal benefit.

Strengthening the Opposition Coalition

The regime is unlikely to implement significant reforms if those outside its ranks do not put it under serious pressure to do so. There is no specific set of legal changes that would facilitate growth in the power of political parties because the obstacles they face are not legal in nature. Again, they stem from the discretionary distribution of favors and punishments. The opposition is in a position to demonstrate—as it started to in the 2006 electoral campaign—that it is both unified and committed to the types of reforms needed to prevent Yemen from descending into a serious economic crisis. If this commitment is viewed as ongoing—not something that is only required when elections are scheduled—then there is potential for significant change. Because the lack of executive political will is one of the biggest obstacles to reform, the opposition may begin to recognize its potential to exploit this and make reform seem the least worst option for the president. If this does not occur before the 2009 parliamentary elections, there will be little room for optimism that Yemen will move beyond a system of pluralized authoritarianism in the foreseeable future.

Strengthening Local Administration

Nearly three-quarters of Yemenis live in rural areas, and yet power is heavily centralized in the capital, Sana'a. Democracy advocates have been keen to strengthen Yemen's local councils, but the changes required to grant them genuine power and independence from the central authorities have been continually obstructed. Yemen's local councils, which were first established in 2001, are inexperienced and lack the internal capacity to fulfill the tasks the constitution outlines for them, and they must also contend with serious obstacles from the regime. However, they still hold the possibility of expanding their role and effectiveness in the future, the popularity of which is indicated by the strength of demands for elected council leaders, who are currently appointed by the president.

The president's ability to appoint all governors and council directors is seemingly permitted by the ambiguity of an article in the 2001 constitution, which refers to "the nomination, election and/or selection and appointment of heads of these administrative units." The question of whether the local heads are to be elected or selected is unanswered, and the government has erred on the side of selection.

Moreover, all funding to the councils must be approved and granted by the ministry of finance, which is subject to strong unofficial executive control. In practice this means that the councils have no control over their budgets, which greatly undermines their potential for autonomy. And the central government is only minimally committed to covering operational costs of the local councils. The Local Administration Law states that local councils can only spend their money on capital investments, thus while they can build infrastructure, there is no recurrent budget to operate or maintain the facilities that they build.

Despite these very real hindrances, the idea of effective and decentralized local councils in rural areas is widely supported in Yemen. Some councils have started to demand more rights, gaining the respect of their local communities, and in several instances local councils adopted creative strategies to counter the limitations placed on them. Although councils are not authorized to hire and fire local government employees, a number of council members have begun to "withdraw confidence" in members who were appointed by the central government in an attempt to wrest some political influence from the regime. After the 2006 elections, President Saleh reiterated his promise that governors and local council heads would soon become elected posts. He may have done this because he felt that the GPC's electoral sweep at both the district and governorate levels gave him little cause for alarm, and he may have also have seen it as a low-cost political card to take away from the opposition, which has long called for direct election. Either way, if implemented, this would be a positive step toward greater government responsiveness to its citizens.

The process of decentralization poses a considerable problem to the regime, however. Despite the rhetoric of unification, Yemen is still significantly divided politically, economically, and, some argue, culturally between the mountainous highland region that surrounds Sana'a—where the vast majority of the regime's power brokers are from—and the rest of the country. The centralization of political administration and control in the resource-poor highland region largely hinges on the fact that virtually all of the country's natural resources are located elsewhere. Roughly 80 percent of Yemen's oil is located in the former South, and the remaining 20 or so percent is in Marib, a strongly tribal area not short on animosity for the Saleh regime. The coastal region, with its fisheries and strategically located seaports, is also outside of the landlocked highland region. For the regime, devolution of power to local councils risks ceding control over the resources that drive the country—a possibility it does not take lightly.[5] This said, because the direct election of local council leaders was one of the president's key postelection promises, it would be worth the opposition and foreign donors attempting to hold him to his word.

Obstacles to Significant Reform

One of the biggest obstacles to reform in Yemen is the catch-22 that President Saleh would hit were he to seriously change his regime's approach to governance. If Yemen is to remain a viable state, aggressive political and economic reform must diminish the patronage system, and the legal inconsistencies and personalized power that stem from it. However, the president has built his regime's political survival on the same system that undermines its future. Any progressive changes that he implements will necessarily distribute resources and power away from the narrow circle of elites that form his strongest support base, and such changes are likely to be met with resistance from the elite.

Economic Decline

Yemen is one of the poorest countries in the Arab world, and the grim economic situation means that it will be some time before the issue of democratization can become a pressing issue for most Yemenis. Low per capita income is not a guarantee of an authoritarian political system, but research shows that it makes democratic consolidation much more difficult. It also greatly increases the temptation to accept government offers of financial assistance in return for political obedience, undermining the establishment of independent political forces capable of influencing the executive.

The precariousness of Yemen's economic situation cannot be overstated. Poverty levels have nearly doubled since unification in 1990, and by 2005, GDP growth was estimated to be significantly lower than population growth. Yemen is dependent on oil revenues for about 75 percent of its budget, but these look set to decline rapidly in the near future. In early 2005, the Yemeni government estimated that the country had only 750 million barrels of "proven (and fully recoverable) oil reserves" remaining. At current extraction rates, this leaves enough oil to last around three-and-a-half more years. It is likely that new discoveries and improved extraction methods will extend this period somewhat, but a 2005 International Monetary Fund report doubted that this would more than double the extractable amount of oil remaining.

The report warned that even with dramatically slowing production, Yemen's oil revenue and exports are likely to "be virtually depleted by 2018."[6] With so much of the population directly dependent on the government for employment, stipends, and subsidized goods, the political repercussions of oil depletion are serious and would likely overshadow the possibility of greater political reform. Even if natural gas exports begin as quickly as the government hopes, many local economists are predicting a partial economic crash at best. On top of these urgent predicaments, Yemen also faces rapid population growth and freshwater depletion—the per capita availability of which is already just 2 percent of the world average. These very real resource crises bear heavily on the country's future and diminish the likelihood that political reform will be a top priority for the government for quite some time.

Yemen urgently needs to diversify its economy to reduce its dependence on resource rents, but the regime has simultaneously undermined its means of generating alternative sources of income. A recent study by Yemen's ministry of planning and international cooperation and the World Bank showed that regional investment in the country had dropped by nearly three-and-a-half times between 2002 and 2004, and that other international investment had fallen nineteenfold in the same period.[7] The ministry acknowledged that corruption, bribery, and a "lack of government" were among the main reasons for the flight of investors. That so many of the obstacles to investment are imposed by the government is concerning. However, it also means that they are at least partly avoidable, and that there is the potential for change if the regime removes some of the obstructions it has put in place. As oil revenues diminish, the regime will find itself short of the money that it uses to incorporate people into its patronage networks and in need of a more stable source of legitimacy as well as new sources of income. This venture will require some serious changes to the way that the regime approaches governance.

Weak Institutions

Exacerbating the challenge of transforming the structure of power is the fact that state institutions that could help reduce the strength of the patronage system do not exist. Loyalties to Yemen's various patronage networks undermine the potential for loyalty to other formal and informal institutions. Power is the domain of personalities, and the regime has neither built strong institutions nor maintained those that existed in the former South. Contrary to what one might expect of a state, Yemen has actually encouraged the move away from its own institutions and into the hands of individuals linked to it through patronage. The World Bank estimates, for example, that only about 30 percent of Yemen's population relies on the formal judiciary, while the rest call upon tribal sheikhs to settle their disputes.[8] People prefer the efficiency of the tribal system to that of the state system, where courts are inaccessible, corruption is rampant, and verdicts are poorly enforced. The use of traditional dispute resolution is not necessarily a barrier to reform, but it becomes one when the regime encourages the selective use of tribal mechanisms to settle political disputes with its opponents. The regime's use of such methods has undermined its own legitimacy and convinced citizens that neither the state nor its institutions can be trusted, which has in turn reinforced the desire for independent and usually informal institutions that function outside state control. Moreover, there are still some pockets in the country where tribes operate with virtual autonomy from the state.

Desire for Tribal Autonomy

One frequently cited prerequisite to democratization is that the vast majority of citizens must agree they belong to the same political community. Although most Yemeni citizens do not dispute their identity as Yemenis per se, the link between this identity and a sovereign Yemeni state is more tenuous. Yemen has a complex array of subnational tribal and regional identities, some of which receive more loyalty from their members than does the state, which is seen as feckless and corrupt. Yemen's tribes are often referred to, and often consider themselves, as a state within a state. Tribal leaders do not always grant the government access to the territory under their control, and the number of government soldiers killed for entering an area without the permission of the tribe provides good reason for the state to heed these restrictions.

The strength of Yemen's well-armed tribes at times inhibits the government from carrying out the normal functions of a state, such as extracting natural resources, punishing criminals, constructing government buildings, or controlling the use of scarce water reserves. However, these actions are based on more than a traditional preference for autonomy. Like other Yemenis, the tribes perceive the corruption and inefficiency endemic in Yemen's state institutions, and many believe that independence from the institutions is the only way to defend their interests. Against a weak, mismanaged, and sometimes fierce state, tribal structures and institutions provide a network of social security for their members. This lack of trust between the tribes and the state is a serious obstacle to coherent development and reform. While the desire for tribal autonomy remains, the state will be limited in the ways that it can exercise authority over and therefore govern its citizens. As long as the tribes outside of the relatively narrow group that benefits from the current system feel excluded by the state, they have limited reasons to accept the state's sovereignty.

Divisions Among Oppositionists

The difficulties with initiating reform are compounded by the fact that Yemeni society is still too weak in relation to the regime to mount a coherent challenge to it. Alongside the manipulation to which oppositionists are subjected by the regime, these groups also repress each other. Yemeni opposition groups exist within a complicated web of regional acrimony, kinship loyalties, tribal/non-tribal and north/south splits, all of which are further convoluted by state patronage and funding from other authoritarian Arab states. Foreign funding has meant that most of Yemen's political parties are based on imported ideologies (such as Marxism, Nasserism, Baathism, and Wahhabism), none of which were developed in response to the country's own political circumstances.

In this fragmented environment, rumors are rife surrounding which oppositionists are co-opted by the regime and which are actually aligned with ideological opponents—a situation that severely undermines trust between activists. This distrust provides fertile ground for the type of divide-and-rule leadership at which the regime is so adept. Furthermore, where a margin of free expression and association coexists with the regime's propensity to repress political action, debate tends to be reinforced as the most viable form of opposition. In this environment, oppositionists are sufficiently free to disagree with one another and define the problems that they face but are generally too restricted to act upon possible solutions. Disagreeing with each other is thus made easier than creating a coherent mandate with which to press upon the government.

Divisions in the Islah Party

Like many in Yemen, the West also has some lingering uncertainties regarding the democratic credentials of the dominant opposition party, Islah. These concerns may be overstated but are not completely unfounded because of the lack of clarity in Islah's public discourse and the diversity of its leadership. Islah is a party of hazy power centers and somewhat ambiguous public intentions. The majority of its leaders are centrists, but there is also a powerful though informal hard-line Salafi group within the party. Islah's leading hard-line conservative, Abd al-Majeed al-Zindani, has, for example, been historically useful for attracting Salafi supporters, many of whom reject party politics but may still vote for Islah or support its social programs for lack of a better option. Al-Zindani has publicly contradicted the moderates' message that democracy is compatible with Islam. He also runs a university that is widely believed to breed intolerance and radicalism, which has sharpened international concerns over the intentions of the party. The moderates within the party have had a tense though broadly accommodating relationship with this group, although the rift between the two has become more pronounced recently, particularly since early 2007.

Al-Zindani's presidency of the Shura Council was not renewed in Islah's internal elections of February 2007, which was seen as a victory for the members of the Muslim Brotherhood within the party. Al-Zindani was not removed from the party but he was certainly pushed closer to its periphery. While some other hard-line Salafi members retained leadership positions in the council, their positions are more precarious than at any other time in the party's history.

Although Islah is in a state of flux, it is reasonable to presume that its ambiguity has served the party's political purposes.[9] Maintaining ideological hard-liners in prominent leadership positions has achieved two things for Islah: one, it has widened its support base to include members who would otherwise be unwilling to support a party with a purely moderate platform (or perhaps even party politics at all); and two, it has provided an obvious contrast between Islamist hard-liners and Islah's mainstream moderates. However, by creating what is essentially an Islamist umbrella, a loose coalition that provides a home to a sweeping variety of competing ideological strains, Islah has contributed to public (and also international) uncertainty about its real intentions. Islah's lack of coherence has strengthened the concerns of Yemeni liberals, fairly or otherwise, that it is a fundamentalist party operating under a veneer of centrism, which has made the party's position within the JMP subject to considerable scrutiny. Such levels of distrust among local groups limit the impact that outsiders can have in promoting significant reform.

What Can Outsiders Do to Facilitate Significant Reform?

Foreign donors' margin for maneuver is hampered by their own concerns with combating terrorism. This is not likely to change in the near future, particularly if the potential for a serious economic or resource crisis is realized. In the prevailing climate of heightened security concerns, foreign governments tend to prefer reform and funding initiatives that do not squeeze the Yemeni regime too hard, lest it retract its support in combating anti-Western terrorist threats. It is by no means just the Yemeni side that is cautious about provoking rapid political changes, democratic or otherwise. Security is the key objective of many donor countries, particularly the United States, and the Yemeni regime is adept at marrying its domestic policies—however antithetical to genuine reform and decentralization—to this concern. President Saleh's tacit warning about the link between Yemen's stability and the preservation of his own leadership was writ large across his recent electoral platform. Responding publicly to the outcome of the elections, the president reminded his audience that stability under authoritarianism is preferable to state collapse: "Which is better, the dictatorship of Mohammed Sayeed Barre or the situation in Somalia now?" Elsewhere, he played on Western fears that democracy could put Islamist extremists into power: "Our democracy will not be as [the] US wants it to be in Palestine, yes some Islamic movements are extremist and not qualified to take power but we all must accept the result whatever it is." The U.S. administration's overly congratulatory statement that the elections were "free and fair and will set an example for the region" probably demonstrated to the Yemeni regime that the United States did indeed value stability over greater democratic competition. These types of public statements only reinforce the types of reforms used by pluralized authoritarian states to maintain their positions of power. In the future, the United States and other donors should place more emphasis on differentiating between significant and cosmetic changes, so that the Yemeni government does not continue to treat the ornaments of democracy as though they were its substance.

Despite these limits, there are some steps that donors could still take. Yemen has shown in the past that it does take account of donor perceptions of the country's political and economic trajectory. To this end, electoral politics have been an important element of Yemen's efforts to secure donor commitments, but they are not sufficient. The crude connection between seemingly democratic reform and aid money was articulated by Yemen's prime minister days after the 2006 elections: "Yemen today presents itself to its neighbors, friends and development partners as a civilized and democratic country. [The] donor countries' conference will create more positive attitudes for the sake of developing the Yemeni people, particularly following the success of presidential and local elections."[10] The desire of the Yemeni government for international acceptance gives donors some degree of latitude to apply pressure to the areas where it is needed most: the devaluation of the patronage system, institution building, better management and governance, and the greater devolution of power to local authorities. Donors' preference for working with the Social Fund for Development over other Yemeni government ministries might also be emphasized to the government to underline the fact that with greater transparency comes greater donor willingness. Donors interested in democratic reform should also concentrate on working with opposition political parties and providing them with training to build their capacity to place pressure on the regime for greater reform. However, funding from Western donors in Yemen is very limited compared with what is given by the Gulf states, which tend to have different political priorities for the funding they provide to their neighbors. Western donors should attempt to coordinate and negotiate their funding priorities with the Gulf states to increase the impact of the programs they support.

Negotiating With the Executive

President Saleh is central to any reform process, and if he chooses to act, considerable reform can be achieved in a reasonable time period. There is good reason to believe, however, that some at the top of the regime still do not perceive the urgency with which genuine reform is needed. One indication of this was President Saleh's left-field announcement in late 2006 that he intends to solve the country's dire water and energy problems by generating 20,000 megawatts of electricity from nuclear energy. Outsiders should try to press the importance of creating more achievable solutions to Yemen's problems, such as those discussed above. Given that the regime's own survival is inextricably bound to this process might increase the prospects of the regime being receptive to this message, provided that discussions are conducted with sensitivity.

Many Western donor–funded political party, civil society, and journalist training programs have been well received by the participants, but the success of programs targeting the grassroots has limited usefulness in the face of such heavily centralized executive control. These programs can assist in providing information and building the internal capacity of the groups they focus on, but alone they cannot do much to convince the regime to include these groups in political decision making. Without simultaneous pressure on those in power, these initiatives are unlikely to do more than chip away at the outer edges of centralized power.

It appears that while outsiders can facilitate the endurance of pluralized authoritarianism and the curtailed margins of free speech and association that it entails, there is probably not a great deal that they can do to dislodge the dominant political balance of power. Pushing too hard for aggressive reform is likely to be counterproductive to the West's security concerns and also to the Yemeni government domestically, which must emphasize its sovereignty in its dealings with the West, lest its opponents use this for political advantage. If significant political changes are to occur in Yemen, it is primarily for the Yemeni regime to choose. The West, however, should still apply consistent pressure in this direction and work to build the capacity of domestic actors who share this goal.

The likelihood of Yemen charting a course from pluralized authoritarianism to democracy is not high in the near-term future. However, the postunification reforms have changed the dynamics of the relationship between state and society in a more than purely superficial manner and have had an impact on the ways that the state and social forces relate to and interact with one another. Elections may be manipulated and opposition groups hindered and co-opted, but the use of a democratic façade represents a political shift, even if it is not necessarily a democratic one. The location of legitimacy, the modes of political discourse, and the expectations of the citizens are all being remolded to fit within a new political environment in which there is still room for some creative maneuvering for those in Yemen who seek change.

Notes

1. Quoted in Abigail Lavin, "Democracy in Yemen? The Arabian Peninsula's First Contested Presidential Election," *Weekly Standard*, October 11, 2006.

2. This term was coined by Marsha Pripstein Posusney, "The Middle East's Democracy Deficit in Comparative Perspective," *Authoritarianism in the Middle East: Regimes and Resistance*, ed. Marsha Pripstein Posusney and Michele Penner Angrist (Boulder, CO: Lynne Rienner, 2005), p. 17, note 20.

3. *Yemen Mirror*, "I am not a Taxi, Saleh Says," June 22, 2006. Available online at: <www.yemenmirror.com/index.php?action=showNews&id=53>.

4. Quoted by Brian Whitaker, "Salih Wins Again," *Middle East International*, May 2, 2003. Available online at: <www.al-bab.com/yemen/artic/mei92.htm>.

5. For further discussion of the impact of these divisions on the regime's concerns about empowering local councils, see Stephen Day, "Barriers to Federal Democracy in Iraq: Lessons from Yemen," *Middle East Policy*, vol. 13, no. 3 (Fall 2006), pp. 121–39.

6. International Monetary Fund, *Republic of Yemen Country Report* No. 05/111, March 2005, p. 5.

7. Reported in *Yemen Times*, "Foreign Investment in Yemen Declines," April 4, 2006.

8. The World Bank Group, *Comprehensive Development Review: Judicial and Legal System Building Block*, 2000, p. 7. Available online at: <http://lnweb18.worldbank.org/mna/mena.nsf/Attachments/Judicial/$File/BB-5.pdf>.

9. For discussion of the use of ambiguity by other Islamist parties in the Arab world, see Nathan J. Brown, Amr Hamzawy, and Marina Ottaway, "Islamist Movements and the Democratic Process in the Arab World: Exploring the Gray Zones," *Carnegie Working Paper*, no. 67 (Washington, D.C.: Carnegie Endowment for International Peace, March 2006).

10. *Yemen Times*, "Stage Set for Yemen's Donors," September 28, 2006.

MOVEMENT IN LIEU OF CHANGE

Julia Choucair-Vizoso

Most Arab states experienced ferments of political reform and widespread murmurs and discussions of democracy over the past twenty years. Today, Arab regimes increasingly employ the idea of unfolding democratic transitions as a legitimizing platform domestically and internationally. As the ten country case studies in this volume indicate, however, no Arab state ventured to fundamentally change the existing political system or introduce the core features of democracy, which would give citizens the ability to choose powerholders and create genuine checks and balances between state institutions.

The cases discussed demonstrate the great diversity in both Arab political systems and the nature of ongoing reforms in the region. The Syrian regime remains fully autocratic, having prevented the formation of organized opposition groups. Saudi Arabia is still autocratic, but is currently experiencing some progress toward a more open political system. Citizens in Lebanon and Palestine enjoy much greater freedom of expression and association, but weak institutions and unresolved conflicts continue to undermine democratization. In the semiauthoritarian states of Algeria, Egypt, Kuwait, Jordan, Morocco, and Yemen, the space for popular participation increased significantly over the past two decades. Yet even in these countries, positive changes do not guarantee further opening.

Why have the changes and reforms in the region failed to bring about fundamental political reform? Why is democracy in the Arab world so elusive? The different experiences and trajectories of the ten countries explored in this book offer insights into the continuing obstacles to democratization, the sources of potential change, and the challenges for democracy promotion.

The Limits of Top-Down Reform

Reforms introduced in Arab countries in the past decades for the most part have been orchestrated from the top by governments that were not forced to embark on drastic measures to stave off dangerous political and social discontent. As a result, political elites steered a risk-free course toward reform, careful not to undermine their own power or to traverse the slippery slope of uncontrolled change. A surprisingly large number of reforms were introduced in the countries studied here. Arab ruling elites demonstrate no aversion to change, particularly economic and social change aiming at modernization. But they have proven deeply averse to real political openings that would alter the distribution of power. The top-down reforms enacted in most Arab countries are not intended to transfer political power from monarchs and presidents to elected institutions but to consolidate political power in the executive in light of the challenges posed by economic stagnation, high unemployment, rampant poverty, and mounting social tensions. The ultimate objective is to develop more efficiently governed and economically successful versions of the existing states.

Among the rulers who adopted the rhetorical mantle of political reform, Morocco's King Muhammad VI is the model of the authoritarian modernizer. Since assuming power in 1999, he has cast himself as a progressive, modern monarch, prompting speculation that he would move the country toward constitutional monarchism. Under his rule, Morocco has witnessed improvements in overall human rights, women's rights, and economic reforms, but no progress toward genuine political participation or increasing the capability of institutions that could check the monarchy's absolute power. The king furthermore asserts that he intends to remain an "executive monarch." Jordan's King Abdullah II, who assumed power the same year as Muhammad VI, has called for amending legislation and introducing initiatives to increase political participation. He has only introduced piecemeal measures, however, designed to increase participation within limited parameters—increasing the participation of women and youths and expanding the capacity of civil society to address development issues—rather than tackle the opposition's core demands for a fairer electoral system. Syria's Bashar al-Assad, the third young Arab leader to come to power in this period, has focused on economic and administrative reforms. By cracking down on political dissent, the regime revealed that maintaining stability is its highest priority in the political sphere.

In other countries, self-proclaimed reformists in the ruling establishments—such as in Egypt's National Democratic Party—identify more efficient, modernized government and economic reform as their principal goals. They advocate streamlining bureaucratic procedures, fighting corruption, forging partnerships between the public and private sectors, and creating jobs. In Kuwait, many within the emir's circle even see democratization as an obstacle to more rapid and sustainable growth, blaming the parliament for Kuwait's failure to match the growth experienced in other parts of the Gulf, particularly Dubai, Abu Dhabi, and Qatar.

Many Arab rulers strive to present themselves abroad as enlightened leaders with a vision for transforming their societies, starting by modernizing the economy and culminating in democratization. Putting aside whether or not the smooth trajectory from modernization to democratization is theoretically possible, the reform record of the countries discussed here does not suggest that it is happening in practice. For Arab states to move toward actual democracy and not just more efficient governments and economies, the initiative, or at least the pressure, will have to come from domestic political forces outside the ruling elites.

Mixed Opposition Picture

The abundance of discontent across the Arab world does not always translate into effective, organized opposition. In the past decade, opposition groups slowly have expanded their role, and some parties in Egypt, Kuwait, Morocco, and Yemen have become better organized and more popular. Most opposition political parties in the region remain weak and divided, however, restricted by structural conditions that are unlikely to change in the near future. In the case of secular opposition movements the problem is compounded by their own failure to rally constituencies.

Most opposition parties in the Arab world only have a small space in which to maneuver. For example, parties are illegal in Oman, Qatar, Saudi Arabia, and the United Arab Emirates. They are also illegal in Bahrain and Kuwait, but in those countries candidates across the political spectrum compete in elections with the backing of political societies, which are political parties in all but name. Other countries embrace multipartyism in theory but function effectively as one-party states. Syria, for example, allows only candidates vetted by the ruling Baath party to run for office. Strict and arbitrary licensing procedures as well as laws restricting their ability to organize and even hold meetings constrain political parties in Tunisia and Egypt.

In some cases, electoral systems rather than political party legislation are the real cause of party weakness. In Jordan, the electoral laws for the lower house of parliament are designed to overrepresent segments of the population allied with the regime. This undermines political parties because they are perceived as ineffective and unable to field winning candidates or influence government. Lebanon's electoral system promotes competition among individual candidates rather than political groups. Finally, emergency laws and limits on freedom of association allow some regimes to keep opposition parties in check.

It is undoubtedly difficult for Arab parties to operate in the face of legal restrictions and government harassment. Secular parties, in particular, have been plagued by inefficacy due to internal schisms, weak organizational and financial bases, and above all the failure to articulate a coherent agenda and vision for transformation in their societies. Liberal parties consistently fail to develop an appealing social agenda to match their abstract political demands. Even socialist parties have failed to renew themselves despite their historically solid bases of support. As Ottaway and Riley show in the case of Morocco, opposition parties are often as much in need of reform as the political system itself.

Moderate Islamist parties and movements demonstrate greater success, in part because of their strong organizational cohesion and simple message, in part because as religious organizations they are more able to circumvent restrictions on gatherings. As a result, they have emerged as the only truly organized opposition movements in many Arab countries. They include Egypt's Muslim Brotherhood, Jordan's Islamic Action Front, Yemen's Islah party, Palestine's Hamas, Morocco's Party of Justice and Development, and Kuwait's Islamic Constitutional Movement. These parties, along with the civil society organizations associated with them, have been able to develop service networks. Their religious character allows them to use mosques to build and organize constituencies and, in some cases, avoid regime repression. In Jordan, for example, the Muslim Brotherhood remained legal during the thirty-six-year ban on political parties because it was considered a social organization, not a political group. Islamist movements were also more tolerated by regimes—in Kuwait, Egypt, and Jordan, for example—that were seeking a counterweight to the influence of communists, Baathists, and pan-Arabists in the 1950s and 1960s.

The emergence of Islamist parties as the only viable opposition force in many Arab states has polarized the political scene in a manner that does not bode well for democratization. First, Islamists' ideological strength and superior organization intimidate many secular parties, who also distrust the agenda of long-term societal Islamization. In fact, in many Arab countries, non-Islamists regard Islamist movements as a greater adversary than the ruling regime. Morocco's Istiqlal and Union Socialiste des Forces Populaires (USFP) have chosen the regime's protection from Islamist parties over pushing for reform. Similarly, legal opposition parties in Egypt have a vested interest in allying themselves with the regime in an effort to marginalize the Muslim Brotherhood. In Kuwait, many liberal opposition forces perceive Islamists as a threat to the future of Kuwaiti society.

Second, the weakness of non-Islamist parties could lead to a dangerous head-on confrontation between Islamist parties and ruling governments. Evidence of this is already emerging in Egypt and Jordan, both of which recently saw worrying setbacks in liberties. In Egypt, politics is polarized between the ruling party, which uses a combination of patronage and intimidation to win support, and the Muslim Brotherhood, which is legally barred from becoming a party despite holding 20 percent of seats in parliament. Following the strong showing by Muslim Brotherhood candidates running as independents in the 2005 parliamentary elections, the regime launched a massive campaign against the movement, employing mass arrests, lawsuits against Brotherhood supporters and financers, and a barrage of constitutional amendments designed to weaken the movement's influence. In Jordan, the Islamic Action Front's inability to move beyond a political battle with the regime has created a stagnant political life marked by periodic confrontations. Finally, many repressive Arab regimes have garnered permissive tolerance from the United States and Europe by invoking the specter of democratically elected, anti-Western Islamist governments.

The Difficulty of Cross-Ideological Coalitions

Arab opposition movements rarely join forces to demand change, although the rewards of combined pressure on regimes would be substantial for all groups. In Morocco and Syria, for example, even a modicum of coordination would be essential in allowing the opposition to push for change. In Kuwait, further liberalization largely depends on the ability of different groups to collaborate on a common reform agenda.

The obstacles to joint action are often ideological. Opposition groups' recent attempts to find common ground in a number of Arab countries highlight the enduring hurdles. Deep disagreements on the vision for change and the nature of the reforms needed hinder cooperation between disparate movements. In the rare instances when groups from all sides of the ideological spectrum agree, however, the impact can be substantial. In Saudi Arabia, for example, the partial convergence of the platforms between liberal reformists, moderate Islamists, and conservative religious scholars, combined with the support of moderates in the royal family, gave new momentum to the reform process, leading to small, incremental yet significant measures. It is vastly premature to talk of a paradigm shift, but combined pressure from many groups has made a difference.

Syria, in contrast, demonstrates how deep schisms between opposition movements in the region lead to political paralysis. Despite concerted efforts since 2001, Syrian opposition groups have failed to find common ground due to divergent goals, ranging from an expressly secularist, democratic regime to an Islamist caliphate. They also differ, according to Lust-Okar, in their willingness to accept gradual reforms rather than a more dramatic and risky regime overthrow. Opponents are also fragmented by regional divisions, sectarian splits, and personal animosities.

Even cooperation on specific, limited goals can lead to positive results. Kuwaiti Islamist and non-Islamist forces, traditionally pitted against each other, worked together on electoral reform in 2006, forcing the ruling family to accept their proposal. This alliance, however, was short-lived. To sustain joint action, Kuwait's opposition movements must overcome both normal political rivalries and deeper tensions about the nature of the political system, as Paul Salem argues in his chapter. Nathan Brown's account of the reform experience in Palestine shows that even cooperation on narrow goals proves impossible when the ultimate ends of various reform coalition members sharply diverge, often contradicting each other. In the case of Yemen, the unusual cooperation between Islamist and secular parties convinced the president of the need to introduce reforms. Yet this coalition's self-perception as a political lobby has become a self-fulfilling prophecy: The government, too, does not view it as an alternative power center.

Opposition movements have to overcome not only ideological differences, rivalry, and distrust but also the regimes' capacity to exploit these weaknesses. Arab regimes demonstrate aptitude in dividing their opponents, for example, by offering some parties incentives at the expense of other parties. Mubarak's regime most recently illustrated this divisive strategy when the government enacted constitutional amendments offering registered liberal and leftist opposition parties limited opportunities to expand their activities while making it even more difficult for the banned Muslim Brotherhood to operate. This is probably the reason that the legal parties did not object strenuously to the controversial constitutional amendments.

The Unfulfilled Potential of Parliaments

Even in the Arab countries reforming most successfully, parliaments lack the powers enjoyed by legislatures in democratic countries. Constitutions placing too much control in the executive branch restrict their authority. In Morocco, the king has the power to appoint a prime minister and government without taking election results into consideration, to terminate the government and parliament at will, and to exercise legislative powers in the absence of parliament. In other countries, parliaments are given formal powers only to have substantive power encumbered by executive branch interference. The perpetual threat of suspending parliament in Kuwait and Jordan provides a powerful check to the body's ability to challenge the executive. In Egypt and Jordan, flawed electoral systems or fraudulent elections further decrease the parliament's public legitimacy.

Some parliaments experienced a new sense of empowerment and greater political dynamism in the past few years. The victory of many opposition candidates in the heated 2006 legislative elections emboldened Kuwait's active and defiant parliament (by regional standards). Opposition deputies agreed to a detailed reform plan and were quite aggressive in questioning key ministers—some of whom hailed from the ruling family—on public spending and corruption. In Yemen, some members of parliament have started to see their institution as a potential vehicle for change and a forum to voice dissent and raise public awareness. Constitutional amendments in Egypt expanded legislative powers in March 2007, allowing parliament to vote article by article on the state's general budget and withdraw confidence from the cabinet.

Although these changes are important, the distribution of power remains fundamentally unaltered. In Egypt, the same amendments increasing parliament's control over the budget give the president the right to dissolve parliament without a referendum while confirming his authority over the appointment and dismissal of the prime minister. The Kuwaiti parliament's power is severely constrained by the possibility that the ruling family will suspend it once again. Furthermore, smaller opposition groups do not even want a true parliamentary system in which the cabinet would be fully responsible to the parliament: Fearing their rivals will get the lion's share of parliamentary power, they prefer to cut deals with the ruling family. Parliament's function in Yemen continues to be primarily cosmetic. Sarah Phillips finds that this situation could change if popular discontent increased sharply or if enough members of parliament became convinced that their interests are different from those of the regime, but this has not yet happened in the country.

That members of parliament occasionally exhibit bold attitudes is not enough to transform Arab legislatures into genuinely independent and effective institutions. The case of Kuwait further demonstrates that parliaments can be feisty and obstructionist for decades without achieving a breakthrough. Cooperation among opposition members of parliament can help sustain the qualitative changes in parliamentary activity occurring in several countries. Ultimately, however, the promise of parliaments is contingent on institutional changes such as the legalization of a broader array of political parties, the introduction of competitive elections, or the transfer of greater power from the executive to the legislative branch.

The Limits of Civil Society

The potential role of civil society as a driver of democratization has become an important theme in both scholarly work on democratic transitions and in regional democracy promotion programs. In reality, however, civil society organizations play a limited role. In an earlier Carnegie study, *Uncharted Journey: Promoting Democracy in the Middle East,* Amy Hawthorne argued that for civil society to play a democratizing role, a critical mass of organizations and movements must develop three key attributes: autonomy from the regime, a prodemocracy agenda, and the ability to build coalitions with other sectors of society (such as political parties) to push for democratic change. Although some civil society associations have acquired these attributes, the case studies discussed here provide no evidence that these associations constitute a critical mass yet. The state of civil society varies across the region, but many countries share similar problems: restrictive legislation; few prodemocracy nongovernmental organizations (NGOs) compared with those focused on development or service functions; vulnerability to cooption by the state; deep fragmentation between different sectors of civil society; lack of a unifying vision for social and political transformation among key civil society actors; dependence on foreign funds; and lack of internal democracy.

In Kuwait, for example, many NGOs are dependent on government cooperation or funds or are dominated by members of the statecentric elite. Similarly, proximity to the ruling leadership largely determines the effectiveness of actors in the Yemeni civil sphere. In Jordan, legislation prohibits civic associations from engaging in any political activities and requires them to abide by tedious and complicated administrative and oversight requirements. Furthermore, the government directly interferes with their leadership to remove members it deems threatening to state interests. In Morocco, civil society organizations have done impressive work in human and women's rights and have fostered debate on other major issues, but they lack the clout to compel the regime to implement reforms it does not want. Ultimately, there is no substitute for political parties in forcing the palace to open the way to a democratic process.

Even in Palestine and Lebanon, where civil society has thrived historically due to the collapse of state institutions, civil society has been unable to give reform the support it needed. Palestinian civil society was initially a key supporter of the reform movement but its dependence on external donors undermined its ability to deliver organized political support. In Lebanon, vibrant civil society organizations proliferated during the civil war and were crucial in the economy's survival and in providing services during the collapse of the Lebanese state. Due to the Lebanese state's persistent weakness and the nature of the confessional system, however, civil society organizations are organized primarily along confessional lines and serve as patronage vehicles for members of their own communities. Some cross-confessional prodemocracy organizations exist, but their capacity to push for change is severely limited.

Many civil society groups in the Arab world have managed to survive and have sometimes even become active within the limited space regimes grant them, but these groups have not expanded this space or affected the political game more broadly. Thus, civil society has not emerged as a key actor in promoting a democratic transition in Arab countries. Of course, current limits do not preclude the possibility that civil society organizations will develop into effective political reform advocates. One of the promising signs in some countries is the emergence of electoral commissions and nongovernmental domestic election monitoring groups. Although the semigovernmental electoral commissions currently have neither the power nor independence required to make a critical difference in the conduct of elections, they legitimize political activism by civil society groups, as Michele Dunne and Amr Hamzawy elucidate in the Egypt chapter. These developments constitute an indirect government acknowledgment that civil society organizations have a legitimate role in political affairs.

The Weak Link Between Economic and Political Reform

Many of the case studies in this volume attribute ruling regimes' tremendous ability to coerce through cooption or outright repression to their near-monopolistic control on the country's economic life. First, regimes use this control to develop efficient patronage systems in which benefits are doled out on the basis of political allegiances. In Morocco, for example, the monarchy's control of economic resources makes being part of the *makhzan* a key to social mobility and even security. In Yemen, the regime buttresses its patronage system by encouraging citizens to be financially dependent on the state, whether through government employment or reliance on personal connections to the regime to succeed in business. According to Salem, the monolithic and statist nature of the Kuwaiti economy gives the state ultimate control and influence over society. Increasing oil revenue allowed the Sabah family to shed its original dependence on the big trading families for financial support and thus to suspend parliament, which was the seat of the families' power. Parliament has been reinstated, but Kuwaitis' economic interests tie them firmly to the state, dissuading them from more openly challenging the system. Hugh Roberts makes a similar argument regarding Algeria, where high oil prices and resulting buoyant revenue gave the "distributive" state a new lease on life.

Economic control also allows some regimes—in particular, Algeria, Egypt, and Jordan—to sustain excessive expenditure on their security apparatuses and therefore enjoy well-funded and loyal security agencies. These agencies play a critical role in suppressing reform around the region. In light of this reality, many argue that economic liberalization measures would facilitate democratic transition. The logic is twofold: first, economic reforms (and particularly privatization) would create new winners and losers among political elites, leading to the emergence of new coalitions of independent economic players pushing for an independent political role as well; second, economic liberalization would bring about economic growth, which is strongly correlated with the viability of democracy in most countries.

This logic, however, is not supported by any evidence in Arab countries, which still lack an empowered and prodemocracy business class despite ongoing privatization programs. Lust-Okar shows that while economic and administrative reforms in Syria provide more space for private sector growth, there is no indication that this produced change in the balance of political power, forces independent of the government, or greater political pluralism. Instead, a revitalized private sector creates new monopolies controlled by members of the governing elite. Similarly, the powerful private business elite in Jordan, long-time supporters of Hashemite rule due to their own economic interests, is becoming more influential without making political demands. Furthermore, the losers in the economic reform process call for the restoration of their old privileges rather than political change.

There is no solid evidence demonstrating that economic growth leads to democracy. In the previously mentioned Carnegie study *Uncharted Journey*, Eva Bellin showed that there is no statistical proof that economic growth will help initiate a process of democratization. Rather, twenty-five years of research suggests not that prosperity delivers democracy, but rather that democracy (which develops for any number of reasons) has a better chance of surviving if a country has a higher gross national product. Certainly, the case studies here do not offer evidence contradicting the general findings on the relationship between economic growth and democratization. In fact, they do not even offer clear evidence that economic liberalization is leading to economic growth.

Furthermore, the partial economic liberalization launched by Arab states is unlikely to compromise their ability to maintain robust security services in the near term. Resource-rich states will continue to receive substantial revenues from both oil and gas industries, which are unlikely to be fully privatized. Resource-poor states like Egypt and Jordan capitalize on their geostrategic usefulness to the United States and receive substantial amounts of U.S. economic and military aid.

The Obstacle of Regional Conflict

The West often accuses Arab countries of using the unresolved conflict with Israel as a blanket excuse to avoid dealing with shortcomings in their own political systems. Although the criticism is often justified—in that the conflict has no bearing on a wide variety of issues—the studies in this volume show clearly that, in some countries, the regional situation is a significant hindrance to democratic development. Palestine and Lebanon are the countries most affected by regional conflict, but Jordan, Syria, and Kuwait are also impacted.

The Palestinian case illustrates most clearly the difficulty of reform in the midst of an ongoing conflict. As Nathan Brown remarks, "for a brief but critical moment, the circumstances favoring political reform in Palestine seemed more propitious than they ever had in any Arab context." The turn of events after the 2006 legislative elections, however, demonstrated that reforms will not lead to a qualitative change in Palestinian politics in the absence of a broader political and diplomatic context favorable to institution building. Reform in Lebanon also cannot be extricated from the wider regional context. Fragmentation in the Lebanese system invites the disproportionate influence of outsiders. As a result, Lebanon has always been a microcosm of regional dynamics. Most recently, U.S.–Syria and U.S.–Iran tensions contributed to the stalemate that has paralyzed Lebanon since early 2006. In turn, the stalemate over the composition of the government froze any attempts to discuss the underlying structural flaws of the political system preventing Lebanon from becoming a truly democratic state, such as the need to amend the electoral law.

In Jordan, the regime is unlikely to take steps to open up the system as long as the regime feels threatened by the situation in Palestine and Iraq. The presence of a large population of Palestinian origin whose allegiance to the monarchy is not as firm as that of the original Jordanians creates an element of instability that delays the path toward greater political freedom. The conflict in neighboring Iraq has exacerbated the regime's feeling of vulnerability, further relegating political reform below security considerations. In Syria, as Lust-Okar shows, sectarian violence in neighboring Iraq invoked fears among regime elites as well as average Syrians that quick reforms could be destabilizing. According to Salem, Kuwait's generally positive trajectory is more threatened by regional instability—especially the overflow of Iraqi sectarian violence and the possible eruption of hostilities between the United States and Iran—than by domestic reversal.

Regional conflict's negative impact on political reform serves as a convenient excuse for regimes to postpone all reforms while the conflict over Palestine remains unresolved. Countries and organizations seeking to promote democracy in the Middle East, however, should not ignore the conflict's real impact in many countries and the extent to which it hinders, or at least greatly complicates, internal transformation.

The Uncertain Role of Outside Actors

U.S. rhetoric since 2002 has accorded new prominence to political and economic reform and democratization as policy goals in the Middle East. Though more understated, the European Union's Barcelona Process has been promoting similar transformation in the Arab countries of the Mediterranean basin for over ten years. Most Arab citizens are deeply skeptical of outside actors. They are unconvinced of the EU policy's effectiveness and indeed often are unaware of its existence altogether. They believe that the new U.S. democracy and freedom rhetoric was simply a cover for the old U.S. policy of imposing its choices on the Arab world. The concomitance of new rhetoric and preparations for invading Iraq is a major reason for this skepticism. Democracy promotion in this view is simply an excuse for the United States to forcefully remove regimes it does not like. In the years following the invasion of Iraq, U.S. human rights violations in Iraq, Afghanistan, and elsewhere further undermined the United States' image as a democracy promoter.

Adding to this skepticism, the case studies here indicate that the United States did not effectively or coherently integrate democracy promotion into its regional policy agenda despite the dramatic shift in U.S. rhetoric. The Palestinian experience between 2002 and 2007 is the most telling example of continuing inconsistencies and contradictions in U.S. policy. As Nathan Brown argues, between 2002 and 2006 there were significant accomplishments in Palestinian institutional reform. A well-formed reform agenda, a strong and experienced group of Palestinian activists supporting the changes, and a vocally supportive international community contributed to this success. The victory of Hamas in free and fair elections in 2006, however, led the United States to withdraw its support from all Palestinian institutions in the hope of forcing Hamas to relinquish power, greatly undermining the earlier progress on institutional reform. The U.S. approach to democracy promotion as a means of achieving short-term goals (such as backing particular leaders or parties) rendered the international effort to bolster Palestinian institutions hypocritical in the eyes of many Palestinians and Arabs.

Dunne and Hamzawy highlight the same U.S. fickleness in the case of Egypt. In 2004–2005, the United States showed an active interest in democratization in Egypt, publicly putting pressure on the regime to introduce change. By 2006 the Bush administration was already backing off, however, worried by the electoral success of the Muslim Brotherhood and anxious to maintain the support of the Egyptian government in confronting mounting regional crises.

Conflicting U.S. interests and the country's credibility deficit in the region will continue to detract from its potential as an advocate of democratization in the foreseeable future. The ongoing and deteriorating Arab–Israeli crisis, the U.S. dependence on oil, and U.S. reliance on Arab security services in counterterrorism activities are unlikely to disappear soon. The ten case studies explored here recognize the reality of conflicting interests and the limitations of external actors to bring about political reform. Nevertheless, the studies draw some lessons about what could make international democracy promotion less controversial and more effective.

Lesson 1: The Importance of Context

The clearest lesson that emerges from the country studies in this volume is that each country's experience with reform is unique. Outside democracy promoters need to recognize the uniqueness of each situation and develop separate country strategies rather than promoting regional initiatives. Any effort must begin with a realistic evaluation of the current situation in each country, the main hurdles to democratization, and the probable impact of the measures being advocated.

The case of Algeria illustrates the dangers of incorrectly diagnosing political problems. As Hugh Roberts elucidates, the United States and European countries greeted the introduction of formal pluralism between 1989 and 1991 with unwarranted enthusiasm, predicated on a misconception of the nature of Algerian authoritarianism. They assumed that these problems were rooted in the National Labor Front's (FLN) formal political monopoly and that the introduction of political pluralism was the indispensable point of departure for democratic reform. That assessment ignored the preponderance of the executive branch over the legislative and judicial branches and the fact that the executive as a whole was subject to military hegemony.

Considering specific country contexts will aid external actors in distinguishing between cosmetic and significant reforms and avoiding excessive praise for minor reforms that do not lead to true political competition. Rulers in the Arab world are adept at introducing piecemeal reforms, arguing that this type of partial liberalization is a necessary middle ground on the way to democracy. Most often, these reforms are a way for regimes to consolidate their rule and avoid real reforms.

Accounting for the uniqueness of every country's reform experience will also discourage the use of standardized democracy promotion toolkits that have failed to inspire real change in Arab countries despite successful applications elsewhere.

Lesson 2: Embracing the Role of Facilitator

The inability of domestic actors to build mass-based organizations to challenge dominant political structures is a major contributor to the endurance of Arab authoritarian regimes. External actors can play an important role in facilitating an environment conducive to domestic actors building their capacity to push for reform. Three strategies can aid in this process.

First, democracy promotion agencies and donors should recognize the real weaknesses of non-Islamist parties in the Arab world today. Conventional party assistance methods employed by various U.S. and European political party foundations are designed to help already-functioning parties overcome organizational weakness and improve election campaigning. The problems of the non-Islamist political organizations, however, are much deeper. As Ottaway and Riley demonstrate, Moroccan secular parties are uncertain of their identity, ineffective in reaching constituencies, and pessimistic about their future. In this context, the most important contribution to true democratic reform that the United States and Europe could make would be to facilitate the transformation and renewal of the major secular parties by pressuring their leaderships to launch internal reforms, with a focus on long-term rather than immediate results.

Second, while Western actors will always be more comfortable dealing with secular parties, they cannot afford to ignore the fact that moderate Islamist parties are currently the strongest political organizations in the Arab world: They have successfully built grassroots support, developed political machines, and adopted the reform mantle in the region. Ignoring this reality will not decrease the influence of Islamist movements across the region. Foreign institutions and governments need not actually support these groups or collaborate with them as closely as they do with liberal parties. Nonetheless, they need to recognize that they are legitimate and important political actors, that they are here to stay for the foreseeable future, and that developing contacts and understanding their positions are imperative.

Third, the United States and Europe can help by pressuring governments to keep open the political space needed for productive dialogue among all actors in the society—Islamist and non-Islamist alike. Western donor–funded political party and civil society training programs can be helpful, but they have limited influence on the centralized executive control in most Arab countries. Coordinated external pressure encouraging elites to heed internal calls for change will give reformists greater latitude to voice their demands. This pressure can be exercised through public statements, direct private engagement with Arab government officials, economic and military assistance, and trade relations. In all cases, pressure must be consistent and sustained.

Lesson 3: The Need to Align International Pressure With Domestic Agendas

External actors advocating reform will be more successful in their efforts if they align their agendas with the demands articulated by reformists in those countries. The benefits of such an approach can be seen in the Palestinian experience of 2002–2003, when international support provided a vital source of leverage for Palestinian reformers by focusing on demands expressed by domestic reformers. By pressing Arab governments on the issues demanded domestically, external actors will also allay popular suspicion of and apprehension toward their intentions. In Jordan, these domestic demands would include expanding legislative powers, adopting new press legislation, decreasing regulations on NGOs, and undertaking electoral system reform. In Saudi Arabia, support for the demands of Saudi reformers would include broadening the power of the Shura Council, choosing some of its members by election, and legalizing more NGOs and professional syndicates.

How Significant Is the Change?

The introductory chapter in this book argues that significant reforms, "are those that have the potential for leading to a democratic paradigm shift in a fairly short time period, without the interference of a long chain of intervening variables that may or may not materialize, and equally without the interference of unforeseen circumstances." By this definition, it is impossible to talk about a democratic paradigm shift in any of the countries discussed here. Despite the intense political life documented in this book, the governments are unwilling to introduce changes leading to a paradigm shift and the opposition has been incapable of forcing such shift. The greater degree of pluralism, the signs of cooperation among opposition groups, and the emergence of more vocal parliaments are still counterbalanced by regimes that retain the tools to disperse, placate, and exclude dissenters. Incumbent governments have shown great resilience in maintaining the system as it is, slowing down or reversing changes when that status quo appears threatened—as Egypt did in the wake of the Muslim Brotherhood's gains in the 2005 elections.

This reality, however, does not imply that no paradigm shift will occur in Arab countries. Sudden shocks to political systems in the region—wars, economic crises, leadership successions—may lead to paradigm shifts, but not necessarily democratic ones. In fact, the only real paradigm shifts that are occurring now or may occur in the near future are negative: the collapse of the Palestinian authority and the possible collapse of the political balance that has enabled Lebanon to survive precariously. The country studies in this book do not speculate about these possible shocks since they are by their nature unpredictable. The studies do, however, reveal that there is no evidence that the incremental reforms of the past two decades will lead to further openings, let alone democratic breakthroughs.

INDEX

terrorism, 2, 155
torture: abolition in Morocco, 167
"town square" test, 96–97
Trade and Investment Framework
Agreement (Egypt/U.S.), 41
trade relations: democracy assistance
and, 40–41
trade unions: in Jordan, 59
Transparency International (Morocco),
169
Trans-Saharan Counter-Terrorism Partnership, 157

al-Ubaid, Abdallah Salih, 203
Um al-Qura University, 197
Uncharted Journey: Promoting Democracy
in the Middle East (Hawthorne), 268,
270
UN Interim Forces in Lebanon
(UNIFIL), 131
Union Nationale des Forces Populaires
(UNFP), 163, 165
Union of Palestinian Medical Relief
Committees (UPMRC), 111
Union Socialiste des Forces Populaires
(USFP), 165–66, 173–75, 184, 264;
socialism of, 175
United Arab Emirates: political parties
banned in, 263
United Arab Republic (UAR), 214
United Nations Development Program
(UNDP), 1, 84
United Nations Security Council: investi-
gation of Hariri assassination, 75;
Resolution 1559, 71, 75, 120, 131; Res-
olution 1636, 75
United States: Agency for International
Development (USAID), 105; Algerian
policy, 157; Arab skepticism about
democracy promotion of, 272–73;
conflict between political reform and
strategic interests in Middle East,
64–65; democracy assistance in Egypt,
39–41; democracy assistance in Jordan, 67–68; democratization as

strategic goal, 2, 20; economic pressures for reform in Jordan, 50; foreign
aid to Jordan, 65–66; free trade agreement with Jordan, 53, 66; invasions of
Afghanistan and Iraq, 20; limited
influence on domestic reform in
Syria, 89; Middle East Partnership
Initiative, 39–41; Middle East policy
change following 9/11 attacks, 1–2;
policy toward Palestinian-Israeli conflict, 58; pressure for disarmament of
Hizbollah, 133; pressure on Syria for
political reform, 71; public statements
vs. private diplomacy, 38–39; relations
with Morocco, 183–84; role in Saudi
political reform, 209–10; security relations with Jordan, 58; support for
Egyptian political reform, 36–41;
Syria Accountability and Lebanese
Sovereignty Act of 2003, 71, 74–75;
viewing Palestinian reform as opposition to Arafat, 99; war on terrorism,
64, 138, 151, 155, 157; withdrawal of
support for Palestinian reforms,
94–95, 104. See also Bush (George W.)
administration
United States-Jordan Free Trade Agreement (2001), 66
USAID (United States Agency for International Development), 105

voting age, 128

Wafd Party (Egypt), 18, 19
Wahhabi religious establishment: antireform stance of, 192–93; balance of
power with royal family, 192–93;
enforcement of religious laws, 192;
institutions under, 192; Islamic Awakening movement and, 196–97; jihadist
groups emerging from, 197; moderate
Islamists targeted by, 196; opposition
to educational reform, 202–3; as political actor in Saudi Arabia, 191–93;
role under Saudi Basic Law of

CONTRIBUTORS

NATHAN J. BROWN is a senior associate at the Carnegie Endowment and is also professor of political science and international affairs and director of the Middle East Studies Program at the George Washington University. He is the author of four books on Arab politics, including *Palestinian Politics after the Oslo Accords: Resuming Arab Palestine*. His past work has focused on Palestinian politics and on the rule of law and constitutionalism in the Arab world.

JULIA CHOUCAIR-VIZOSO is a former associate at the Carnegie Endowment for International Peace in Washington, D.C. She is currently a Ph.D. candidate in Political Science at Yale University. Her research focuses on the possibility of democratic change in the Arab world, with attention to political, economic, and social reform trends in the region. Prior to joining the Carnegie Endowment in 2004, Choucair-Vizoso assisted with research at the Center for Strategic and International Studies in Washington and the United Nations Economic and Social Commission for Western Asia in Beirut. She has also worked as an independent consultant on Middle East issues, including human rights, Lebanese politics, and the European Union's approaches to reform in Arab countries.

MICHELE DUNNE is a senior associate and editor of the Carnegie Endowment's *Arab Reform Bulletin*. A specialist on Middle East affairs, formerly at the State Department and White House, Dunne is the author of *Evaluating Egyptian Reform, Integrating Democracy Promotion Into U.S. Middle East Policy*, and *Libya: Security Is Not Enough*.

AMR HAMZAWY is a senior associate at the Carnegie Endowment and a noted Egyptian political scientist who previously taught at Cairo University and the Free University of Berlin. His research interests include the changing dynamics of political participation in the Arab world and the role of Islamist opposition movements in Arab politics.

ELLEN LUST-OKAR is an associate professor in the Department of Political Science and chair of the Council on Middle East Studies at Yale University. She received a Ph.D. in Political Science and an M.A. in Middle East Studies at the University of Michigan. Her publications include *Structuring Conflict in the Arab World* (Cambridge University Press, 2005), as well as articles in such journals as *Comparative Politics, International Journal of Middle East Studies, Middle Eastern Studies,* and *Politics and Society.* She is currently working on projects examining the politics of elections in the Arab world and the relationships between national and transnational Islamist movements.

MARINA OTTAWAY is a senior associate in the Democracy and Rule of Law Program and director of the Carnegie Middle East Program. Her most recent book, *Uncharted Journey: Democracy Promotion in the Middle East* (co-edited with Thomas Carothers), was published in January 2005.

SARAH PHILLIPS received her Ph.D. from the Centre for Arab and Islamic Studies, Australian National University, in 2007, and her doctoral thesis has been accepted for publication. She is currently working with the National Democratic Institute in Yemen. Phillips specializes in Yemeni politics, political party development, democratization and reform in the Arab world, and the role of Islamists in these processes.

MEREDITH RILEY is currently Elisabeth Luce More Wellesley-Yenching Fellow at Chung Chi College at the Chinese University of Hong Kong. She was a Junior Fellow for the Democracy and Rule of Law Program at the Carnegie Endowment 2005–2006. She has worked with the Asian Human Rights Commission, United Nations Association of the U.S.A., and the office of Senator Hillary Rodham Clinton.

HUGH ROBERTS is an independent writer and consultant and a specialist on North African politics. From 2002 to 2007 he was the Director of the North Africa Project for the International Crisis Group. From 1997 to 2002 he was a Senior Research Fellow of the London School of Economics. Between 1976 and 1997 he lectured at the universities of East Anglia, Sussex, UC Berkeley, and the School of Oriental and African Studies in London. His book, *The Battlefield: Algeria 1988–2002. Studies in a Broken Polity*, was published in 2003. He is currently working on books on the Berbers of Algeria and on Islamism and violence.

PAUL SALEM is the director of the Carnegie Middle East Center. Prior to this appointment, Salem was the general director at The Fares Foundation and from 1989 to 1999 he founded and directed the Lebanese Center for Policy Studies, Lebanon's leading public policy think tank. Recently, Salem was a member of the Lebanese National Commission for Electoral Law Reform, a blue ribbon commission tasked with revising Lebanon's electoral laws and proposing a new system. In 2002, Salem was a member of the Senior Review Committee for the UNDP Arab Human Development Report. He also has held various positions at the American University in Beirut. He is a regular commentator on television, radio, and in print on political issues relating to the Arab world.